TRANSITION
MANAGEMENT

A Practical Approach to Personal and Professional Development

SANDRA L. McKEE

BRENDA L. WALTERS

Prentice
Hall

Upper Saddle River, New Jersey
Columbus, Ohio

Library of Congress Cataloging-in-Publication Data

McKee, Sandra L.
    Transition management : a practical approach to personal and professional development
/ Sandra L. Mckee, Brenda L. Walters.
      p. cm.
    Includes index.
    ISBN 0-13-061051-8
    1. Life skills—Handbooks, manuals, etc. 2. Success—Handbooks, manuals, etc. 3.
Self-actualization (Psychology)—Handbooks, manuals, etc. I. Walters, Brenda L., 1945-
II. Title.

HQ2037 .M34 2002
646.7—dc21

2001053683

Vice President and Publisher: Jeffery W. Johnston
Senior Acquisitions Editor: Sande Johnson
Assistant Editor: Cecilia Johnson
Production Editor: Holcomb Hathaway
Design Coordinator: Diane C. Lorenzo
Cover Designer: Jeff Vanik
Cover Art: Corbis/The Stock Market
Production Manager: Pamela D. Bennett
Director of Marketing: Ann Castel Davis
Director of Advertising: Kevin Flanagan
Marketing Manager: Christina Quadhamer

This book was set in Janson Text by Aerocraft Charter Art Service. It was printed and bound
by Maple Vail Book Manufacturing Group. The cover was printed by Phoenix Color Corp.

Pearson Education Ltd., *London*
Pearson Education Australia Pty. Limited, *Sydney*
Pearson Education Singapore Pte. Ltd.
Pearson Education North Asia Ltd., *Hong Kong*
Pearson Education Canada, Ltd., *Toronto*
Pearson Educación de Mexico, S.A. de C.V.
Pearson Education–Japan, *Tokyo*
Pearson Education Malaysia Pte. Ltd.
Pearson Education, *Upper Saddle River, New Jersey*

Prentice Hall

10 9 8 7 6 5 4 3 2
ISBN 0-13-061051-8

Contents

CHAPTER 2 Moving Toward Your Goals 21

CHAPTER 3 Organizing Time and Tasks 39

CHAPTER 4   Maintaining Growth   59

CHAPTER 5   Creating a Positive Attitude   77

CHAPTER 6 Improving Your Communication Style 97

CHAPTER 7 Problem Solving 117

CHAPTER 8   Confronting Conflict   137

CHAPTER 9   Self-Nurturing for Survival   157

CHAPTER 10   Self-Advocacy   177

CHAPTER 11   Developing a Support Network   203

CHAPTER 12   Maintaining Personal Relationships   223

CHAPTER 13   Launching Your Career   245

CHAPTER 14   Lifelong Career Management   271

Preface

Reaching the goal of personal and professional satisfaction requires many transitions throughout a person's life. The constructive management of transitions will yield success on both levels. This book provides critical-thinking skills and behavioral tools that should be as much a part of the repertoire of the new professional as those listed on the resume.

In any life transition, but especially in the transition from student to professional, priorities, communication systems, time-management patterns, finances, and goals all will be challenged. Skill in navigating the requirements and expectations of the new milieu of work *and* of changing personal situations is necessary for a satisfying life. For this reason, we address both personal and professional development issues side by side.

Readers will be challenged to conduct ongoing self-assessment to facilitate the goal-setting and transition process. Because behavioral testing is a particularly helpful tool toward this end, two resources for this type of assessment are available. One is the *Prentice Hall Assessment Library*, which is a CD-ROM for students; instructors can request copies through their Prentice Hall representative. The other is an on-line resource, www.queendom.com. Both of these sources provide tools that cover the areas of personality, relationship, and career. In the appendix of this book is a listing by chapter of the tests that most closely apply to the material.

Another recurring element is the theme of *self-nurturing* (taking responsibility for one's own physical, emotional, and relational well-being) combined with *self-advocacy* (cultivating constructive and beneficial skills and approaches in order to manage one's career). Each chapter ends with an activity that asks readers to commit to goals in self-nurturing and in self-advocacy as they relate to the specific focus in the chapter.

Because the "rules of the road" are very different in industry than in academic environments, the behaviors, talents, skills, and priorities that create success in the academic world do not all necessarily transfer unchanged to industry. As a guide to the other side of the college career transition, this book goes into some detail on the conditions and challenges the new employee in a professional environment might find. (*Note:* The term "professional" is used throughout the book to refer to any career-type job as opposed to part-time or temporary income sources.)

Recommendations for handling many potentially difficult and uncomfortable situations are given both by the authors and by professional coaches in their particular subject area.

Chapter Features

- **Transition tips.** These consist of brief **statements** from individuals who have recently made the college-to-career transition. Some will be successful transitions, in which the groundwork was laid and the movement to the new challenges of professional life was a positive experience. Some are stories of less successful transitions in which insights gained from the mistakes will be shared.

- **Cases for applying chapter concepts.** Each chapter provides opportunities for readers to apply **critical-thinking and behavioral skills** to situations adapted from real experiences. Short scenarios with thought questions punctuate each chapter and allow students to apply the concepts just learned.

- **Links to or lists of on-line resources.** These Web sites and organizations will help support the graduate during the transition to professional life.

- Conceptual models presented in the form of **charts, diagrams, and illustrations to accommodate different learning styles.**

- **Activities.** These occur throughout the chapters and require students to evaluate their own situations and set goals.

- Specific references to types of **self-assessment tests** to help students evaluate their professional attributes.

- A **conversational style** that puts students at ease and draws them into the material.

- Discussion of **skill, knowledge, and attitude elements** of the college-to-career transition.

- Preparation of graduate expectations for the world of industry in order to **enhance first-year productivity.**

This book's style and straightforward approach make it a good fit in career orientation, personal development, and professional development courses, as well as a valuable resource for anyone entering the career world for the first time.

Of the many job search books on the market, very few even attempt to prepare the student for life on the other side of the college-to-career transition by sharing pictures of what to expect. Many graduates jump blindly into a job. This book serves as a "portable mentor" and strives to give students insights and skills they may not yet know they need. We hope to help sutdents make the career jump and land on solid ground.

Acknowledgments

The authors would like to thank all of the professional industry coaches who kindly shared their insights with us as well as the many former students we interviewed for their comments that appear in this book. We would also like to thank our editor, Sande Johnson, for believing in an idea whose time had come and for supporting us as we developed this book. In addition, Cecilia Johnson, assistant editor, was the "left brain" who kept all of the details together. Many clients, patients, and students over the years have encouraged the pursuit of this project, and it is our hope that it will meet the needs of many more.

We would like to thank the following reviewers who offered insightful and constructive comments on the manuscript: T. Clifford Bibb, Alabama State University; Bruce Bloom, DeVry Institute of Technology–Chicago; Linda Bush, ITT Educational Services; Linda Googe, Mt. San Jacinto College; and Allyson Tanouye, University of Hawaii at Manoa.

S.Mc. and B.W.

I would personally like to thank Gene Minor, my mentor, coach, and guide over many years, whose help and support have contributed so much to what I am and know today. I hope you will be proud of this book, as it received much of its inspiration from you and from the role model you have been for me.

In addition, I thank my co-author, Brenda Walters, who for the second time agreed to the rigors and all-consuming demands of developing a book with me and contributed not only wisdom and experience, but also creativity and insight. I am the richer for the experience.

Finally, I acknowledge the patience of my children, who endured my many hours glued to a computer keyboard.

S. Mc.

About the Authors

Sandra McKee's second book, *Practical Project Management*, is out under the Prentice Hall name. Just returned from her third industrial sabbatical, McKee keeps close tabs on the types of environments and situations the new graduate will find and has fresh, first-hand information on what is required to be successful in those situations. Her professional speaking, coaching, and consulting experiences continually present new situations and challenges in diverse fields, so she has regular exposure to a broad range of industry conditions. Her recent focused research and work with retired military persons making the transition to the civilian corporate world and with adults wrestling with attention deficit disorder bring valuable insights and conclusions to the content of the book. Sandra is a Senior Professor at DeVry Institute in Atlanta, Georgia.

Brenda Walters (B.C.S.W.) provides advice to hospitals and treatment centers as a consultant for their mental health patient operations and personnel issues. As a private therapist, she works with clients at all levels, from high-ranking executives to line workers and service providers, giving her superior insight into interpersonal and relational issues in those environments. Directly tied to employee assistance program directors in large and small companies, Walters is regularly called on to address employee performance problems on both an individual and group level. She has been interviewed on television and radio regarding her work, especially in the area of addictions, and has contributed to publications on the topic of stress management in sports competition. Brenda is a board-certified therapist in private practice in New Orleans, Louisiana.

CHAPTER 1

Transitions and Life Changes

The average person today is expected to live approximately 80 years. During the 80 or so years of your life, you will experience many potentially life-changing events. These events will present you with many opportunities; each of which is a choice. A life event is an opportunity that brings you to the threshold of a new place, a new way of life. At each threshold you are faced with a choice. You can stay safely where you are or you can choose to pass through these doorways and establish yourself at a new level of maturity and satisfaction. This process, crossing the thresholds of life changes and settling into a new place in your progress toward a satisfying and fulfilling life, is a *transition*.

Once you learn a positive and constructive approach to life's challenges, you become the maker of the map that leads to the treasure of a full and happy life. Acquiring new skills to deal with life transitions allows you:

- To learn how to focus on solutions rather than problems.
- To feel in control of yourself and your life.
- To improve your self-esteem.
- To build future successes in managing your life transitions.
- To gain the respect of others.

We define the process of *transition* as **a shift in operating style that allows** *successful adaptation* **to a new set of life conditions.**

An example of a fairly difficult, but successful, transition process was Scott, a student at a small Georgia college. An athlete and a typical, active young male, he had a large circle of friends and a fiancée. In an instant, his whole life changed. A car accident caused injuries that resulted in brain damage, and suddenly, nothing in his life was familiar or doable. Family support and months of therapy to relearn simple things, like walking and talking, still did not return him to his former robust and active self. His fiancée broke off their engagement. Life had to start over for Scott on very different terms. His successful transition was predicated on his will to adapt. His new role has taken him all over the country as a motivational speaker. It has inspired him to make a valuable contribution to his community and has brought him a new life.

Scott's story, and others like his, might be summed up with the following: "We are not owed the right to an easy voyage through life, but instead are presented with opportunity to achieve some level of greatness. The real regrets in life only come from not doing our best. All else is out of our control" (Phillips, 2000, p. 10). What we can control, however, and improve on significantly, is our ability to manage transitions into more satisfying levels of fulfillment in our lives.

A transition is precipitated by a change—brought about either by you or by an external event. Learning to manage change and its effects ensures you continual forward movement with your life.

Face the Changes

"New stuff is a cause of confusion and a source of creativity" (Lowe, 2000). That quote sums up the effect and benefit of change in our lives. Anything that is different from what we have experienced before is a little confusing. Different conditions also give us the opportunity to be creative about the way we use or play out the change.

There is no escaping the fact that we will go through many transitions due to life changes. Some of these changes are unexpected, while some of the changes we create ourselves. Some allow us to merely add new elements to our lives, while others demand that we close a door on something (or someone) familiar. Choosing not to change in the face of changing conditions has implications of its own. Some changes we create because we see advantages in going through the change process, and others we choose in order to remove ourselves from circumstances that are unhealthy or unpleasant.

Any type of change has been described as an "upending of expectancies" (Shaw, 1957). This is what happens when what is expected does not occur at all; rather, something entirely different takes place, requiring us to be creative and enlarge our view, to stretch ourselves beyond our original boundaries to new and different horizons. Even good changes and changes we drive ourselves can leave us feeling "upended." But they allow us to make transitions that we might otherwise not have chosen.

To successfully navigate the transition process that change creates, you must:

- **become proactive**
- **overcome loss and fears**
- **engage reason and creativity**
- **take action**

Even if you are one of the lucky ones and have avoided major upheavals in your life, you should now begin to acknowledge that change is both continual in its occurrence and continuous in its effects. This means that:

- Change will occur over and over throughout life.
- Change forever alters conditions and people.

Because of these two facts, you must develop a repertoire of skills that you can use when change occurs in your life.

Ben was in special forces in the military for 10 years and saw some pretty heated action in foreign domains. When he chose to separate from the service to pursue a steadier, less dangerous life and have a family, he was faced with several challenges. Though he had acquired a degree in mechanical engineering during his years in the military, what he felt most confident of was his special forces skills. However, he wanted to make a clean break and move into a completely new life.

Because change is likely to be common in your life, you must learn to develop strategies to manage change, rather than resist it. By developing these strategies, you prepare to take control and return to equilibrium quickly. These strategies give you a firm footing in the change journey and help you enjoy regular successes along the way.

1. What might be Ben's first obstacle to overcome as he attempts the transition to a kinder, gentler life?

2. If you were to write a statement of redefinition, a new way for Ben to think of and describe himself, what would it say?

3. List three behaviors that Ben may have to learn to change in order to begin the transition to a new life.

Become Proactive

Cultivate Resilience

The first strategy, then, in managing change is to cultivate resilience. Resilience is the ability to bounce back, to get past the rough spots in life. When we become less agitated and more adaptable in the face of change, we reduce our stress level. Dealing with life events at a lower stress level gives us the opportunity to focus more readily on solutions and action. Therefore, we are better able to move through the crisis unencumbered by an excess of emotional baggage.

The most resilient people are those who:

- are in good health
- have solid support systems
- are on good terms with some sort of belief system

Good health creates a feeling of strength; this includes a good diet and enough sleep to maintain a stable emotional state. Connections at all levels—family, community, clubs, or social groups, even pets—provide additional emotional support. A belief system, whether you call it religion or a spiritual set of truths you live by, allows you to be a part of a larger world and gives you some assurances.

You can also cultivate resilience by "practicing" to be flexible. Taking different routes home, experimenting with new foods, associating with people from other cultures, or even changing your office around can all help to desensitize you to changing conditions. Something as simple as thinking of "what if" scenarios can be beneficial. In your day-to-day life you can become stuck in predictable patterns, consciously or not. By breaking the pattern regularly, you will find yourself adapting more quickly to new conditions—large and small.

TRANSITION TIP   *Jeff Tillilie, Buyer*

Travel takes you to see what other places have to offer and how other people look at things. You get a bigger picture of life if you live several months in another country. When you realize that there are lifestyles and values different from yours, then you become more relaxed about changes and differences. I would advise anyone to travel to another country, even live there for awhile, and you'll get a better understanding of what you like because you have some comparisons.

Increase Perception

Another part of responding positively to change is to increase perception. If you are aware of what is going on in your work or personal world, you are less likely to be taken by surprise. If you understand that business and industry are continually looking for ways to cut costs and downsize, you will be more likely to invest your time in careers that fit into the current trends, rather than follow more traditional careers.

From a personal perspective, if you understand what factors affect your relationships, you will be able to short-circuit crisis and beef up emotional connections to withstand stressful conditions. When you become more observant and begin to see patterns of cause and effect in relationships, you can plan changes in your life that will help you adapt to new conditions as they evolve.

Overcome Loss and Fears

Whether a change has an immediate positive or negative flavor to it, a first reaction might be a feeling of loss: the loss of the familiar that has gone before or has always been. Another could be fear: second-guessing the future, an inability to control how events will unfold. Even a potentially positive change requires you to leave the familiar behind and enter a new and unknown situation.

Loss

Strong feelings are especially acute in cases of unexpected catastrophic or traumatic events. When catastrophic changes occur, movement through a grieving process is required in order to separate from past events and move on. Those who refuse to acknowledge the feelings and, thus, squelch this process can become stuck emotionally, maybe even geographically, unable to transition to the next level or place of their lives. Comments from people who are stuck might include, "I'm just an unemployed assembler. There's no point in learning a new career now," or, "I can't leave here; it's just too painful."

By acknowledging the feelings of loss (you are having them at some level whether you admit it openly or not), you give yourself the chance to work through them and move on. The grieving process takes time because there is a myriad of emotions involved, such as:

- denial—"This isn't really happening."
- bargaining—"If I just had another chance . . ."
- anger—"I hate the person (or event) that caused this."
- depression—"I might as well just give up."

- acceptance—"My life will be different, but I will go on." (Kübler-Ross, 1997)

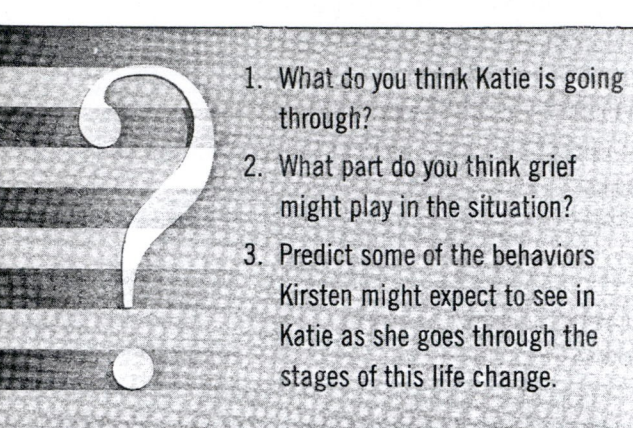

1. What do you think Katie is going through?

2. What part do you think grief might play in the situation?

3. Predict some of the behaviors Kirsten might expect to see in Katie as she goes through the stages of this life change.

Kirsten and Katie, identical twins, had been inseparable while growing up. Both had chicken pox at the same time, lettered in basketball in high school, enjoyed the same concerts, and disliked the same foods. During college, Kirsten met Jake, and when graduated, they decided to marry. At first Katie was happy for her sister and thought Jake was a good choice for her. Eventually, though, Katie began making up excuses to avoid going with Kirsten to wedding preparation activities. She became ill-tempered and withdrawn.

Fear

Those who fare best under unexpected circumstances are those who accept that a certain number of these life upheavals just happen, and they refuse to live in fear of them. For example, refusing to drive a car because of the possibility of an accident is unrealistic. However, cultivating a heightened awareness of how to respond in emergency situations can help you to come successfully out of even the worst scenarios, personal or professional. The key is to avoid handing over control of your life to fear. You do not want to see yourself as a powerless victim of fate.

The fact that you feel some apprehension, even anxiety, about a prospective or occurring change is a good thing; a little fear heightens the thought processes. Too much fear, however, paralyzes. Understanding fear and how people deal with fear will help you as you face the unknown.

For example, it costs nearly $10,000 to fully train a police dog, so a rather elaborate process is used to assess pups for their potential for that kind of work. An important element in the dog's character is how the dog handles fear-invoking situations.

The following test is performed: The dog is brought out into an open area on a leash. At a specified distance, a gun is fired. Imagine the responses of three different dogs:

1. The first dog cowers and frantically tries to get away, even yanking the leash from the handler.

2. The second dog stands there in a blasé fashion, as if to say, "Gun? What gun?"

3. The third dog starts and even cowers for a second or two, then stands up and immediately starts looking around with interest.

Dog #1 is paralyzed with fear and would be of no use in a tight spot, no matter how much training was applied. Dog #2 does not feel fear at all—it is just not in his experience set. (Among humans, some mountain climbers, bungee jumpers, and other extreme sports or daredevil types fall into this category.) He would be worthless in police work because an awareness of danger is an important part of staying alive. Dog #3 is intelligent enough to recognize a dangerous stimulus. It felt the initial, instinctive fear, then rose above it to go to work to discover what the threat was. Dog #3 would likely be chosen.

Feeling fear is not an indicator of an inability to handle difficult or unknown situations. Recognizing that fear should not stop you from consciously assessing a situation and moving forward is the sign of a good transition manager.

Positive Expectation

An effective response to change is meeting it with a positive expectation. Sometimes our negative expectations are the result of past experiences with change that had disastrous or unpleasant outcomes: a parent dying, a best friend moving away, an appearance-altering injury.

ACTIVITY   1.1

List three change events that occurred in your life while you were growing up (until age 18 or so). Beside each event, describe whether it had a positive or negative outcome.

1. _____

2. _____

3. _____

Did any of the events that seemed to have an initial negative result turn out to be positive as you look back on them?

Many of the feelings you have about a present or anticipated change depend on your past experiences or attitudes. Some people view change as exciting. Others feel it is the worst thing that could happen to them. People who fear or dread change may react negatively regardless of the potential benefit of the outcome.

There can be endless argument as to whether positive expectations make positive outcomes, or whether accumulating positive outcomes shores you up and creates positive expectations. You might agree, though, that going through life with an anticipation of things turning out well is better than a day-to-day dread of negative events. If nothing else, a positive expectation makes you feel hopeful, and out of this hopefulness comes clear thinking that can lead the event to a positive outcome.

Engage Reason and Creativity

By definition, transition management, self-development, and effective living suggest a strategy of change, of dynamic movement, of adaptation, and of growth. By using reason and creativity to deal with the world, and the people and events in it, you embrace growth in the direction that will create the most happiness for you.

Reason

Change is the catalyst for who you will become in the future. Rationally, if you aspire to a full and satisfying life, you must respect the very nature of change and allow it to shape you into a strong and vibrant individual.

Rational people are able to see conditions in their lives that require change or can recognize changing situations that require adaptation. However, in many cases, change is likely to begin with the need to eliminate some discomfort in our lives. This discomfort can come from a general desire for more out of life or from crisis and pain that cause a quick and radical change. If you view discomfort as a motivator, as a reason to change to a new, more effective behavior, then it could become a welcome signal.

Though sometimes you might choose a change that can cause you to have temporary pain, you do it through reason, research, and conscious decision making, and you do it to make an improvement in your life.

1. What motivated Thomas to leave his home?

2. What obstacles might have existed to stop him from making the change he wanted?

3. What changes do you think he had to make in his life during the first year in the United States?

After a close friend was shot in a fight, Thomas decided that to make his life better, he had to leave Jamaica. When he was 18, he left the island his family had lived on for over 100 years and moved to a new culture in an American city. After attending a university, he completed a physician's assistant program and soon received a job offer in Dallas. Today, though he has little or no contact with his old life, he is quite happy.

Change requires movement. It is possible you will stay where you are right now in your life unless some sort of discomfort motivates you to make that move. Some of the most successful people owe their motivation to having grown up in poverty or fear. If you experience pain or unhappiness in your life, you might consider it as a signal for change.

ACTIVITY   1.2

Is there a situation or set of conditions in your life that you currently view as painful, disturbing, or unpleasant? If so, describe it briefly here.

_____

_____

Describe what changes this situation might motivate you to make in your life.

_____

_____

Some changes are complex, such as moving to a foreign country, securing an advanced degree, changing careers, or getting married to someone who has children. All of these changes require crossing a number of thresholds before a complete transition occurs and emotional balance is regained.

Creativity

Change can be a creative expression of your life and will. To stimulate creativity, you may want to begin with *visualization*. This is a technique that many successful individuals practice. In a quiet place or just before you fall asleep at night, begin by "painting" in your mind's eye the success scene you want to create for yourself. The more detail you can bring into this scene, the clearer your path to change will be. Each time you do this exercise, add more detail: people, places, specific circumstances.

If you are patient with the process and practice this simple technique over and over, both the scene and the activities required to reach your goal will become clearer. In addition, you will find that your sense of purpose and determination increase with each practice.

The only caution is that you focus on changes for yourself only. Attempts to create change in your life by wanting others to change or by wishing harm to others are ineffective and can be unhealthy. Your unconscious mind can be very powerful, so be certain that you are committed to a positive outcome. You may get everything you ask for. With your visualization, you become more aware of factors that can contribute to your goal—you recognize opportunities.

Reason leads you to see the need for a change or the need to adapt to an external change. Creativity helps you to frame the situation into an effective transition to a new level. Once you have used your reason and creativity to see your path, then you must embrace the change and take action.

Take Action

Remember, if your decision when faced with a need for change is to take no action, that is a choice also. Abdicating from the director's role does not relieve you of your part in the play—it only takes away a great deal of the control you have over what you do. Changes can have far-reaching effects and require that you go through many transitions in order to arrive at a sense of equilibrium. Sometimes these transitions are harder to make because you are not sure of the right steps to take. Sometimes you even procrastinate out of fear of failure and put off a potentially enriching experience.

The key to managing change is to live forward. What is past cannot be viewed as either a monument or a curse. It must, instead, be a springboard, a launch site.

Choose Change

Time and events go forward. People who do not also go forward run the risk of being weighed down by old events and bewildered by new circumstances. Your life will be different every day. You can choose positively: to grow, to learn, to move with change, to become more understanding about events, to develop new life and professional skills, to cultivate new relationships and improve old ones. Or you can stagnate—live a life devoid of growth, accomplishment, self-esteem, and pride in having overcome obstacles.

Albert, who had been with his company through three mergers and four management changes, explained his longevity to a coworker. "I go in the first day and ask the new management what they want me to do." He has chosen change over resistance. There might be many reasons to choose change:

- A change may be to your advantage.
- A change may promise to be interesting.
- A change may be a chance to learn something new and useful.
- A change may help you keep out the "cobwebs" of monotony.
- A change may take you a step closer to your goal.
- A change of your choice makes you feel powerful and in charge of your life.

Commit Effort

The next step is to make a commitment. In order to make your plans materialize, you have to commit to follow through on the work that will be involved in making the change. This commitment is the determination to be persistent, no matter how inconvenient or difficult the task may become. Without commitment, your effort will be halfhearted, leading only to partial success. Commitment is the driving force that steers you in the right direction. It assures you of the reward you seek.

Commitment and follow-through will take you further than any talent or particular advantage. Barry Mitchell, a professional football player for St. Louis, says, "Never quit. No matter if others say your dream is impossible, no matter if they laugh at you for even having such a dream, no matter if what it takes to get there is so hard you feel you can't go another step. Never quit and you'll win over all the others who do."

Operationalize Commitment

The next step is to put into practice the actions or thoughts that are required to get you to your desired outcome. Action brings you back to being in a balanced and stable state with a sense of confidence.

After you get a clear picture of the new conditions you are moving toward, decide what behaviors you must incorporate in your life to bring you to the success point. This part is crucial to your success. You may have to develop new skills; you may have to do some things differently. You may decide you need speech therapy or a new set of friends, maybe a new degree or professional certification. When you begin to practice these new behaviors, they may feel awkward at first. Don't worry about that. Remember your commitment to follow through and be persistent. Allow yourself several weeks to get used to the new way of doing things. Changes do not happen overnight, so be patient with yourself.

An important hint here is that practicing in your mind is often as beneficial as practicing an action. You can practice the skills related to managing changes by rehearsing scenes in your mind and applying your new knowledge to solving problems that may come up. Go back to your visualization technique and create a scene in which you successfully negotiate a raise or have a relaxed conversation with the object of your previously unvoiced affection. No one will see you do this, and you will be preparing yourself for the future.

Relax

The final stage of action is *relax*. Let yourself go through the change process in a calm way. Don't hassle yourself. Be prepared for unexpected occurrences. Above all, don't panic if the desired change does not occur immediately. These things happen in their own time—when you are ready—not when you think you are ready. Trust your subconscious to guide you in the direction you have set.

Wait

Sometimes we have to wait for our plans to unfold. Katie ran a bike and skateboard shop in a small community outside a large city. She was liked and respected by the sports and bike racing community. When a large, new indoor extreme sports park opened just 12 miles away, a competing skateboard and bike shop was invited to set up in the complex, guaranteeing a stream of customers and business success. Katie, disappointed, continued to offer service and support to area enthusiasts. Finally, in just a few months, the owner of the sports park and the management of the shop agreed to end their association after a disagreement. Katie moved in and her business is now thriving.

Observe

Another way you may have to relax is to observe something changing, rather than interfere with the natural evolutionary process. A change may come in a different form than you initially expected. You must be able to recognize that by relaxing and going with the change as it is occurring, you will be able to ride to the other side of the transition—to your new place of satisfaction. If you do not get the job with the advertising agency, you might instead find a contact in a Web page design company—similar environment, just a slightly different end product. Relax and let the process flow as it must without interruptions.

You can be a change agent for yourself. Remember, however, that you cannot change other people. You cannot make your parents suddenly become as you would like them. You cannot make a friend leave an abusive relationship or quit using alcohol or drugs excessively, and you cannot make your boss suddenly become even tempered. In some cases, relaxing means letting go of responsibility for someone else's choices. Focus on your own changes and enjoy the effects of those.

Life can be a creative process of directing your energy, anticipating changes in the world around you, and designing positive outcomes.

Change in the Professional World

Changes you go through as you make a transition to a new job will likely be compounded by changes that take place in your industry and your company. The job you have just secured may have been created due to a market shift or a change in technology. Many models and constructs have been used to describe change and its effects on business:

- systems theory, which looks at the organization as a system that interacts with and responds to forces in the environment
- terms such as *unfreezing* and *refreezing* describe the breakdown of old policies and long-standing procedures and the establishment of new ones
- paradigm shifts, which take place when people recognize that old assumptions and explanations no longer fit newly discovered discrepancies
- the idea that crazy times require crazy management

Today's information brokering has created an industry that has unlimited resources—there is no scarcity of information, and there is not likely to be. In fact, the opposite is to be expected. New distribution channels created by Internet commerce have opened up world markets in a way trade agreements never could. Companies are spawned by technology innovation and within a few years or even months create millionaires out of 25-year-olds, or they fold because they could not get to market before someone else did. Speculation and visions of riches from a technology home run may blind participants to the potentially harsh reality of risk in these industries and inspire new rounds of speculation, much like the lure of the lottery jackpot.

Increasingly sophisticated technical skills are needed to support all of these advancements. For this reason, companies are going outside national borders to find the talent and expertise they need. The influx of people from other cultures has changed the face of whole companies and even cities. Austin, Texas, for example, has recently gained a significant population from India that has come into the community to work in the growing high-tech industry. With these new residents comes their culture, including belief systems, customs, and foods. Larger numbers of foreign students are graduating from American Ivy League colleges and obtaining jobs outside their country of origin.

For these reasons trying to generate a model of organizational change processes in the twenty-first century becomes much like trying to capture fog in a jar or draw wind. But organizations are made up of people, and so they respond to change much as you or I would. Typically, organizations:

- resist change that is forced on them
- seek changes that eliminate pain
- implement changes that promise new vitality or profits

Resist Change

Resistance may come in the form of "digging in"—viewing change as an enemy to be overcome, or at least waited out. This way of thinking assumes that things staying the same is good. There is some logic to this because the company could be getting along quite well, for now, so changing conditions, competitors, or trends are seen as merely blips on the screen or temporary storms to be weathered. Many strong companies with adequate cash reserves can, indeed, get through some fluctuations in conditions. However, a failure to monitor and change with new circumstances can cause irretrievable losses.

Individual managers or employees can argue with upper-level decision makers or exercise power plays to try to circumvent plans that involve change. Ultimately, though, resistance takes considerably more energy and risk than skillfully managing change.

Seek Change to Relieve Discomfort

When competitive position begins to slip, delivery or manufacturing problems hamper the ease of doing business, personnel issues or information system problems cripple operations, or cash flow is in the wrong direction, companies actively seek to make changes to relieve the pain of these problems. There are a variety of ways this might be done, and all directly affect the first-year employee.

Bring in Consultants

Experts in the industry or professional consultants analyze the situation by doing a needs assessment. This involves interviews with employees at all levels of the organization, with customers, and possibly even with competitors. It also includes a detailed examination of the external and internal processes and conditions to find out what the problem really is and what is required to fix it. Then, the consultants make recommendations that could involve process or system revamping, reorganization of functional areas, elimination of certain departments, or even selling off whole units.

You will likely be interviewed in this process if you have been with the organization less than a year. Keep in mind the purpose of the interviews and monitor your assessment of the situation or your take on the best course of action. You may indeed have a beneficial, fresh approach, but it is also possible that you do not have a clear picture of the entire operation, so the scope of your responses should be in your own area.

As a result of the consultants' recommendations, it is possible that new people will be hired to support new strategic directions—while other staff may be laid off to reduce redundancy or costly areas in the existing structure.

Fresh into the workplace with a double major in business and engineering, Benyiata chose a large, stable company that she felt had a lot of opportunity for movement and challenge. After only eight months on the job, her manager asked her to share her "impressions" of the company with a consultant who had been brought in by management. After only 20 minutes, Benyiata had established a good rapport with the consultant, who began to hint to her some changes management was considering. One of the changes would benefit Benyiata directly, but would cause her manager to lose his job.

1. What do you think Benyiata is feeling?
2. Should she agree or disagree with the consultant's view of the situation?
3. Why would a company let go a manager who had been with them for some time and keep an entry-level person?

Reverse Engineering

Reverse engineering looks at processes and results that are central to the company's doing business. It is called reverse engineering because the approach is to go to the end or result, then figure out how to achieve that result. Often processes and procedures become unwieldy due to the repeated addition of short-term fixes as the demands of the business become more extensive and complex. Usually, people in the affected departments are put on a project team, possibly for the first time together, and occasionally an outsider is added for a totally fresh perspective.

Any department can be a part of a change team to improve the company's business, and any employee can be asked to join the team. You might be included on the team to represent your area. It is important that you know and can explain clearly what part your department or function plays in the total process. A change team can be a good way to meet and work with other employees and managers outside your immediate area. Sometimes, it is a way to let you in on the workings and strategies of the entire organization. You may be asked to make specific change recommendations. Ideally, you will be able to develop a well-thought-out formal document or presentation. Report writing and presentation skills are valuable in such situations.

Divest or Sell

As mentioned previously, to fix what a company sees as a drain on company resources, an irretrievable situation, or an irreversible trend, sometimes the board of directors or CEO decides that selling off part or all of the business is the best route. Cutting losses when investors are involved is sometimes chosen as a preferred strategy, even over the objections of management.

The companies with the most integrity tell all employees that this step is being taken and offer outplacement services or generous severance packages to those directly affected. However, in order to look good for a potential buyer or to prevent an untimely drop in stock prices, sometimes this kind of decision is held close by upper management until the very last minute. You cannot always see this kind of change coming, but diligent monitoring of your company's position in the market may alert you to anything drastic that might happen.

Seek Change to Ensure Growth and Ongoing Improvement

Some companies survive by being leaders in the continuous advancement of technology or service offerings. They constantly seek new markets, strive to respond rapidly to market changes, and work to develop new products or services ahead of competitors. Their structure is less rigid than companies that operate in more stable environments. Often, a single employee has duties in several different departments and reports to more than one project manager. In these companies, change is constant and change agents are valued.

Rapid Reactors

Rapid reactors are organizations that can retool or shift resources quickly in response to opportunities or threats in their operating environment, such as the removal of a competitor or the loss of a raw materials supplier. They are lean, without many layers of management; most employees do many different tasks, and everyone works long hours. If you are in one of these companies, be prepared to abandon a project and shift all of your energies and commitment to a new one on a day's notice. Taking too much ownership of a pet project can make you resent the organization's right to direct you wherever it wants. Keeping abreast of the competition and of market trends will help you to avoid being taken by surprise by one of these quick adaptations.

Proactive Leaders

Companies with large investments in research and development seek to maintain solvency by leading the market in some way: cost, time, or quality. Continuous improvement is a term often heard. Employees may be rewarded with cash or other bonuses for suggestions that advance the company's position or improve efficiency and productivity. Staying out in front gives them an advantage, as long as they can do that profitably. They are out on the edge of the technology in their industry and regularly unveil the newest advancements at trade shows and conferences.

To stay on that cutting edge, however, can sometimes be costly, and if your company does not have enough offerings that generate large, steady streams of income, capital reserves can be drained. You may be hired by one of these companies because they want fresh, up-to-the-minute skills and because they perceive you as an idea person. Do not let them down. Continue to develop what you have to offer the company, always meet deadlines, and focus study and thought on ways to constantly improve operations or market advantage.

ACTIVITY 1.3

Either in your current profession or in your intended field of work locate companies that fit these descriptions.

1. Large, stable
2. Small, lean, responsive
3. Cutting-edge technology leader or trendsetter

Monitor the companies you selected for 30 days to see how each plays out its approach. (Reading press releases or investor relations information on the company Web site or looking at industry publications will help provide this information.)

Some changes that may occur in your personal or professional life suggest pleasant or positive outcomes and evoke enthusiasm. Other changes can be extremely painful and require many weeks of adjustment. Both happy and painful change events can be stressful. In the midst of these change events, it is sometimes difficult to remember that those around us are likely undergoing the effects of these events also. Compassion and understanding of those who are close to you should be added to the skills for managing change that you have learned in this chapter.

Mapping Pathways for Change

As you move from the life of a college student to being a working professional, or from one career to another, you will make successful transitions if you internalize and practice the following:

- **Self-nurturing**—accepting responsibility for and taking care of your physical, emotional, and relational self.
- **Self-advocacy**—accepting responsibility for the development, direction, and ultimate satisfaction of your professional self.

Each time you finish a chapter in this book, you will have examined a new area of growth in your life. You will be asked to write down some goals in the areas of your life that relate to self-nurturing and self-advocacy. These goals help guide the transition process through the life changes you are experiencing and driving.

TRANSITION SKILLS SUMMARY

Face the changes

Become proactive

Overcome loss and fears

Engage reason and creativity

Take action

Observe change in the professional world

GOAL SETTING

My self-nurturing goals for managing change in my personal life are:

_____

_____

_____

My self-advocacy goals for managing change in my professional life are:

_____

_____

_____

C O A C H ' S   C O R N E R

"Improvisation is a natural event for all conscious beings."

Improv is the perfect response to the world we find ourselves in today. By definition, it summons up a picture of acting in adaptation to the moment, to whatever is presented to the performer. Thus, its methods certainly fit the world of industry, especially the quickening cycles of change we are seeing today: more changes in ever shorter periods of time. Improv, in spite of the way it may appear to an observer, does have specific guidelines for its application in unexpected and sometimes very surprising situations. Those same guidelines can help anyone, or any organization, that is hurling through the ever shape-shifting space and time.

First principle: Stay in the present moment.

At any given time, we are processing at many levels of complexity and awareness and in many places along the time line of our lives. A smell of bread baking reminds us of our youth in grandma's kitchen; a situation brings back fear of a similar situation that turned out horribly; a smile causes us to speculate about what could be possible with that person. Staying focused, like when an artist is concentrating on the detail of a person's face or when a martial arts or yoga practitioner works to perfect a position and then hold it, is difficult for most of us. In the present moment, change becomes nearly irrelevant because differences are in comparison to what went before and only intimidating in concern about what is coming after. Stress drops dramatically when we can concentrate on now and the events that are occurring, not replaying, comparing, or projecting to some other time.

Second principle: Strive to be completely honest with yourself.

Improvisation is a human occurrence, as is change. Change does not affect buildings or landscape, in that these being inanimate do not choose a reaction. Recognize in

(continued)

yourself what is going on at any given moment: fear, surprise, confusion, delight. The next level of honesty is recognizing the effects of outside influences on the moment. "I am really angry now, but looking at the situation, I can see that mostly I am disappointed that I was not chosen." Honesty with yourself is liberating, much like confession is for some.

Third principle: Be completely honest with at least one other person.

This does not consist of blurting out every thought you have about someone or some situation, but about being straightforward in what you do say. Honesty is related to happiness; if you are not hiding, you are sharing. Choose one person with whom you can be completely honest. This can be useful in the way you relate to others: I agree to tell you if your actions offend me, and you agree to do the same. We are playing the same game at the same time. If a change causes you to be fearful, have one person in whom you can confide this fear and with whom you can practice honesty and candor.

Fourth principle: You must put your work in public view.

This principle requires action, not contemplation or intellectualizing. You participate in the process; you practice your adaptations to the changing conditions. However, it is a step process, one at a time, where you practice being creative about your responses to different and evolving situations. Staying honest, you examine the results of your experimentation and evaluate whether that action achieved what you wanted. If it did not, then another creative approach should be tested.

ROBERT LOWE, coach, trainer, and author of *Improvisation, Inc: Harnessing Spontaneity to Engage People and Groups*, Jossey-Bass/Pfeiffer (2000)

CHAPTER 2

Moving Toward Your Goals

Y ou drive the transitions in your life and are the agent of your own success. A realization such as this can be both freeing and frightening because it implies no restrictions on where you can go and what you can do with your life. The other side of this freedom, though, is that it does not allow you to blame others for any slips or shortfalls along the way.

As you begin to actively manage changes in your life, you can shape each one into a transition that leads you closer to your goals. Change can be defined as merely some event or condition that is different or new. However, when you begin to set goals for your life, you will look at change events differently. Goal setting:

- gives you a direction
- defines areas in which to focus your energy
- requires you to take stock of your situation in some sort of methodical way
- provides a basis for decision making

The process itself has many elements: expectation, goal setting, assessment, plans, resources, and then action.

Expectation

You should have great expectations of your own life. If you expect little that is satisfying or meaningful, you will have little. Expectation is different from wishing and hoping; it is more in the realm of planning and acting. The way you think about your own potential determines the expectations you have. Your expectations define your dreams and your dreams generate your goals.

Though there will always, of course, be different degrees of success with each act and each transition, the critical point is that you start thinking of *yourself* as a success now. Until you do this, you may accept limits on what your life truly can be, limits on your expectations. Thus, the first element in the development of a satisfying life is to perceive the possibility in potential.

Shape Perceptions

When you perceive yourself as a successful person and start adding new skills and behaviors that support that perception, you begin the transition to new successes. Every change you make, every new talent you discover, and every new skill you acquire alters your potential. Thus, even if you have not seen yourself as particularly successful in the past, one change can forever shift your path to a new direction.

One of the key steps to beginning to perceive yourself as successful is to take stock of every important event in your life in terms of the successes. By looking at your life as a history of accomplishments instead of shortcomings, you can begin to change old patterns of criticizing, complaining about, or making excuses for everything that has not gone right. When you begin to accept responsibility for your role in the hardships and mistakes of the past, you also are entitled to claim the personal victories as well. Sometimes, learning gained from a past mistake or insight gleaned in the midst of a miserable experience becomes an important building block for the challenges of the future.

1. Is Star's friend expressing a positive or a negative attitude about her past difficulties?

2. Are there ever good results that eventually come out of a mistake or a failure?

3. Why are some mistakes called "good learning experiences"?

Raised in an angry family that regularly complained how the world had cheated them, Star grew up with little optimism or expectation of joy in life. After she left home, she went to work. She was surprised at how many of the people she met truly enjoyed their lives and felt good about the future. One day, her close friend in the office confessed to her, "You know, Star, I used to get upset over every bad thing that happened in my life, every mistake, every disappointment, every failure. But I know now that those rough times are just passing through. Not much point in getting too excited about them."

Wishing and hoping are not a cure for misery or pain; however, thoughtfully assessing your strengths and options and then acting on them will take you toward what you desire. As soon as you accept a less than satisfying life, you limit your expectations. This is called *resignation*, or in more casual terms, *settling*. Wanting and wishing are passive activities and require no real work or commitment on your part. *Expecting* means that you live your life as if the future you desire *will* happen—not *might* happen—and you direct effort toward that expectation.

Admittedly, expectation can lead to disappointment; that may be why so many of us have abandoned it as a guide for our lives. Many of the life-changing events you are expected to transition through are hard, but "any route you choose in life (and they are all your choice) comes with difficulty as a built-in feature at no extra charge. The real question you have to ask yourself is not what is difficult, but what rewards do you want out of life?" (Phillips, 2000).

When you see yourself as successful, you begin to see transitions, and the adaptations that go along with them, as bringing you ever closer to the life you desire. You perceive an event not as either a success or failure, but as a degree of contribution to your future. A willingness to adapt to new situations is a reflection of your belief that your life is moving in a positive direction. It is an ongoing process of moving, of not just finding a foothold, but making a place for yourself on the other side of life's events.

People who do not see themselves as successful may view any movement or change as necessarily bad and resist making healthy transitions. Their expectation for their future is low. When this happens, they usually become stuck, stuck in old ways of thinking that no longer work in their lives, stuck in the past of what might have been or once was, or even stuck in a pattern of predictable pain, and miss entirely the potential in the new. Once you see the future through the eyes of positive expectation, you will be expanding the way you relate to both old and new aspects of your life.

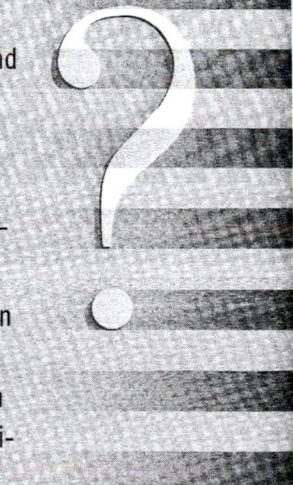

1. What do you think was the biggest adjustment David and Alicia had to make?

2. What role do you think their expectations about marriage will play in making their marriage a success?

3. What do you think will happen if either fails to make a good transition and continues with the same activities and priorities as when single?

When David and Alicia got married, their lives changed. They could no longer relate to the world in the same way they did when they were single. They had to make allowances for new priorities, new goals, and new ways of relating to the world. Although there was great joy in doing so, it still required some adjusting.

2.1 ACTIVITY

1. Describe an upcoming life event in terms of your expectation about it.

_____

_____

_____

2. Now, describe what a successful transition to the other side of the event would be like.

_____

_____

_____

By seeing yourself as successful, you develop a healthy approach to life transitions, which enhances your potential for future success. When you expect a satisfying life, you base your behavior on that expectation. Characteristics of that behavior include:

- flexibility
- a desire to learn
- awareness
- a willingness to take unfamiliar avenues
- a choice to stretch past any boundaries you might have perceived
- a belief that you can manage difficult spots in life

Positive expectation is a way of approaching life as if it were a river and you are cruising effortlessly down the waterway. With this attitude, you generate less resistance and prepare eagerly for whatever eventuality you come on. You free yourself to dream, and out of the dreams come goals to make those dreams happen.

Goal Setting

Goals, like diamonds, have many facets: they must grow out of your dreams, reflect your values and priorities, and always leave room for flexibility and new options.

Dreams

Integrating your dreams into your life helps you frame a *new destiny*. A person's destiny is the end product of what he or she believes can happen and then lives or acts out. The course of history can be, and has repeatedly been, changed by people who believed strongly enough in a dream and who let that belief drive all their actions. An example is the opening up of the former Soviet Union to the rest of the world. That action began with one person who chose to think and live a different destiny. He increased the potential for a successful change for an entire nation.

Very young children see the world as full of promise and delight. Every event is a celebration; every spring a wonder; every door a threshold to a new adventure. But, somewhere along the way some children "get smart." They learn the disappointment of the dream that does not come true. After many disappointments, they learn not to set their sights too high. Their chance for happiness becomes limited by their acceptance of a limited potential. Then, in their minds—perhaps even in your own mind—the world becomes not okay; it becomes a place of unfulfilled expectations.

The "logical" conclusion for us as adults becomes, then, that dreaming is a foolish waste of time. But without the dream of what can be, we have no road map for the journey to our own happiness. We then give the power over our future away to some unguided "fate" that buffets us about with the changing circumstances of the day.

Dreams can become goals; goals can become actions that lead to a positive, satisfying life. Your dreams are the threshold to your potential.

In Activity 2.2, you are asked to put away any negative "reality" limitations that you have learned from your past and, instead, to dream. Your dreams are important, as are the many transitions you will go through to reach them.

ACTIVITY 2.2

Write down the dreams you have about what your future could be. Divide the dreams into professional dreams and personal dreams.

Professional dreams:

_____

_____

_____

Personal dreams:

_____

_____

_____

Priorities and Values

Remember the old adage that says, "Be careful what you wish for; you might get it." At first that seems like such a foolish warning. Why wouldn't someone want what he wished for? Look at the diagram for a model of just this idea.

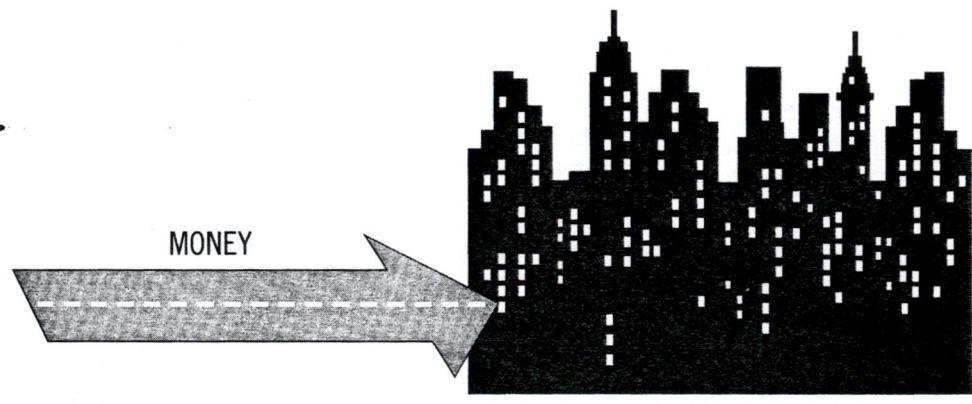

MONEY

For many, prioritizing involves pursuing as much money as possible within a productive lifespan. Though it may seem like a far-off vision to you now because you are just launching your career or are making a major change in your professional direction, the single-minded pursuit of money yields just that: money. You arrive in _Success City_ and find it lavishly furnished with the finest homes, cars, clothes, and all the accouterments of wealth. However, there are no people there; you are there alone because personal relationships cannot withstand the kind of perpetual exclusion created by the demands of money-oriented life pursuit.

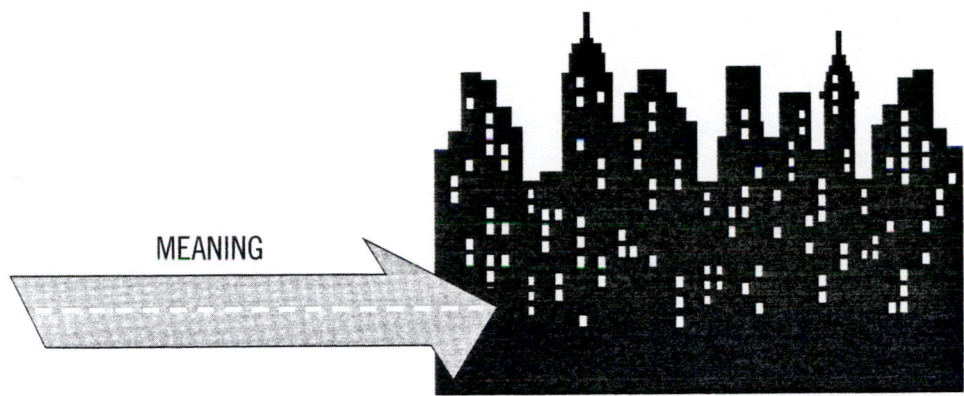

MEANING

On the other side of the priority road is the path of meaning. This pursuit gives great satisfaction and sense of purpose to those who embrace it. Many people on this path relate that they feel a sense of purpose and fulfillment in what they do and the contribution they make. When these people arrive at *Success City*, it is teeming with people, but the cars are often broken, the houses have little furniture, and the people work until they are quite old because they need the money to live.

Before this begins to sound like a discussion on the evils of money or the noble, but financially anemic, life of service, take just a moment to consider the following proposition as you think about setting priorities in your own life.

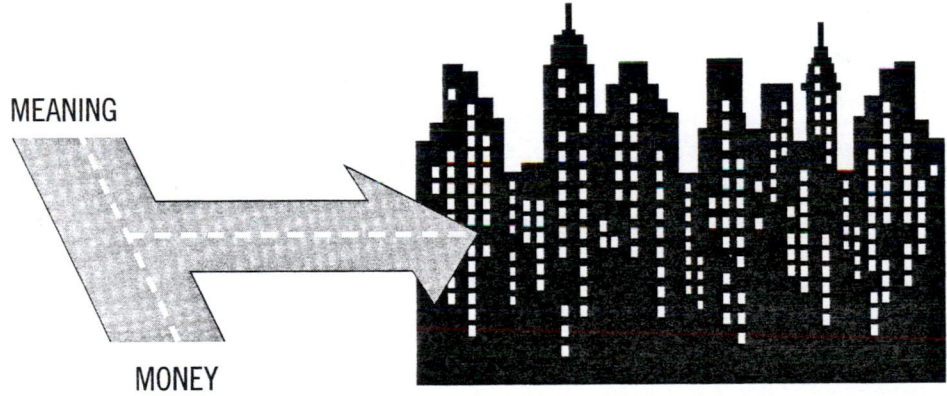

MEANING

MONEY

Making a decent living at something that brings you joy and purpose is not an immoral or self-absorbed pursuit at all. People who are addicted to work have convinced themselves that success is about money, but they have never quite figured out how much money it will take to define that success. So, they step onto the work-more–be-more-successful wheel that rolls right past their relationships.

On the other hand, those who enjoy pursuits that make meaningful contributions too often find they can barely eke out a living. In the case of many service careers, such as social work, teaching, and health care, the burnout rate is tremendous, creating hordes of walking wounded. Individuals may stay year after year in careers that drain them, or they may abandon their original pursuit from sheer exhaustion. These people may end as casualties of the endless need in our society.

As a person draws to the close of her life, the quality of that life is what is remembered. Several elements go into an assessment of the quality of life. Ideally, you find a job that pays you comfortably for doing only what you enjoy and are good at (some people's definition of success). More realistically, though, you come to that position in life after some careful investigation of the career world and some calculated resume building. But the person pursuing success defined by money never quite gets enough. To define and set priorities for your own successful life, you may want to consider the following perspectives:

- The 40–60 years that you have to actively pursue employment leaves time for at least two 20-year careers.
- Honest introspection to differentiate what you *need* to be happy from what you *want* dramatically affects how you define success.
- The job you need to be both successful and happy may have to be created by you or discovered at some later date.
- Understanding and pursuing balance in all elements of your personal and professional life brings joy; a life out of balance often fails in every quarter.

Without setting your physical, emotional, and relational well-being priorities, you can easily find yourself feeling isolated, frustrated, and burned out. Priorities that include both personal and career growth will lead you to the goal of a satisfying and rewarding career position.

Clint and his wife-to-be felt strongly about developing a source for spiritual inspiration in the form of Christian music and messages. Their careers in the technology industry provided a comfortable lifestyle, but not enough money to start a radio station or buy time on a cable TV channel for that purpose. Now, however, the Internet has made it possible for them to achieve their goal through a religious Web site.

Goals

It does not matter whether you are leaving college at the end of 16 or 17 straight years of education, changing your profession after a career dead end, or entering the workforce after having been away from work and school for many years. The challenge is the same for all: set goals that reflect who you are and where you want to go with your life.

- The goals must involve both you and those close to you.
- The goals must have flexibility built into them to allow for unanticipated opportunities.
- The actions required to reach the goals must offer some satisfaction in themselves.
- Goal statements should include benchmarks to note your achievements along the way.

Look at the goals for a small town. The goals grew out of the dream city planners had for a quality life for the citizens.

"The community is safe and feels safe." (vision—dream)

Action items (goals) to make this happen:

- Increased police presence in the neighborhoods
- New strategies to improve the business district
- Improved policies for extended-stay hotels
- Improved commercial environment (including lighting)

"The image of the community is positive." (vision—dream)

Action items (goals)

- Boundaries are defined and attractive
- Landscaped medians, rights-of-way, and sidewalks are well maintained
- Litter is removed consistently

Each goal should have action as its guideline, but include an element of flexibility. Each new skill you acquire and each change you make in yourself or your situation alters your options. A goal you have at one stage in your life, such as maturity or skill development, may be too limited later on. When you achieve growth, you are at a new level and new possibilities are within your reach. A good parallel to this is mountain climbing; each new height you reach gives you a new vista that was unavailable to you from the lower levels.

In a rapidly changing world, you cannot know your options even just five years down the road because new careers and lifestyle choices are emerging constantly. Goals that are evolving and that reflect changing aspirations are not set in concrete; rather, they are malleable to allow for freedom of choice and to reflect growth.

Whichever way you direct your life, the goals you develop should be balanced in two areas:

1. Self-nurturing—goals that relate to your personal and relational life.
2. Self-advocacy—goals that are appropriate for advancing your professional life.

The goal activities should offer some satisfaction or joy in themselves. Great golfers and great musicians know this; they derive pleasure out of the basic activity of their profession. The great golfer still enjoys hitting the ball; the great pianist will seize every opportunity to play, paid or not. Your goals should spring from knowing what is valuable to you and what gives you enjoyment. Remember, define goals as things you will do, not "wouldn't it be nice if . . ."

Finally, some major life goals are so far away that it is easy to run out of steam before you reach them. When you set *benchmarks* or milestones along the way—intermediate and short-term goals—then you have many opportunities to celebrate success. Goals should inspire, not be reminders of how much you have not yet done. When you recognize achievement at points along the way, then you can stay motivated and feel good as you progress; you do not have to wait until you reach the final goal to feel successful.

In an interview, a well-known actor said that he wished his mother had made him practice the piano when he was young. If she had, he would be able to play expertly today.

1. What is the weakness in his logic?
2. Whom does he hold responsible for his lack of success?
3. What do you think makes a person doggedly pursue excellence in her field, whether it is highly lucrative or not?

2.3 ACTIVITY

Write a goal statement that will help you verbalize the specifics of your dream. List two benchmarks you can use as success points along the way. (Be sure that the benchmarks are not longer than two years apart.)

Goal _____

1. _____
2. _____

Assessment

By thoughtfully looking at where you are now, in relation to where you want to be, you are making the first move toward improving the quality of your life and ensuring positive transitions. After you have begun the examination process, you will have a clearer picture of the areas of your life or behaviors that have to be changed. The assessment process helps you recognize the strengths you already have and uncover areas that need shoring up.

TRANSITION TIP   *Major George Kelly (retired)*

Getting out of the military after 20 years, which was my whole adult life up to that point, scared me, stressed me out. But five years before retirement, I started to plan. I did a self-evaluation of skills and qualifications that would translate into private sector terms. I engineered internal moves from weapons, where I had been trained originally, to computers. A move into a new job is stressful; a whole new career is even more so. Just look at the options that will take you where you want to go, then find out what it takes to get there. After that it's just a matter of picking up the skills and knowledge.

Don't be afraid to look at yourself honestly. Don't let the need to be perfect get in your way. Your weaknesses are temporary and can be worked on constructively if you address them realistically now with an eye toward your future.

Lee, a 35-year-old video production assistant, worked for a documentary filming company, but dreamed of actually producing these types of films. He went back to school to get the degree he needed. But as an adult with Attention Deficit Disorder (ADD), he had already lost two prior jobs because of his inability to organize and complete all of his work. When he assessed his situation, he realized that he had to work with professionals who could help him manage his ADD. He consulted a medical doctor and also joined a group of adults with ADD. There he met a producer who had a company that made educational films for children.

1. How do you think Lee's chances for reaching his dream have been affected by his straightforward assessment of his situation?

2. Why do you think he waited as long as he did (losing two jobs) to address the problem that was limiting him?

Periodically doing a check-up on your situation helps you keep your life on track: your WHOLE life, not just your personal and not just your professional life. Keeping a watchful eye on your relationships, looking for potential areas for growth, and monitoring the direction your career is headed are regular check-ups that let you catch and fix problem areas before they have a negative effect on your progress.

Improving relationships just makes everything else in your life go better. By applying the knowledge and skills gained from making successful transitions, you can envision the other side of any troubles or uncertainty. You can see the place where life works both for you and for the people close to you. By remembering to set relationship goals as well as professional goals, you not only improve your present situation, you can also begin to explore future possibilities with confidence.

Increased relationship stability will improve your home life (your self-nurturing support) and increase your professional networking abilities (your self-advocacy opportunities). An added bonus of continually improving your relationships is that you teach any children you may have how to develop good relationships. There is no better legacy to give them for their future happiness.

Once you have determined where you want to go and, based on your assessment of the situation, what is required to arrive there, you have to start gathering the resources you need.

Resources

Any person who is facing life changes has to construct the transition process with the right tools and skills. Hanging a storm door without an electric drill or a screwdriver is arduous and inordinately time-consuming. Knowing the best methods for positioning and hanging the door is also important.

Just as none of us are born with all of the skills we need to hang a storm door, none of us has come equipped with all of the resources we need to go though life in a perfect way. It is necessary for us to constantly discover what could help us along. What each person requires is a set of tools that can be stored and brought out when the need arises. It is like what a carpenter would do when he builds a house.

A tool is a resource that makes it easier to perform a job or manage a life. Obviously, the more tools, the easier it is to address difficult life events and construct effective transitions. Although everyone does not need the same tools, there are general categories.

Information Services

One tool everyone requires to ensure successful transitions is information. Many vehicles exist today that can help you find out what you need to know.

You are exposed to newspapers, books, magazines, computers, and experts in many fields. The Internet, CD-ROM information services, and databases with seemingly inexhaustible sources can be found in public and college libraries as well as in hundreds of thousands of homes across the country. Information is a tool that becomes part of every task you do in your pursuit of a successful life.

Skills and Knowledge

After you learn a new skill, you have to practice it on a daily basis as many times as you can. This includes relationship skills, such as conflict resolution, as well as career skills, such as keyboarding or customer service. Though any new skill you acquire may feel unnatural at first (old ways die hard), the good news is that after a while, the new skill will feel perfectly comfortable, and using it will make things go better for you.

An excellent example of incorporating new tools into your everyday life is vocabulary building. You are expected to have a command of the language of your profession and to express yourself in everyday communication. As you learn a new word, the more you practice by incorporating it into your daily speech, the more natural it feels. Learning new software, a foreign language, or new methods of managing conflict in your family is the same. Once you take the time to learn, these skills become habits that you call up anytime they are needed.

People

You cannot possibly know now all that will be required of you as you move through your career and relationship transitions. Keeping an eye out for others who can help you is always a good practice. Some help you with information, others with support.

Coach

A source of information and career skills is the professional "coach." Coaches are experts in a certain area who share their specialized knowledge with clients. Some do this as a profession; some coaches, though, are just good at teaching their particular skill informally to others and enjoy helping. They may serve as resources for workplace skills, or in the case of a therapist, for relationship skills. If you are interested in hiring a coach, look for a professional who is an expert in the field and who has a good reputation. Networking groups, colleagues, and friends who work in similar jobs or industries can sometimes be called on at no charge for this type of help.

Mentor

If you are lucky and have a mentor or role model in your life or profession, you have someone in your corner who has a personal investment in showing you the path to success. Sometimes a manager or supervisor can become a mentor. However, this is not something that you should automatically expect. You should, instead, be grateful for anyone who chooses to invest their time and knowledge in you in such a way.

Moral Support

The case of Gene is an example of the role of moral support. Gene was the classic "geek" youngster—bright, not socially adept, physically small—who lived in a community that was very sports oriented. His older brother and sister were both athletes and went to college on athletic scholarships. His passion, however, was reading and later, writing, which he kept quiet about for the most part. One aunt always invited him to read his latest writing when he came to visit. "She was my most unabashed fan," he remembered. Her enthusiasm and focused attention carried him through some lonely times and frequent literary rejections. "I probably would have quit writing altogether if she hadn't kept encouraging me."

Dreams, goals, and plans. Even the highest resolve, focus, and dedication need shoring up from time to time. An invaluable resource is the person or group who will go forward with you and support you when you need it.

Media

High-quality audio and video programs can provide skill training and information comparable to that provided by a coach or class. Bookstores and record stores carry these; some can even be rented. Time in a car often becomes dead time; you can make this enriching time by adding to your knowledge with tapes.

You will reach your goals more easily with the right resources. Once you have the resources you need, you can begin to implement your plans.

Action

Once you have researched, improved, and developed your transition skills, you are ready to put the plan you are developing into action. Without action, even the best of plans are worth nothing. You now have to decide how and when to act. Remember, you are learning to be in charge of your future and your happiness. Your goals and plan will become your personal road map for high performance and allow you to approach new thresholds with confidence; confidence that you will make a successful transition to a new level of satisfaction in your life.

One thing that stops many people from acting on their goal-related plans is uncertainty about the effects of the choices they make. When you do not know what a specific outcome will be, you might hesitate. Business decision makers deal with this all the time, and like them, you can thoroughly investigate possible outcomes of the actions you have chosen to implement. Even then, though, you may not be able to allow for all eventualities.

Sometimes, you may just have to take the step, assuming you have designed the step with reasonable care. Besides, outcomes are not always predictable, even with the most seemingly routine actions. Rather than worry about the chance of a negative or undesirable outcome, approach your implementation steps with the idea that you will observe the result and adjust your next step based on what has occurred.

Building a life requires that you act on your plans and use your resources. The events in your life are the materials; the way that you acquire and use tools and skills is your part in crafting those materials into a satisfying life. Have you ever heard the saying, "Don't think, don't try, just do"? This does not mean to act rashly or without planning and care, but it does mean to begin putting into effect what you have developed from your goal and assessment activities.

You can start with the easiest tasks that support your goal, but anything that moves you in the direction you have chosen should be a priority. (See Chapter 3 on time management to help you do this.)

Assessment—Again

Each time you implement your plans and apply new skills, take a moment to assess where you are and what effects you have created. Some actions will take you further than you ever expected; some will either not work at all or not have the desired effect. Stumbling is often part of walking or running. In addition, every time you walk through a different door, you are in a different place. Assessment, a check-up of results against goals, helps you keep your direction or change it if new conditions warrant.

Remember, at each step in this growth process, you alter your potential; you improve your ability to succeed in your own life transitions. The formula is complete. See Figure 2.1 for a visual representation of this concept.

FIGURE 2.1 The assessment cycle.

You've probably heard people say they are *born* to a certain destiny, while others *seek* their destiny. Right here, right now, it is your road, your life. If you like it, congratulations! You have found the key to lasting happiness. But if you don't, you can define your own potential by setting goals. Goals will help you recognize thresholds and manage transitions to new levels. You are where you are today because you wanted more control in the direction of your life or perhaps more freedom in the way you live it.

There are many paths to the same goal. When you have chosen a direction (not even necessarily an endpoint), events, circumstances, and people you meet every day begin to appear as thresholds to where you are going.

The simplicity of this approach to transitions makes it useful throughout your life. Turning loose your limitations allows you to expect a wondrous and satisfying life, the beginning of the process to achieving happiness. Regularly assessing where you are in relation to where you want to be is an important factor in maintaining a workable formula and achieving growth. Any movement forward or any adaptation to a major life event requires that you seek out the pertinent information and learn the new skills necessary for the transition to the other side of the event. Finally, as you enlarge and expand your repertoire of coping and life-managing skills, you find much more freedom of movement, both personally and professionally; movement leading to satisfying results: your future.

Making solid transitions as you move through your professional endeavors and your emotional and relational life ensures your safe arrival in *Success City*, a city you have designed and built.

TRANSITION SKILLS SUMMARY

Expectation
Dreams
Priorities
Goals
Assessment
Resources
Action
Assessment—again

GOAL SETTING

Self-nurturing: My goal statement for my personal and relational life is:

_____

_____

_____

_____

Self-advocacy: My goal statement for my professional/work life is:

_____

_____

_____

_____

C O A C H'S C O R N E R

The move from school to industry is one of the largest a person will make in early adulthood; in some ways it signifies the transition into adulthood. The following general suggestions to those embarking on this stage of life will be useful for the entirety of their career lives, as they will meet challenges all along the path.

- Communications skills should include an orientation to team and close work environments. Almost no one works in a vacuum.

- Remember to take care of yourself and be alert to symptoms of stress or burnout.

- Stability at home is the springboard for launching into any new career direction.

- Learn to solve problems of all types—an absolute necessity for the sometimes crazy world of industry.

- Do a thorough self-assessment: know what you are good at, but also what you might be interested in learning as a growth area.

- Work to situate yourself in a company's culture; be able to work with all kinds of people.

- Attitude can make or break you, attitude determines performance. Attitude is a choice; a positive attitude leads to success.

- A personal mission statement is an absolute necessity. What your intention is as you direct your life should be put on paper in a clear way.

TINA BERRY TAYLOR, L.C.S.W., CEAP, MSW, is an experienced trainer and employee assistance consultant.

CHAPTER 3

Organizing Time and Tasks

John's office is neat in the morning when he arrives, in the evening when he leaves, and even during the day while he is working. Sherry works, drives in a car pool, and is the team mother for the little league team. Both of these people appear organized and in control of their lives. They are also living examples to the rest of us who wish we could be that way.

Though some people are more structured and detailed than others, most of us agree we could improve in this area. The difficulty is that you, like everyone else, have "multiple priorities" in your life; that is, many important things to accomplish and rarely enough time to do them. Whether you are an executive who directs a multimillion-dollar company, an electrician who wires buildings, or an at-home mother who balances parenting with running a household, you know how necessary being organized is. Bringing structure and planning into your life is not to be valued just for its own sake. Managing your time and tasks affects your ability to lead a satisfying life. The benefits are many:

1. Efficient management of job tasks leaves more time, energy, and focus for outside activities and relationships.
2. Accomplishment is emotionally liberating and energizing.
3. Focusing effort prevents the feeling of being overwhelmed.
4. A more relaxed life results from being in control of demands on your time.

Career professionals face challenges that can be clearly defined in terms of the hours in the day.

FIGURE 3.1	Allocating the hours in a day.

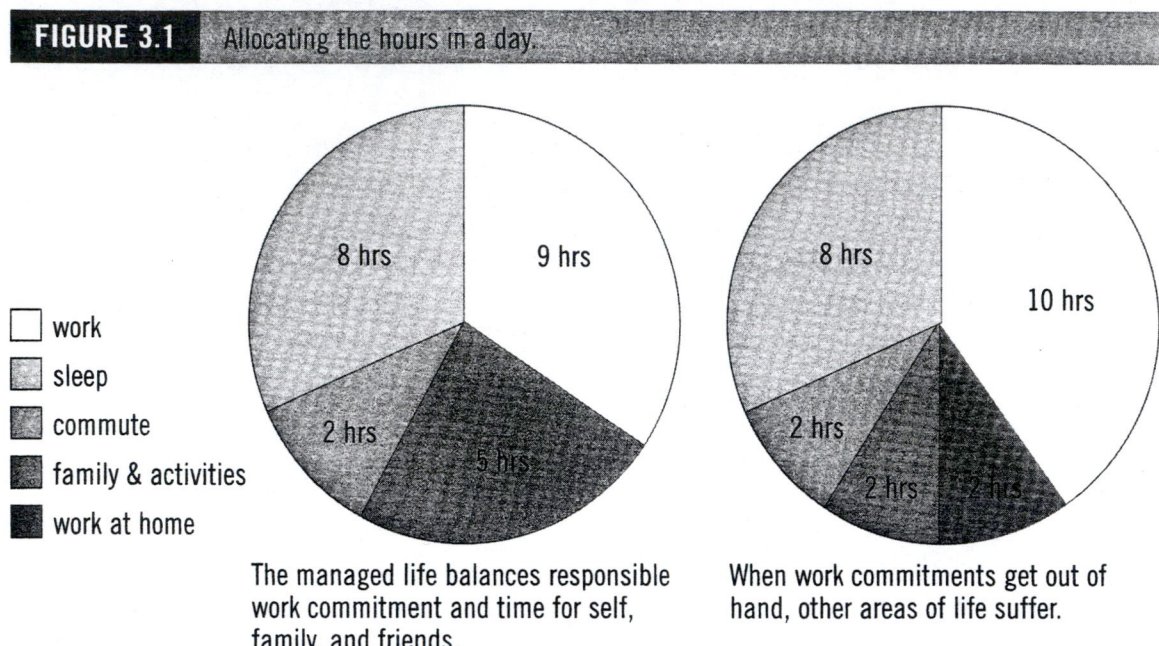

- work
- sleep
- commute
- family & activities
- work at home

The managed life balances responsible work commitment and time for self, family, and friends.

When work commitments get out of hand, other areas of life suffer.

Granted, some people seem to be born to be orderly. A few are trained to be that way, as in the military. Some of us, though, never seem to quite get our lives under control—try as we might. But having a life where you can plan, get things done, and still find time for yourself and for those you care about *is* possible.

In Activity 3.1, you are asked to make a start on the road to organization by choosing those parts of your life you wish to handle better.

3.1 ACTIVITY

I wish I had more time for _____

   I believe that if I could just manage _____ better, my life would seem more in control.

This chapter is about how to manage your life's daily demands. It is not like those books that casually dismiss the problem by saying, "Don't sweat the small stuff." If your life is like that of most adults, you wish there was some "small stuff." It *all* seems like "big stuff." That is why it is difficult to manage. Understanding how you look at organization in general will help you see why some situations are more difficult for you to "get a handle on" than others. In addition, in this chapter you will learn the skills you need to approach life's time and task challenges in a confident and successful way.

Organization Challenges

People who seem like "born organizers" in some respects really are. Just by the way their brain works, some people think and operate naturally in a methodical, structured manner. These people are probably not reading this chapter, so don't worry about feeling intimidated by them anymore. You are going to learn to do the same thing with your life, and no one will ever know you weren't a "born organizer" yourself.

We will explore the difficulty most of us have in gaining a sense of control. There are many reasons for this difficulty besides differences in thinking style. They range from everyone's demands on us to our own inability to manage too many and diverse tasks. Other reasons stem from the value we place on organization, which translates into the amount of energy we are willing to expend to achieve an ordered or more manageable life.

Thinking Styles

The way thinking style enters into our ability to manage our time and tasks is best shown by the example of two brothers: Kyle, 15, and George, 12. Both have the task of cleaning their rooms, which are perfect examples of chaos and disarray. Kyle looks at the mess and sees the room as a gigantic, insurmountable mountain of disorder. Being completely overwhelmed by the immenseness of the task, he becomes agitated, tries picking up a few pieces, then begins to wander around aimlessly. Eventually, he says he cannot do it alone and begs for help.

George, on the other hand, surveys the mess (equally intimidating to the observer) and attacks parts of the task separately: toys, then clothes, then bed, then sweeping. He is done in half an hour. There are a few pieces that did not quite make it to the proper places, but on the whole, the task of making the room look better was accomplished.

On the adult level, we see this in another way. Josh, an electronics troubleshooter, tries the broken hardware, gets a feeling he knows what the problem is, and goes to it. If he is incorrect about his guess, he tries again. His partner, Randy, approaches hardware problem diagnosis differently. When he reports to a customer site, he questions users about the problem, how it occurred and when, goes through a series of diagnostic procedures, and isolates the problem. Both are successful service engineers with high customer satisfaction.

Randy: Careful, methodical   Josh: Quick, creative

Josh makes slightly more errors than Randy on the first try, but he corrects them quickly and is often finished with his calls for the day before Randy. Randy regularly takes longer than Josh, but seldom makes an error. When he does, he usually calls Josh in because the problem is generally some new or perplexing difficulty he doesn't have a procedure for uncovering.

Who has a more effective troubleshooting style? Randy appears to, but Josh likely uses a clear process that isn't apparent to the observer. Josh is a gifted, intuitive, gut-level diagnostician. But sometimes his first impulse is wrong. Randy is a methodical, perseverant, well-trained problem solver. Sometimes, though, the problem is outside the expected, and he can't discover the solution. The success of their business is that the combination of the two styles can handle anything that comes along.

You probably have ways you approach organizing or performing tasks that work quite well. Though successful in some situations, in others these methods don't work at all. By understanding your approach to organization, you will quickly see why some tasks overwhelm and paralyze you and others don't. As soon as you have a clear picture of your style, you can learn additional approaches to apply to tasks that challenge you.

3.2 ACTIVITY

Look at the example of Josh and Randy, and then at your approach to challenges. Identify your task-management style as "quick, creative thinking" or "careful, methodical thinking." Give an example to explain why you chose the answer you did. (Note: This understanding of your style will help you to communicate your style during a job interview.)

_____

_____

Be careful not to confuse a natural organizational style with the conclusions conveyed in the following: "I guess I'm just born to be messy. I know my mother was, so I guess I inherited it." There is not, to the knowledge of medical science, a you-will-be-disorganized gene. Your approach to organization may predispose you, though, to have difficulty with certain situations. Learning organizational skills will help you with those challenges you cannot solve easily.

Value Placed on Organization

How much someone values organization has a direct effect on how much effort the person devotes to achieving order. In your personal life, you may like to have a clean home and spend several hours each week to keep it that way. Your spouse or housemate may appreciate a clean house, but not enough to work to keep it that way. In Activity 3.3, rate the value you place on different areas of organization in your life.

ACTIVITY   *3.3*

Circle the number that most accurately describes the value you place on the following items:

1. Orderly physical space at home and work

    (Not at all)   1   2   3   4   5   (I work to keep things orderly)

2. Time scheduled in a careful way

    (Not at all)   1   2   3   4   5   (I schedule my day carefully)

3. Time versus physical organization

    (Physical space)   1   2   3   4   5   (Time)

What conclusions can you draw about your natural tendency in regard to organization?

_____

_____

_____

In your personal life you are free to be as organized or disorganized as you like. Perhaps throughout your education you managed just fine, made it to most of your classes and finished reports on time. Once you begin your job in the corporate world, the number of things you have to keep track of and complete increases dramatically. You are expected to be able to manage tasks, such as:

- be at meetings on time and prepared
- deliver projects and reports within deadlines
- apprise management of project status
- locate important information quickly

Fortunately for professionals, many organizational tools and aids are available.

Lack of Skills

When we are young, life is relatively simple. One reason is that when we are young, we don't have as many "things," in the way of personal property or responsibilities to keep track of or maintain. Car ownership, for example, brings with it car payments, insurance payments, oil changes, tire rotation, and washing. None of this exists for the young person. So, as young people, we rarely develop good organizational or planning skills. The most visible evidence of this difference lies with mail and phone.

When you were a child, you managed your school life and your social life with help from mom and dad and maybe a brother or sister. When you become an adult, you manage your own life and you must assist those with whom you interact. You counsel a friend, coach an employee, help your boss, haul the kids, meet a coworker for lunch, call your aging parent, or visit your sister.

Whew! How do you do it? Many of us feel like we end up not handling any of what we do well. Some of your success at managing your tasks depends on the skills you have learned. In Activity 3.4, you will report any skill training from your childhood or adult life that has helped you to handle multiple tasks.

3.4   ACTIVITY

Write down organizational techniques you were taught while growing up. For example, "My father taught me that paying bills as they come in helps to prevent a pile-up at due dates." "My brother kept a small cassette recorder in the car to record things he wanted to remind himself to do."

1. I remember: _____

2. I remember: _____

Now, write down an example of the way you have organized your responsibilities as an adult.

_____

_____

_____

If you are like most people, unless you have attended seminars, read books, or received specific instruction on methods for managing multiple tasks, you probably do not have a good set of skills to apply. But even the most skilled person cannot use that training until he learns to be assertive about the need to organize.

TRANSITION TIP   _Scott Davis, Business Development_

The first realization that hit me about time is that suddenly I didn't have summers off. Fun had to come in short weekends. Also, the importance of time management really hit when I realized the organization required in a flexible collegiate environment was very different from the requirement of the 60-hour work week that ran six days. The advice I would give the person just out of college is this: Now you are completely free to make all of your decisions and manage your own life. You are also accountable for all of those decisions, so you have to police your life yourself if you are going to make it.

Like any other challenge, time and task management is addressed at two levels: defining the challenge and developing skills to meet it. So far, you have begun by defining the challenges.

For the skills, we can draw from the experience of professionals who manage complex tasks and deadlines for a living. These people are called project managers, and they have some helpful approaches you can use in your daily life as well as on your job. They accomplish their goals by keeping three issues in focus regardless of the size or complexity of the job:

- setting priorities
- securing necessary resources
- completing tasks

You can move one step closer to successfully organizing the activities in your life by learning what these professionals know and use every day—methods for organizing time and tasks.

Setting Priorities

Figuring out the most important and productive ways to allot time is a challenge for most people. Everyone has limited time; most of us work hard. Yet, some people accomplish a lot, while others just get tired. How is it that with the same number of hours in a day some get more done than others? Successful organizers plan. They take the time to think about their tasks or goals to decide what is most important to finish. Then, they direct their time and energy there. They understand the notion of the critical path. The *critical path* is the set of steps you have to go through, in proper order, to accomplish your goal. For example, if the goal is to get to work on time, specific activities must be completed in order:

MORNING ROUTINE
1. Get up at 6 A.M.
2. Shower
3. Dress and make coffee
4. Eat breakfast
5. Feed dog
6. Set burglar alarm
7. Lock door

Parts of the process must occur in order, and you must complete all of the steps necessary to reach your goal satisfactorily, but some tasks can be done simultaneously. Chris wants to build a fence for the dog. He knows that he has to have his property surveyed, draw out the plan for spacing the posts, buy what he needs, and put the fence up.

He cannot buy materials until he has the survey because he has to measure to see how much he needs. He cannot put up the fence until he has all of the materials. If Chris does not prioritize the specific steps and allow time for each one in order, he will not reach his goal.

The critical path helps to set priorities. Prioritizing helps Chris plan the best use of his time in other ways. If he has two hours to wait for a plane or an hour to wait at the doctor's office, he can use this time to make up his list of materials or draw his fence plan, instead of sitting in the airport bar or reading a magazine at the doctor's office.

Remember, stress can occur in your life when you fail to do what you think you really should be doing. If you get distracted, your priority plan reminds you to keep focused. Completing each step toward your goal is easier when the steps are clearly defined and priorities are set for their completion. *If someone seeks to involve you in an activity that is not on your critical path, you have the right to decline.*

Setting Priorities at Work

Every employee should understand the priorities of the workplace. All too often, however, employees, especially new ones, fail on the job by spending time on tasks that are not priorities. Employers complain about this relatively common problem.

> Duane took a new job at the Blue Rock Farm. His supervisor directed him to the field where he would be performing his job, which was picking up rocks. To make a good impression his first day, Duane diligently went about his work. He picked up rocks: blue ones, yellow ones, green ones. He even dug up some silver and gold ones he saw barely protruding from the ground. At the end of the day he had filled an entire dump truck and drove it proudly into the yard for his supervisor's inspection.
>
> The supervisor walked around, looked at the load Duane had gathered so painstakingly, shook his head and said, "What is this?"
>
> Puzzled, but still enthusiastic, he explained, "I filled the entire truck like you said. I picked up pink rocks, green rocks, and I even dug up some of the silver and gold ones, see?"
>
> The supervisor looked right at Duane and said, "Son, what's the name of this farm?"
>
> Realization hit Duane, and his enthusiastic look disappeared.

Unlike school, where compassionate teachers give credit, and maybe even a passing grade, for "effort" or "trying hard," in business this is not true. Working late, coming in on weekends, taking work home; none of this matters if you do not advance company goals with your activity. Pushing on a sitting elephant all day would be considered inconsequential if your job was to move the elephant. This is why status reports are often set up with two headings: *Accomplishments* and *Goals*. No one cares what you did, just what you accomplished. And no one cares what you accomplished if it was not related to the goals of the company. (The status report and its role in demonstrating your work to your manager is discussed in more detail in Chapter 10.)

This is why if you are asked to stay late to help a fellow employee on a project, your best choice might very well be to decline. If the request does not relate to the activities for which you are held accountable, then the time might better be spent with your family. That is not to say that you never help coworkers. The truth is, however, that your salary and performance reviews are based on the goals set for *you*.

Ideally, you and your manager have a conversation about the role your job plays in the overall success of the organization. This conversation takes place both at the start of your new job and periodically over the first year with a new company. Unfortunately, this is more likely *not* to happen than to happen. Some organizations and some managers will prove to be excellent support for your success. However, a great many will not. Thus, the process of determining the best way to prioritize your time may very well be left to you. Following are some guidelines for ascertaining the path to accomplishment.

1. Read the financial or stockholder's report to get a clear picture of the company's vision, strengths, markets, and competition.

2. Secure from your manager a description of how your position fits into the company's goals. (You may have to ask many questions to get this information.)

3. Observe those who receive promotions or bonuses—see what kinds of projects they are working on.

4. Be aware of what activities you prefer to do and how those relate to your overall duties—are you spending all of your time "picking up blue rocks" or are you doing other things you enjoy more instead? (If you find that many of the things you enjoy are not part of the duties for which you are accountable, then it may be time to change jobs.)

Securing Necessary Resources

You have probably driven down the road behind an old pickup truck that is loaded with pine straw, bags of grass seed, small shrubs, and an assortment of shovels, rakes, and brooms. There may even be a lawn mower balanced tentatively on top of it all. This truck is an example of good resource planning. Lawn care businesses send out their workers in the morning loaded for the day's work. A trip back to the storage site to pick up supplies or tools is time consuming and unprofitable. Planning, based on the jobs of the day, prevents extra trips or unnecessary purchases.

Materials and Tools

At a technology research lab, the failure to have the necessary parts on hand can delay the development and delivery of a million-dollar product to a customer. In your own life, you have probably been frustrated more than once when the pen by the phone is out of ink or there is no paper to take a note on. This is a simple problem, but it illustrates that having the resources needed to perform a task is necessary to make your life flow smoothly.

Gathering the resources for any task requires that you think about what you need to achieve, what you want to do. In the example of Chris building a fence, he had purchased a booklet that suggested the types of fence pullers and other tools he would need. So, with about two hours' planning, Chris saved himself nearly a day's time because he wouldn't have to stop to get something he needed. He also avoided the irritation of needing something he did not have. As part of the planning, Chris also discovered that he was lacking another important resource—help. As you do your planning, don't forget to include the human resource factor—people to help you do what needs to be done.

People

People can make the difference in whether you can accomplish a task or not. A lack of child care can prevent you from having adequate time for work and home tasks or even certain recreational activities. Friends or hired labor can provide an extra set of hands and contribute to the timely completion of a job. Once you decide what help you need, then you can determine where that help will come from.

Remember that you might not be a "planner" by nature. If you are not, then you probably have quite a few tasks that frustrate you because you cannot seem to get them out of the way. Resource planning, like any other planning, takes time. This is why so many people don't plan. They get into the frenzy of "I have to get started." What they don't realize, though, is that people who don't plan frequently spend a great deal more time on their tasks than those who do plan—including planning time.

The most important people resource is you. The place to start assessing resources is yourself:

1. What do you already know about this project or challenge?
2. What skills do you have that you can apply directly?
3. What do you need to know that you do not know?
4. How can you fulfill that need? Learn? Ask or hire someone?
5. How much time can you allot to this task?

6. Is it better delegated to someone else because of the value of your time or the availability of skilled people?

If you use people resources, you should consider the following:

1. What are the skills and knowledge of those in your immediate sphere?
2. How committed are they already to other tasks and priorities?
3. How dependable are they? What is the quality of their work?
4. Is this a project they would be interested in helping with, learning about, working with you on?
5. How can their time be freed up for your project? Negotiate a barter of time, resources, or pay.
6. How much of your budget for this project can you devote to paying people?
7. Is the deadline important? (Note: budget and deadline are directly related in business. The longer something takes, the more it costs in terms of resources. For personal projects, if you are not in a hurry, this is not necessarily the case.)

Organization Support Tools

Organizing in your head may work with small projects or daily planning demands, but for anything complex or for lives with numerous activities and obligations, tools specifically designed for organization are almost a necessity. Following are some tools that you might find useful.

1. Computer software can record and remind you of tasks and appointments.
2. Records or data-management systems can automatically sort and organize information to make it easy for you to use.
3. Day planners or appointment books allow you to record important information and deadlines.
4. Personal digital assistants that fit into a pocket, purse, or briefcase allow you to record appointments, phone numbers, and so on, so you don't have to remember them.
5. Reminder services call or e-mail you to let you know that a loved one's birthday or other occasion is coming up.
6. In those cases where the luxury of an assistant is available, a person who sets a high value on and has considerable skill with organizing can be a lifesaver.

7. Project management environments have forms or software into which you enter the status of activities as well as deadlines. These programs can prompt you when something is due.

8. Color-coded folders placed in a tiered rack on your desk or in a file drawer make your organization system visible and easily accessible.

9. Meeting notes and phone messages kept in one spiral-bound or hard-bound notebook are there when you need them. (Yellow sticky notes can disappear precisely when you need the information on them. Get into the habit of putting written notes of any kind in a notebook.)

10. A large calendar that hangs on the wall in a conspicuous place can serve as a planning tool.

Bill has to prepare two proposals for clients of his company by Friday. His children have a baseball game on Thursday night, and he has promised to attend. Bill's goal is to accomplish both by the end of the week without sacrificing one or the other.

1. What are the activities required for Bill's tasks?

2. Can any be done simultaneously or are they all in a critical path?

3. What resources would you suggest Bill use to complete the tasks?

Completing Tasks

The final step in organizing is completing the tasks. This seems like a natural conclusion, but many things can interfere with your efforts. We will look at two common impediments and help you develop strategies to deal with them: time just gets away and there are too many things to do to finish any. How many days have you started the morning with great intentions? You may even have taken a day of leave from work just to "catch up." For both barriers to completing a task or reaching a goal, the solution is *awareness*.

Time Just Gets Away

Often when a distraction comes along—phone, office talker, someone with a problem—we find ourselves redirected from our goal activities. If we are not aware of the time we are spending on these distractions, we can end the day without completing anything. What's worse, we seldom remember exactly how we got off track. *Be aware of distractions and keep them temporary.*

Two hints will help you. *First, make sure phone calls meet your needs and not someone else's.* Our adolescence left us with a priority of always answering the phone because of the teenager's need to communicate. As an adult, you have to separate that urge from a real communication need that supports your goals. In other words, use a machine or let the phone ring during the times you are working on your necessary items. Sales people and chatty friends have a high need to communicate with you. This may not support your need to complete your priority tasks.

Second, throw away junk mail without opening it. The time it takes to wade through all of the worthless "stuff" could be spent meeting your own goals. Time is allotted to each of us in the same way each day. How you use that time sometimes makes the difference between accomplishment and frustration. By eliminating some activities, at least for the time you are pursuing a specific goal, you make yourself available for your priority items.

Each one of your goal steps takes time. Carefully assessing the time required to perform each step helps you plan more successfully. One of the biggest hurdles for anyone trying to plan activities based on time, though, is that in many cases you truly have no idea how long something will take. Especially on a new job, you have no prior experience with the tasks and thus no good estimate of the time needed. In this case, you can ask people who have done similar tasks. For future reference, it is a good idea to keep notes on how long activities actually take to perform.

3.5   ACTIVITY

Choose one goal you want to accomplish in the next two weeks. Develop the necessary steps to complete it and decide the order in which they must be done. Also, estimate the time needed to complete each one.

Goal: _____   Completion deadline: _____

Necessary steps   Time needed

Step 1: _____   _____

Step 2: _____   _____

Step 3: _____   _____

Step 4: _____   _____

(It is a good idea to return to this exercise after you have completed the tasks and compare estimated time to actual time.)

Now, you have drawn a clear picture of the tasks required to reach your goal because you have written down the goal, the steps, and the time required. You are able to develop a realistic plan for making those steps happen. (A time and task organization sheet is included at the end of this chapter to help you.)

Too Many Things to Do

If you are doing too many things, you are probably not doing any of them very well. Then, you get angry with yourself for not performing as well as you know you can. At work, your job may be too much for one person, in which case you might have to ask your boss for help.

Be careful with this though. You may be perceived as not being able to manage your time well. Be certain that you are truly overcommitted and that you can document multiple, overlapping tasks. Sometimes your manager will "lend" some of your time to a manager for another project. When you become overloaded, go to your managers and ask them to decide which tasks they feel your time is best spent completing. That way, you are not put into the position of being unable to meet deadlines.

In your home life, on the other hand, just the sheer number of people in a family multiplies house cleaning, bill paying, repairs, shopping, cooking, laundry, and errands, and these needs don't stop just because you work.

Saying "No"

Too often our lives become overloaded not by those tasks required to maintain ourselves at home and at work, but by those tasks "required" by others. Those tasks may appear to be "required," but in reality, they may not be. Are these pictures of your life? Look at the following examples.

> "Stephanie, we need someone with your experience to manage the fund-raiser for the new fellowship hall."

> "Mom, would you drive Zack and me to the ballgame and pick us up at Benny's at nine? Oh, and can you change my orthodontist's appointment to next week? A wire broke on my braces."

> Mack is a newly-employed accountant with a cleaning services company. He is heading out the door at the end of the day in order to attend a professional meeting on behalf of his company. A coworker calls to him, "Mack, the Jackson account says their software has bugs in it, and they're not able to process their payment on Thursday. Can you help me with it?"

Other individuals felt entitled to ask that Stephanie, "Mom," and Mack help out. In each of these cases, these individuals could have said, "No, I'm sorry, I have another obligation." This response might have kept them from feeling over-loaded. Other people's priorities can become yours very quickly if you let them. Have you fallen into this pattern with those you live and work with?

3.6 ACTIVITY

1. If you did something recently that you didn't have time for, but did anyway, what happened?

   _____

   _____

2. How did it affect your ability to do what you needed to do?

   _____

   _____

3. What might have happened if you had said "no"? Describe the positive and negative impacts on you and on the other person.

   Effects on you: _____

   _____

   Effects on the other person: _____

   _____

Your survival depends on taking action to get yourself off the merry-go-round of a hectic life. In case you haven't noticed, the horses on the merry-go-round are wood; you are not. *The best reason for managing your multiple responsibilities better is your own well-being.*

Your family can do their own laundry, coworkers can survive without your help on every task, and your friends will understand if you can't meet them for every gathering. Stop doing everything and train others around you to support what you do. Find a baby sitter who can help the kids with baseball or home-work. Locate a temporary agency that can supply short-term help for your work. Look at your responsibilities and find ways to delegate some things.

The workplace and the home are, of necessity, team environments. Use the team. Analyze the tasks, the steps, and the resources, then decide how you will complete the undertaking.

Eliminating "Dead Air"

A big productivity loss can occur because of "10-minute dead air." This is wasted time. The minutes just before an appointment or an important phone call or the time spent waiting for someone become dead air, a term used in broadcasting to describe those moments of silence that occur due to a technical failure or operator error.

ACTIVITY 3.7

Review your activity plan for a major project you have coming up. After you have written down all of the major tasks and their time requirements, describe at least four activities that can be done in 10 minutes.

Example: *"I need to get involved in a networking group to advance my career potential."*

10-minute activities:

1. *Look in phone book or on the Internet for networking organizations.*
2. *Determine two or three that seem most likely to target.*
3. *Review notes from conversation with leader of networking group.*
4. *Send e-mails to a networking organization requesting information.*

Goal: _____

_____

10-minute activities:

1. _____
2. _____
3. _____
4. _____

Eliminating Time Wasters

To complete your goals, you must be aware of time wasters. Following is a list of time wasters that you might encounter when you try to accomplish goals:

- Focusing on minute tasks instead of larger, goal activities.
- Hurrying, which causes mistakes that can sabotage success.
- Becoming distracted or paralyzed by worry.
- Not taking time to read instructions, then having to start over.
- Spending time trying to "do it yourself" when assistance is really necessary.
- Not planning, which creates delays (not having tools needed).

An example of a time waster that may be difficult to deal with is the friend who asks for your time. "Bill often sees me outside when I am doing a landscaping or building project and asks me to help him with something he wants to do right then." A good response that is respectful of everyone's goals might be, "Sure, Bill, but right now I'm going to finish this deck. Why don't we plan to look at your project tomorrow. I'll be finished by then."

Building the well-managed life is not easy, but the necessity and the rewards are undeniable. Changing your old habits of being everyone's best resource or of plunging into work without planning requires discipline at first. But, like other skills you are learning, time and task management can be learned. The reward is a happier and more relaxed *you*.

TRANSITION SKILLS SUMMARY

Address organization challenges

Set a value on effectively managing time and tasks

Define specific time and task priorities

Secure resources

Complete tasks

GOAL SETTING

My self-nurturing time and task organization goals are:

_____

_____

_____

My self-advocacy time and task organization goals are:

_____

_____

_____

C O A C H ' S   C O R N E R

The operative word is clutter; clutter that builds up more quickly than most people can deal with it. But clutter is just delayed decision making—too much stuff due to an ineffective decision-making system. Think instead that every piece of paper that comes to you must be put into a specific category. This is the basis of the *Clutter-FREE*™ system.

File

Refer or delegate

Eliminate or toss

Execute or take action

Surviving on the job, especially a new job, requires that you focus on organization from the first day. Your setup is the key to heading off clutter problems before they become so huge they are intimidating. Start with four trays on your desk, credenza, or cabinet. Label them "in," "out," "file," and "read." Every piece of paper goes into one of these trays and is acted on accordingly. E-mail can be handled the same way:

F—create folder

R—refer or forward

E—eliminate by deleting

E—execute by reading, replying or acting

There is no reason to store endless streams of e-mails in your computer's inbox. Because your system administrator will notify you that you are overloading the network, you will have to deal with your e-mails eventually. (Ms. Wilkowski's company offers software, "Taming the Paper Tiger," that allows you to catalog data through keywords and cross-reference words. This allows you to "find anything in five seconds or less.")

BETSY WILKOWSKI is a professional organizer and founder of The Organized Executive, Inc. (www.organizeyouroffice.com).

Time and Task Organization Sheet

Goal to be completed: _____ Deadline: _____

Necessary steps   Time needed

1. _____ _____

2. _____ _____

3. _____ _____

4. _____ _____

5. _____ _____

6. _____ _____

Resources needed:

Supplies: _____

Tools/equipment: _____

Human resources: _____

Additional help or expertise needed. Hire? Friend or favor? Delegate?

_____

_____

Potential time wasters:

_____

_____

Strategies for time wasters:

_____

_____

Timeline:

By / / _____ should be completed

By / / _____ should be completed

By / / _____ should be completed

CHAPTER 4

Maintaining Growth

Trying to keep up with business or just trying to stay informed about important aspects of your own life is becoming an ongoing challenge. Most of what you knew five years ago is past history now, and if you haven't added new ideas, skills, or information to your knowledge base, you are probably behind in your profession. In your personal life, you are perhaps learning and growing too: finding out about health issues relevant to your age group, studying travel or investing, maybe even becoming more involved in religion or world events.

Lifelong learning is not just a buzzword or catchy phrase. It is necessary for us to thrive; our well-being is enriched when we constantly challenge our brains with new information and ideas. The world is changing quickly, but information about that world and the forces affecting it is readily available *if* you know how to find and process it. By finding and using good information, you can live and work more effectively. When you make continuous growth a priority,

- your work becomes more interesting.
- you are able to respond quickly to requests for information.
- you become more assured in challenging circumstances.
- you have career security.

Finding Information

Finding information is often confusing, frustrating, and overwhelming to people who have no idea how to go about it. If you have not been exposed to the wealth of resources in your community or if you have recently moved to a new city, you might be lost as to how to find services and suppliers. In your work life, you are expected to be able to gather and report information on competitors, products, and other pertinent subjects.

Information Literacy

Information literacy is the term used to describe the ability to locate information. The term "literate" refers to someone who can read well enough to shop for food, follow simple directions, and maintain mobility (e.g., by reading bus schedules). Computer literacy is the ability to perform the basic computer functions that may be related to your work or personal affairs. Information literacy may well be the next divider of the population into "have" and "have not." As more and more information becomes available via the Internet, databases, satellite transmissions, and electronic communications, those who are unable to access certain information sources will be impaired in their survival in this information-rich society.

Further, the free availability of such huge amounts of information puts greater responsibility for discernment on the user. Filtering devices, such as editors who check material for validity and sources for credentials, exist for published information, but may not be a part of the electronic information age. Anyone can post information on the Internet without any editorial checking for validity or integrity. No longer can news and fact seekers accept wholesale and unexamined what they gather even from sources that may appear flashy and professional. Thus, the information-literate person must be able to:

- Use a variety of avenues to gain knowledge for the everyday requirements of work and personal business.
- Apply critical analysis and filtering techniques to discriminate between valid, useful information and frivolous, unsubstantiated material.

Thus, a critical approach to information gathering is a necessary skill and a personal responsibility.

A helpful book, *Teaching Information Literacy Skills*, guides the Internet researcher through this process (Iannuzzi et al., 1999). The authors discuss a system, or checklist, for evaluating information from the World Wide Web using the acronym **S T A R T.**

- **S**cope—does the article have all aspects of the information you need?

- **T**reatment—is the evidence provided consistent, logical, and free from bias?
- **A**uthority—is the author qualified and how do you know? (Note that URL addresses that end in .gov or .edu are generally considered to be reputable.)
- **R**elevance—does the article provide information that verifies or supports your point?
- **T**imeliness—is there a date on the material and is it current enough to be helpful?

Dirk and Sissy moved from their hometown to a city 100 miles away. They felt sure that they would be able to find all that they needed simply by picking up the phone directory. Although the directory was an essential tool in the beginning, problems arose for them that were complicated and could not be answered simply by looking in the Yellow Pages.

For the pain Sissy had developed in her left shoulder, options included an orthopedist, a neurologist, a chiropractor, and a general practitioner. In her former home, she could count on advice from the network of professionals that she had grown to trust.

Dirk and Sissy discussed the situation over dinner and came up with a plan that would not only solve the physician dilemma, but would also set a precedent for finding other resources they might need.

The steps they came up with are logic based and take into account such elements as need, desire, finances, and ability:

- State what you want to find or accomplish.
- List what you already know about the subject.
- List all resources that might be helpful, such as county agencies, reference librarians, the human resource department at work, police departments, the Red Cross, churches, and local information agencies.
- Make inquiry calls and gather information.
- Sort the information into options.

1. What three information sources would be helpful for Dirk and Sissy?
2. What approach could they use to determine the most trustworthy information?

Using this formula, Dirk and Sissy made a list of actions that would help them gather information about physicians in their area who might be good choices to treat shoulder problems:

1. List doctors located on our side of town.

2. Check with the nearest hospital's physician referral service for doctors that seem to fit.

3. Check insurance list for specialists.

4. Get recommendations from others at work.

5. Would this one be good for Dirk too?

6. Can we manage the insurance deductible?

They picked one that was in the company insurance directory and was also recommended by Dirk's boss. For them, what had been a difficult task in the beginning turned out to be a learning experience that would benefit them when a need for other resources arose. They acquired a skill to help them in future transitions. Because job changes are becoming more and more common and moves to new cities can result, you will benefit from knowing how to find information in a new town.

Sources of Information

Vanessa and Fitzgerald want to work in the same city when they graduate, but they also want good career opportunities. They could research cities that have several large companies or look at individual firms that have many openings in their fields.

Sometimes, finding out about important things in one's life is often a matter of asking the right person. A popular television game show calls this a "lifeline," where contestants may call someone for help answering a difficult question. If you are a college student, besides the library, a major source of knowledge is the student services department. If you are employed, you can call on your company's human resources department or the employee assistance representative. Others may simply check with state human services departments, clergy, police departments, telephone directories, 1-800- directories, and local chambers of commerce. Services agencies also have Web sites.

If you are in an emergency situation, call 911; however, in a large city where the emergency system could become overloaded, have the number of the hospital emergency room or trauma center handy too.

 4.1 **ACTIVITY**

When you have to know something in a hurry, where do you usually look? Do you have a friend who is particularly knowledgeable about certain issues? Write down the names of people you know who are good sources of information.

1. Name: _____

   Source of information on: _____

2. Name: _____

   Source of information on: _____

Whatever your need is, you can find information if you know where to look. Information gathering is most often a matter of knowing where to go to find answers to questions. On-line services, such as databases and the Internet, give you access to information on every topic you can think of through e-mail, downloading services, bulletin boards, and interactive systems. Some sources of "how-to" classes or even sophisticated job-skill courses on the Internet are:

- www.learn2.com: Everything from free tutorials to fee-based classes. Some video feeds; good range of topics.
- www.ehow.com: Free classes on hobby and consumer topics.
- www.smartplanet.com: Classes for a low fee. More like a distance-learning site than general interest.
- www.hungryminds.com: General interest classes for a fee and some credit courses from various postsecondary schools.

Some cities are starting to list all of their services on local Internet exchanges, and many colleges and universities are also on the Internet. Anyone with a computer and a modem can use the phone lines to gather and exchange all types of information. If you do not know how to use the Internet, you would do well to find a course about it or visit a library that has it. Your future on the "information highway" depends on your understanding this helpful and powerful tool.

You can find information on the Internet or in books or magazines. Remember, too, that you do not need to retain or commit to memory all that you find. According to an anecdote, a reporter once asked Albert Einstein "How many feet are in a mile?" The reported response was, "I don't know." The interviewer expressed surprise that one of the greatest minds of the century did not know that piece of information. Einstein said, "Why should I clutter my brain with something that I can look up in a few seconds?"

Whether the story is true is irrelevant. The point is that the quick access to information may be equally as important as retention. Saving and storing information can take many forms:

- *Books*—as you read keep a piece of paper nearby. Write notes or impressions as you read, and when finished, record what you thought was the most important concept, item, or quote. Then, if you want to refer to the book, you can use your notes.
- *Articles*—can be scanned onto a disk, torn out, or copied.
- *Internet material*—bookmark sites to make them available any time you need to find them.

A note about retention: we retain what we use. People complain about not being able to add or divide because they use calculators all the time. You only need to retain what you use and use what you retain. Otherwise, knowing where to find information is more important than being able to retain it.

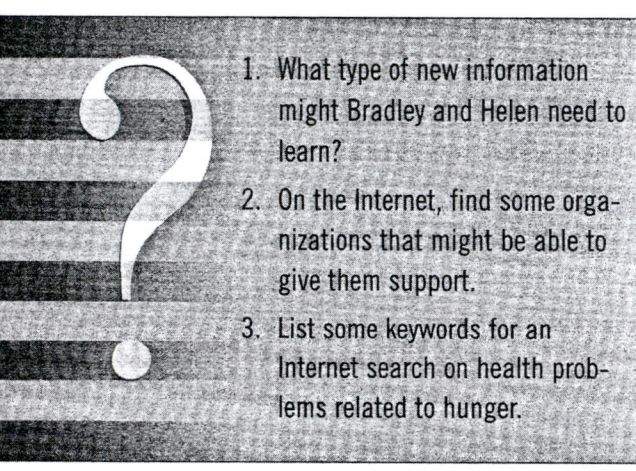

1. What type of new information might Bradley and Helen need to learn?
2. On the Internet, find some organizations that might be able to give them support.
3. List some keywords for an Internet search on health problems related to hunger.

Bradley and Helen want to adopt an orphaned child from a foreign country. They have never had children before, and this child has some health problems related to poor conditions and malnutrition.

You can also learn more about your world and the important ideas and events in it by attending seminars, classes, or lectures. Because the purpose of such classes is to add to your knowledge or skills, you want to retain this material.

If you do not have good information-processing skills, you may not retain much of what you find or hear. Information of this type is only as useful as your own ability to remember and apply it. Learning to program your brain for the maximum retention will help make you better prepared for work or school.

Information Processing

Each of us remembers sitting around the reading circle or at a desk in school and being called on to read aloud. If we did well and read every word correctly, we learned two things: that reading every word is important and that reading is a good thing. If we didn't do well, we probably came to the conclusion that reading was difficult and that learning would have to come from other sources.

Schools tend to offer very little guidance about information gathering after the first few years of teaching us to read (about second grade). Thus, some children figure out the "secrets" of fact finding in an efficient and time-effective way on their own. Other children grow into adulthood with an aversion to reading and a difficulty with locating information quickly and retaining it.

Whether you enjoy learning new ideas and procedures or not, you are living in an age where aggressive, lifelong learning is the key to career survival. Knowledge is indeed power, and the lack of knowledge about your job or the world is most certainly the opposite. Whether you are a student or a professional in a company, you have a daily need to process information.

In college that information may be the answers to assignments in a textbook or the data required for a research project. In industry, though, you are more likely to have to deal with a troubleshooting guide for a new piece of equipment, steps to perform a work-related task, or facts about your company's products or market trends. Whatever the information, you are expected to gather and process it quickly and to retain it for future use. If you learned a method to do this while you were in school, you may have forgotten it by now. If you didn't learn it in school, now is the time.

As adults, we process information from the inside out, instead of the outside in. We take impressions, facts, perceptions, skills, and knowledge and apply them all day, every day to solving life's problems. We are expected to come up with creative solutions for work and home crises. Our brain begins to process in primarily one way. In a world that doesn't change much, this is not a problem. Unfortunately, ours is not that world. In the face of change, we must constantly update our intelligence on the world around us. This intelligence gathering makes us better equipped to meet the challenges that come at us daily and to recognize and capitalize on opportunities.

To do this requires us to program our brains for a new approach. Instead of screening out the myriad of impressions that come to us each day in ads, on the news, in conversation, and from our experiences, our minds have to be told to retain certain things because we need them. For example, if Kirby is to avoid going into overload, he must ignore and discount the many phone numbers that he hears on the television, radio, and other media. But if he is looking for car repair, and someone he knows offers him the number of a friend who is a reputable mechanic, he must program his information system to pay attention to and retain that number (see Figure 4.1). This works much like a computer or a filing system.

If you tell your brain that you have to remember something, it will oblige you and not screen out important facts. If you do not have a reason to remember individual facts or ideas, your brain will select on its own with no useful pattern.

So, to accomplish efficient data gathering, you are going to have to engage in an interactive process of listening and reading that meets your adult information needs. The techniques for this process are different from the ones you may have used for your childhood tasks.

FIGURE 4.1	"Filing" needed information.

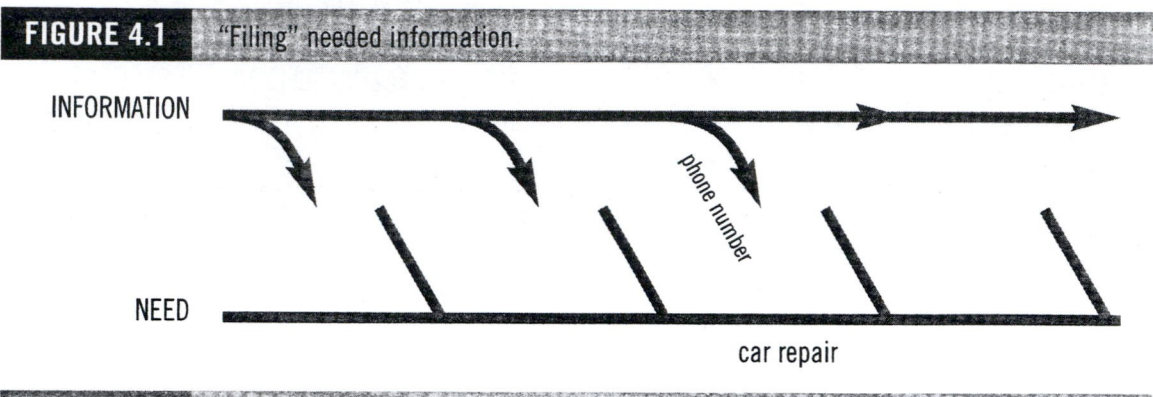

Interactive Listening

If your boss sends you to a training school at company expense for you to learn a new procedure for work, you had better learn it thoroughly. You may be asked to teach the others you work with what you have learned. For this task, you have to use active listening.

Step 1. Make sure you understand the purpose of the listening situation and the value of the information to you. Write down ahead of time the purpose and your information need.

Step 2. If you are a written-information processor by nature (you learn best by reading), then set up columns on a piece of paper that are labeled by your information need. For example:

The purpose of this seminar is to help us set up a local area network.

My need is to find out what trouble-shooting help might be given for our system.

Problems	Solutions	Help Available

If you are a visual person (you learn best by seeing pictures or diagrams of things), then set up a picture to help you collect the information and remember it (see Figure 4.2).

If you are a student who has to study for tests, or a business person wanting to give a presentation, you should use one of these approaches. The reason these note-taking methods help is that your concentration begins to fade about two-thirds of the way down the page you are reviewing.

So, if you try to store information by only reading your notes, you will likely miss some items or forget important facts that come from material found in the bottom one-third of your note pages. Pictures and columns help

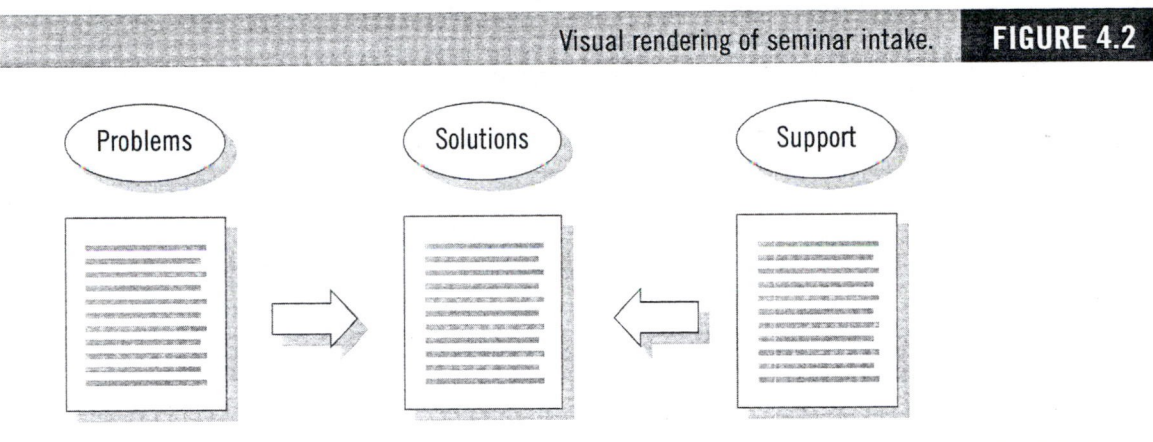

Visual rendering of seminar intake.   **FIGURE 4.2**

focus your eye and help you record what you want to remember. This technique helps you use the whole page without losing the bottom third.

Step 3. Wonder about what is being said. Your brain processes much faster than people talk, so it is easy to get bored. This is how you suddenly find yourself returning your attention to what is being said after several minutes of being "somewhere else." By actively wondering about what is being said, you keep focused on the topic. Also, this technique causes you to process the information, so you are more likely to remember it. For example:

> "I wonder about the types of cable we will need for the network."
>
> and
>
> "She mentioned a technical support staff. Are they by telephone or do they come out? If she doesn't say, I'll ask the question later."

Step 4. Take notes as you go, but don't let it interfere with listening. If you listen actively, you will understand the concept being discussed, and you will retain the idea long enough to write it down after the point is made.

Step 5. Repeat each main point in your head several times before moving on to the next one. As was noted earlier, your brain processes very quickly and you will be able to do this in a second or two.

Step 6. Ask questions whenever the speaker says it is okay. This could be during or at the end of a presentation. Either way, make sure the questions are relevant to your information needs, but also be mindful of the needs of the group. Don't get too far afield with questions about your particular situation.

Step 7. After the presentation is over, immediately review the main points in your mind or in your notes to make sure you got the information you came there to receive.

> Thomas works in the new regional sales office of his company. With many new salespeople, the manager wants to have a sophisticated training program to orient them. The money ($1,000 apiece) is not in the budget yet, so she decides to send Thomas. He is instructed to plan to train the new people in the techniques he will learn at the seminar.

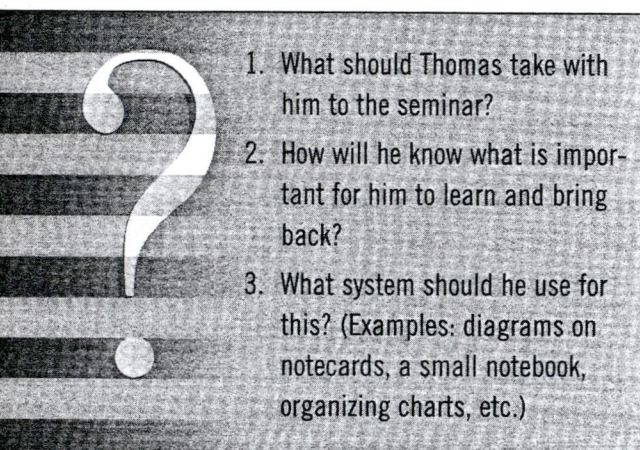

1. What should Thomas take with him to the seminar?

2. How will he know what is important for him to learn and bring back?

3. What system should he use for this? (Examples: diagrams on notecards, a small notebook, organizing charts, etc.)

Use the listening skills to teach yourself to be a better communicator. Observe political speakers, informative speakers, seminar leaders, religious speakers, salespeople, and television commercials. Look for not only the content of their communication, but also the techniques they use to make what they say sound believable and to make you want to act on or take in the information. Then, begin to use the same techniques in your own oral communication. Lifelong learning takes place every day if we avail ourselves of the information that is offered over the many media in our society.

Interactive Reading

Approaches to adult information gathering from print media are slightly different from "regular" reading. The first consideration is whether you have the time to devote to reading regardless of the importance of the information. Most adults read fewer than 350 words per minute. If you have three textbook chapters, or two procedures manuals, or several long business proposals to read in a day, examine the practicalities of the situation. There isn't enough time at that rate to read it all. Consequently, most people rely almost exclusively on verbal media—talking and listening. Considering that we retain less than 25 percent of what we hear after three weeks, this is a risky proposition. We are usually accountable for much more than that.

There are many techniques to improve reading speed and comprehension: machine methods that flash lines of print at a set and increasing speed on a screen for you to read; courses where you learn to use special approaches to reading a page; and books about a psychological approach to reading. All of them have one thing in common: they address the inefficient approaches we have learned and the bad habits we have developed. But, if you understand certain things about information-gathering needs and human thinking patterns, you will quickly see how you can make dramatic improvements in a short period of time. Take a moment now to determine your own reading speed.

ACTIVITY 4.2

Time yourself for 30 seconds while you read the passage below at your normal reading speed. Then, circle your reading speed at the point where you stopped. (Note: It is much easier to do this if someone times you.)

Begin timing now.

Research Summary for Zero Emission Background Study

As a summary of the work of several people, the information following is an overview of some of the research done to determine the degree of success

60   expected in marketing / zero emission (electric) vehicles.

"Research studies say this . . ." "Research studies say that . . ." For every topic or forecasting need there is some sort of research done. The

120   purpose of research is / to add to information available for making decisions. It should never be the sole basis for strategic planning or for forecasting. Products

180   have succeeded with the help of marketing research / and products have failed with it. (Don't ask Coca-Cola how much they spent on researching the disastrous "New Coke.") Forecasts alone, by their very nature, can completely

240   deny the / effect of sound marketing strategy on consumers' willingness to buy and are limited in their ability to fully determine risk or potential.

300   A good example of this is the decision / for paint color on a car. Looking at the figures for largest amount of paint sold, one would naturally conclude that

360   white was the best color to paint a car / to make it sell well. In reality, though, white is the choice for fleet vehicles in many areas and is not necessarily the first

420   choice of the buying public. In / a quick survey of night students, ages 20–50, at a local college, the color blue was the most popular, immediately followed by

480   black. The sample was largely male and / largely engineers: both factors that affected the interpretation of the outcome.

Interestingly enough, even in this nonscientific poll, an unexpected result

540   occurred: 31 percent said that stopping to put gas / into their car was the most bothersome element of having a vehicle. (The engine was second with 27 percent.) So,

600   being open-minded to a wide range of consumer responses / often can lead to clear and helpful information.

Write your words-per-minute score here: _____ wpm.

Barriers to Speed and Comprehension

When we read at 300 words per minute, our brains get bored and our attention drifts, so that our eyes can actually arrive at the bottom of a page, but our brain doesn't remember reading any of it! Our own boredom becomes a barrier. Thus, it is certainly logical to expect that reading faster improves your retention.

The concentration required to push yourself to read quickly all of the time keeps you focused on what you are doing. That way, your brain doesn't have time to play. So, the notion that reading faster decreases your ability to remember is invalid.

The second barrier is a bad habit that most of us have developed over years of reading. Eye-movement studies of people reading show that the eye constantly moves back up the page and goes over material time and time again. Keeping the eye moving down the page at a steady rate may double your reading speed the first few times you try it.

The third barrier is "soup-can reading." This is similar to the old reading circle; you read every word, and somewhere in all of those words you happen across something of value—eventually. You cannot afford to wait for "eventually" in our fast-paced world.

The final barrier is non-interactive reading. As was explained earlier, if you do not read for a specific *purpose*, then what you read may not be retained.

The word purpose has a meaning here. "My boss told me to get through these specifications for Monday's job by tomorrow" is not purpose. Real purpose is convincing your brain that what you are about to read has value to you. This is an act of conscious reading, of interacting with the material. You accomplish interactive reading by improving your concentration, using physical focus cues, quizzing yourself, and scribbling. Following are some techniques to improve your reading speed.

Improvement Technique #1. Push yourself to move your eyes quickly across the lines and down the page. The constant push keeps your concentration up. It may feel uncomfortable at first, as if you are not "reading" at all, but just getting your eyes to "hurry up" will improve your speed.

Improvement Technique #2. Use an attention getter to guide your eyes along the page. Some people use a small, colored ruler to slide down the page as they read. Some books, such as textbooks and magazines, are very "busy" in their format. There are pictures, ads, and other articles on the page. These can be very distracting and draw your concentration away from what you need to read and absorb.

A good technique to prevent interference by distractions on the page is to cut a square hole in a plain, white piece of paper. The size should be the width

Reading a "window" of text.   **FIGURE 4.3**

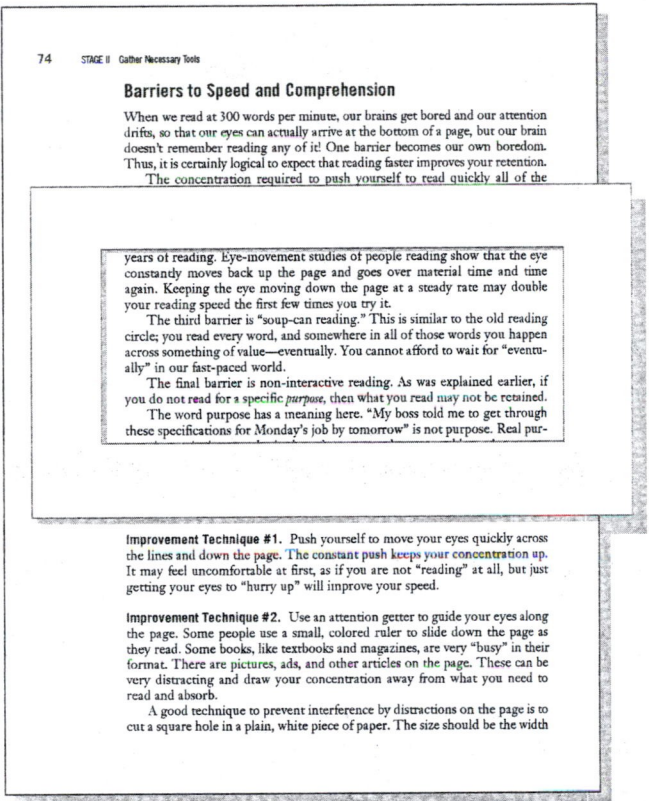

Reading a "window" of text.   **FIGURE 4.3**

of the columns of print you are reading and about three inches deep. Sliding this down or across what you are reading gives a "window" effect, so you are drawn to the only thing in your field of vision, the print.

Even holding a pen on the page and moving it down while you read will help. The purpose is to keep your eye moving down the page and not going back up all the time.

Improvement Technique #3. Quiz yourself before, during, and after you read. A difficulty that we, as adults, have with learning new written material is that we seldom retain anything that we do not have to process immediately for a purpose. If someone asks you a question about a political issue, for example, and you are embarrassed by not having any knowledge of the issue, then you will purposefully correct that situation. You will look up an article or ask someone. You will remember the answer to prevent further difficulties that could arise if you are asked again about the same topic.

A technique to help you gather information efficiently from printed material is quizzing. Before you read, think of questions you hope to have answered by the reading material. Then, read for the answers. Proof that this works is looking up a phone number. You do not read every name on every page until you find John Smith on Halvern Lane. Instead, you program your brain to find the name on the street, then scan the page, skipping all names but his. Your eye automatically passes over all of the other Smiths and John Smiths and comes to rest on your friend's name and address.

Quizzing after reading a fact you want to remember causes you to process the information through an additional path in your brain (the outgoing path as well as the incoming path) and increases your retention. Quizzing after each important idea reinforces in your mind that you *want* to know that information, and that your brain should not screen it out like it would an ad or a piece of unnecessary information.

Improvement Technique #4. Reading with a pen or pencil in hand and scribbling reactions to written material as you read it is an important part of effective information gathering. In elementary school, you couldn't write in your books because they had to be returned and used the next year. Now, you are grown and can buy your own books and magazines or photocopy a few pages at a time. So, scribble away in the columns, above the title, around pictures and charts. Underline or highlight critical ideas. Add sticky notes. These notes can be questions, disagreements with the facts or ideas proposed, expressions of confusion, or personal notes. What you write is not important. What is important is that you process by using the "wondering" technique suggested earlier. Wonder on paper.

4.3 ACTIVITY

Look over the short selection below. From the title and the headings, create a diagram of the way you might set up your note taking.

Planning a Working Budget

What People Don't Do

So many working people handle their daily tasks on the job quite well and responsibly, but their budgeting of personal finances lacks the same diligence.

This problem is common to both younger and older adults. Interviews with employees of a large consumer products company show that fewer than 20 percent have a savings or investment plan outside whatever their company provides. And, of those who use the company plan, few put aside the maximum amount allowed. In addition, there are only 18 percent who use any kind of consumer comparison guide or research to help them when purchasing products—even those purchases as large as a car. So, wage earners are not saving aggressively, and they are not using important and easily available reference material to ensure they obtain the best value for their money.

What They Should Do

It would appear that the best recommendation for anyone who wants to improve personal finances is not to become involved in get-rich schemes or austere "buy nothing" purchase plans. Just saving a regular amount of money each month, no matter how small, will generate enough funds to finance a nice investment program that can grow into a hefty future source of income. In addition, just an hour or two of research into the quality of products in a given category will prevent money from being wasted on poor or overpriced products.

You will find that as you pattern yourself to read with a purpose and a plan, your concentration and memory for facts improve. You will be able to program yourself to remember more of what you read in newspapers, professional publications, and general information sources. The tools you have developed thus far can be applied to any listening or reading situation to help you gain the most from what you see and hear. If you practice the skills regularly, they will become natural, and you will be able to use them without thinking. Practice with newspapers, radio and TV newscasts, magazines, books, and other listening or reading situations. Your job, however, will require other types of learning.

Professional Development

Once you have stepped into your job, what you have learned in college is already beginning to become obsolete. As disconcerting as that sounds, especially when you think of all those study hours and review sessions, it is true. Not only is current technology hardware roaring down the obsolescence turnpike, the information needed to survive on a day-to-day basis must be updated constantly. New employees will find this especially true.

> **TRANSITION TIP**   *Brandon Davis, Network Engineer*
>
> I came on at the busiest quarter of the year, so an official orientation session was out of the question. No one had the time. I could have sat in my office, but instead, I found out what my department was working on specifically, researched the products, and even dug out manuals for the new systems. By the time anyone got around to showing me what I would need to know, I had already learned most of it.

The kind of information gathering Brandon Davis describes shows *initiative*—learning because there is something you need to know, not because someone has told you to learn it. What working people often miss are the many sources of new knowledge that are easily accessible. You will not necessarily have to take a class to keep up. In this book we use the term "professional development" to describe any activity that enriches your knowledge, skill, or attitude for the work environment. As a self-advocacy plan, you can advance your career by learning skills and knowledge that make you worth more to your company or some other company.

Some examples of avenues of professional development are:

- Reading—for example, this book—you gain knowledge and learning skills that will help you in your career.

- Observation—you can watch people who are good at something you feel you might need to know and pick up some new practices.

- Apprenticeship—this term is usually used in union-type jobs, but the concept of attaching yourself to a "master," an acknowledged expert in your field, always applies.

- Ferretting—many people do not want to go to the trouble of learning new procedures, equipment, or software. By digging into manuals, user guides, and technical or product specification sheets, you can quickly become the "expert" in a new area.

- New product training—every tool used in business was developed and sold by a company that may offer half-day or day-long introduction seminars on their newest products free of charge; an excellent way to stay up to date.

- Trade shows—volunteering to work in your company's booth at a large industry trade show adds to your knowledge in two ways: you see what others (both customers and competitors) think about your company, and you gain exposure to the very latest trends and "players" in your industry.

- Internal, company-sponsored training—formal classes developed by specialized areas of your company or the human resources department cost you nothing and often help you earn promotion "points" or credit for your self-improvement.

- Professional organizations—meetings and publications of professional organizations in your field can provide an entire education if you will become involved.

Personal Development

Just as you pursue professional development, you can improve your personal life through development. If someone wants to put in a brick patio, she might attend a seminar at the local home improvement store, read a book or article about the activity, or even ask someone who is knowledgeable how to do it. In short, she would actively go about learning in order to carry out the improvement project. If she buys a new computer, or upgrades the one she has, she has to work to learn the new capabilities and operating protocols in order to get the best use out of it.

Ample information on relationship building is available from workshops, articles, books, experts, Internet sites, and television programs, but too many people ignore the need to develop in this area. Few people put effort into learning if there is no urgency or an immediate need to know.

The passive person sits and waits to "see what happens." This person is either the victim of a failed relationship or the lucky member of a winning relationship. The active person sets a priority on relationship building. He commits to continue to work at growing and improving the relationship's ability to adapt to new situations and conditions.

There is a lot to know about building fulfilling relationships. The ever-changing world, as well as the constantly evolving dynamics of people, demands constant growth and learning for successful adaptation. Thus, lifelong learning should not just be a professional growth goal area, but a personal one as well. For this reason relationship skills are the focus of two chapters of this book.

TRANSITION SKILLS SUMMARY

Develop information literacy

Use interactive information processing

Keep up with professional development

Apply lifelong learning to personal development

GOAL SETTING

My self-nurturing goals for applying my new information-gathering skills:

_____

_____

_____

My self-advocacy goals for applying my new information-gathering skills:

_____

_____

_____

COACH'S CORNER

Research requests may come in any form, something as specific as a patent search or as nebulous as, "I saw an article in an old copy of *TV Guide* by Robin Williams, I believe. Can you find that?" In some cases, marketing might hear about a company releasing a new product or about an EPA ruling concerning a chemical that my company manufactures. Following up keeps me aware of specifics in the industry.

Databases, such as Dialog or Lexis-Nexis, are paid services, and every industry has vendors like those with information specific to the industry. A single vendor may package 200–300 databases. The information varies in quality, so some screening has to be done, but you eventually learn which are the best for your company.

We subscribe to 600 professional journals, many of which we access on-line. Journals posted on the Internet require a subscription to access more than a few articles in each issue that are made available to the public.

My company uses the Internet primarily for document delivery. We use it to get information about companies we are not familiar with and for press releases about industry news. LISTSERVs® keep us up to date on what services are being offered. We have discovered sources for translated patents through a LISTSERV®; previously, we had to pay for the document and pay for a translation.

ROSANA MEADOWS, Technical Information Specialist

CHAPTER 5

Creating a Positive Attitude

We seek out positive attitudes in friendships, intimate relationships, employees, and sales people because people who are energetic, optimistic, open, and happy are just naturally attractive. We do this because they:

- radiate a sense of satisfaction about life
- seem centered, calm, and in control
- are pleasant to be around
- tend to have many friends
- have a spirited enthusiasm
- expect positive outcomes even in the most difficult times
- infect us with their upbeat spirit.

With all of the benefits of positive-attitude living, you might find it hard to imagine anyone who wants to view the world and life any other way. But, attitudes and behavior are learned over time. We are, after all, the sum total of our experiences and our attitudes about those experiences. Thus, a negative attitude can grow out of too many failures, hurts, and disappointments. Eventually, the negativity becomes a pattern; whining, despair, and helplessness win out over perseverance and expectancy.

In the same way, happy experiences lead to expectations of positive outcomes. But a pattern of happy life events is not the only reason a person develops an optimistic viewpoint. The world can be a hazardous, treacherous, and often frightening place, but it is also exciting and rich with gifts, heroism, and joy. Optimism is a choice—do you choose to see the poverty or the compassion, the hope or the depravity, the loss or the potential? Whatever you expect to see, you will.

The truth is, no one wants to be around a person who spews out negative thoughts and feelings. It makes others feel uncomfortable and it throws a damper on the general mood. If you find that you are in the group of people who use negativity excessively, you can, and should, disconnect its effect on you before you fall into the pattern or habit yourself. If you are one of those who view the world and the people in it with distrust and negative expectation, you can consciously change, creating a life of joy and satisfaction for yourself and those around you.

Understanding the Value of a Positive Attitude

The effects of a positive outlook are far reaching. It can make the difference between a life of dread and a life filled with peace. A positive attitude can have a dramatically beneficial effect on one's health also. Seeing the world as being full of opportunity and potentially good experiences prevents many of the physical effects of stress and the ensuing wear and tear on the body.

Characteristics of a Positive Attitude

Positive people are easier to be around and tend to uplift others around them, especially if they are in a leadership position. They are better to work with and for. Through their attitude, they generate confidence and help others stay calm in crisis situations. Because positive people are optimistic, they create opportunities for themselves by believing that solutions are just around the corner. They know that every problem has a point where a resolution lies. They see themselves as being able to get to that endpoint quickly. This attitude rubs off on others and fosters a constructive circle of friends, family, and coworkers.

A positive attitude is associated with high self-esteem. People with high self-esteem are desirable in the workplace for several reasons:

- They take responsibility for their work and future, including mistakes.
- They make good team players and are able to share success with others.
- They can commit because they are confident they will be successful.
- They are slow to anger because they do not carry grudges.

- They are candid, giving constructive criticism.
- They manage conflict well, valuing resolution over winning.
- They can take risks because they respect failure as a learning process, not a reflection on their essential value.

A positive attitude is powerful. It can help you realize your dreams because with an optimistic expectation, you feel free to dream.

Characteristics of a Negative Attitude

There are two kinds of negativity we deal with in our lives: our own negativity and that of others. We often are not aware that the troubled, uncomfortable feeling that nags at us is really negativity and its effects. Low expectations in our careers and relationships cause us to settle for something less than a satisfying life. The negative spiral downward is reinforced by the lack of real joy and inner fulfillment, further adding to the misery.

The characteristics of a negative person are as follows:

- They experience worry and fear almost daily.
- They often see themselves as victims of life.
- They feel powerless and overburdened by their circumstances.
- They are often described by their friends and coworkers as "naysayers" or "wet blankets."
- They approach tasks, aspirations, and relationships with low expectations.
- They project their negative view on others: "You'll never get that promotion; someone else has seniority."

The cumulative effects of negative thinking on us are dramatic. We become stressed out, self-esteem decreases, confidence fades, and we are unable to stay focused on our goals (see Figure 5.1).

Negative people "stomp" on ideas and possibilities.   **FIGURE 5.1**

No way.

This job stinks.

You don't have enough seniority.

That will never work.

Negative persons may experience an underlying hopelessness about life. Feeling powerless, they may struggle to gain some control. This struggle is emotionally draining and can actually cause situations to go badly. Adverse thoughts often become self-fulfilling prophecies, and the cycle of negativity continues.

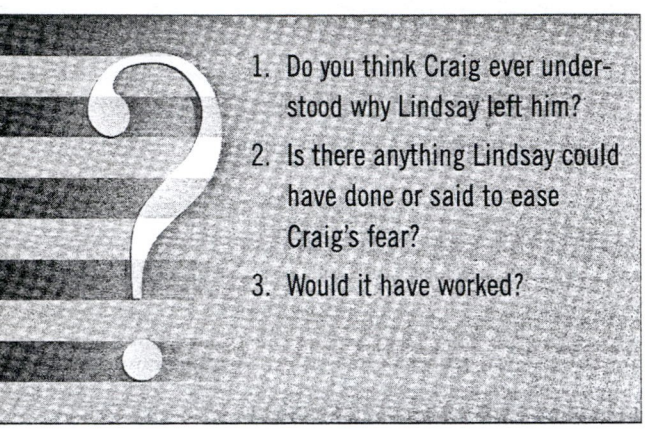

1. Do you think Craig ever understood why Lindsay left him?

2. Is there anything Lindsay could have done or said to ease Craig's fear?

3. Would it have worked?

Though Craig and Lindsay had been best friends since junior high school and dated all through college, Craig worried that Lindsay would leave him when she went to work. She had matured into a quite beautiful woman and drew admiring glances wherever they went. Though she was seriously committed to Craig, she began to be put off by his insistent jealousy and self-deprecating remarks. Eventually, his behavior led to several arguments, and Lindsay sadly broke off the relationship.

Negative communication with yourself and with others can become a habit that causes you to talk yourself into a dismal view of the world at large. It destroys expectations, and it alienates other people who don't want to hear pessimistic talk all of the time. The original cause for this doleful approach to life may have been a disappointment or even a tragedy. Though probably long forgotten, the initial life event left behind a pattern of negativism.

Alex, a computer specialist at a bank, was a worrier. He had come from a family who criticized him in an effort to make him improve and work up to his potential. He obsessed over his work and worried that he was not good enough for the job. He was very hard on himself if he made the slightest mistake and was openly critical of others' work as well.

Stephany was an executive secretary at a hospital that had just been bought by a managed health care organization. Stephany was still relatively new to her position and liked it very much. Her coworkers and the medical staff constantly expressed their fears and resentment over the changes that would be coming. Over the next several months, she felt more and more stressed and overwhelmed by her job even though her duties remained the same. When she got home in the evenings, she was exhausted. She had already been to her physician and he had found nothing wrong with her. She just could not figure out what was making her feel so bad.

Obviously, these examples are about negativity, but in Stephany's case the negativity was coming from her environment.

Negative thinkers usually have had much practice. Also, they probably are not even aware of the source of their own misery. They tend to blame their unhappiness on everything but their negative thinking. They use such statements as, "If only this would happen, I could be happy."

Those who communicate negatively also have negative expectations. They wait for life to change rather than beginning to change what they can. They usually wind up "waiting" most of their lives. Those few who have good fortune often cannot enjoy it because they don't know how.

ACTIVITY   5.1

Are you subjecting yourself to negative talk? Give some examples that you have used or heard others use.

1. Negative things I say to myself or others.

    a. _____

    b. _____

2. Negative things I have heard others say to me or around me.

    a. _____

    b. _____

Negativity in the office group dramatically inhibits productivity. The word *toxic* is often used to describe this effect. The stimulus can be a disgruntled, toxic worker who complains or criticizes constantly or it can be an organizational climate of fear or distrust. Even the rosiest personalities and the most highly motivated employees will eventually be adversely affected.

Improving Your Attitude

Although it is true that there is effort involved in changing old patterns, the effort is well worth it. You will find yourself feeling happier about life because you will feel a greater sense of control over your thinking. When difficult things come along, you can look for the silver lining, rather than lament about how you have been victimized.

Recognize Negativity as Learned Behavior

Both positive and negative thinking are most often a product of past experiences. We learn these patterns as children and continue to repeat them. These experiences usually occur when we are very young and do not have the intellectual capacity to question them. The critical judgments or the unflattering comments that we heard as children may have shaped us in directions we did not want to go. Young children's thought processes do not question or sift messages that come to them. Because of this, they do not have the ability to assess the accuracy of damaging statements, and, consequently, internalize them as truths. Because at some level in the child's mind the information is absolute fact, he proceeds to think about and operate on these ideas for many years.

The total effect of this is the development of a negative self-image. It is impossible to look constructively and positively on the world through eyes shaded by a negative self-image. These patterns become ingrained in our unconscious thinking and control our lives.

Conversely, those who have emerged from childhood with a generally positive self-image seem to be able to weather difficulties and experience less stress in adult interpersonal situations and life events. Contributors to this attitude might be anything from success as an athlete or with some hobby, excellence in schoolwork, or even the constant support of a doting grandparent or other "fan." This is why the way adults speak to children is so important. Regardless of the external reality of a child's life, positive and respectful treatment and communication can have lifelong beneficial effects.

5.2 ACTIVITY

Try to remember some negative comments made about you or to you when you were a child. See if you can come up with a positive statement that refutes the original comment.

1. Negative comment: _____

   Positive statement: _____

2. Negative comment: _____

   Positive statement: _____

Identify Worry Styles

Some of our negative learned behavior is worry. We spend far too much time feeling concerned about the potential for disturbing life events. Interestingly, the value we attach to something—whether it is interpreted as a good thing or a bad thing—is a learned identifier. For instance, eating less than the average person may be viewed by some as positive, a way to control weight and maintain good health. To someone else, not eating much suggests a loss of appetite and poor health—a cause for worry.

Our worry topics and style are often developed in very subtle ways during our youth. Your neighbor, for example, may have expressed concern about a drought and its effects, such as the local lake or river drying up. Or your brother worried about his appearance and whether people liked him. These examples are all filed away and emerge when some stimulus similar to the worry stimulus occurs. When you ask yourself why you are worried about your car breaking down even though you have an auto club, a cell phone, and a new car, you might remember a parent or relative worrying about such things.

The way people worry is learned as well. If your mother smoked when she was worried, you might have a strange desire to smoke when you are upset, even if you are not generally a smoker. Some people cannot sleep; some sleep a lot when worried. Some get quiet; others talk incessantly. Think about your behavior in the dentist's chair—a good indicator of one element of your worry style.

As soon as you understand why you identify an event or situation as a reason for worry and where you acquired your worry style, you can start disconnecting irrelevant and irrational responses. Constructive positive approaches to problems or dramatic life events is empowering and more effective than worrying.

When was the last time you remember your worry having any effect whatsoever on the outcome of a situation? Worry is taxing and interferes with clear thinking. Also, some worry behaviors can be extremely dangerous (e.g., a woman who drives when she worries could find herself in a very bad place at three in the morning, or a person who becomes cross or ill-tempered when worried may find himself alone or out of a job very soon).

Monitor Internal Dialog

We all talk to ourselves at some level, consciously or not. We play messages in our heads that we have received from others or we fill our thoughts with messages of our own choosing. Often, we are not immediately aware of this self-talk, and that is one reason why it controls our attitude and behavior so regularly—we never question what is coming into our heads. Once you begin to notice your internal dialog, you can act to change what is detrimental or pessimistic. No one has to live with negative thinking or its effects.

The more you talk to yourself in negative ways, the more you wind up frightening and agitating yourself. This kind of talk can:

- Create stress and panic attacks that can be debilitating.

- Make you feel that you are going crazy.
- Make you sweat profusely.
- Cause chest pains and make you feel you are about to die.

To maintain emotional and relational health and to progress in life, get a handle on your thinking patterns. Learn how to be kind to yourself and refute any unkind observations or comments that sneak into your thoughts. In addition, cultivate the habit of saying something positive or kind to someone each day.

When you take the step to notice what goes on in your head, you have begun the task of changing any negative internal programmed tapes to positive internal dialog. The change is not difficult if you maintain your awareness and short-circuit anything that you do not like. After all, you are the one in control of your thoughts. Even when negative thoughts float through your mind, you do not have to keep them there. You can learn to eliminate them and avoid the disturbing and taxing results. You might not be able to control what comes into your head, but you can certainly control what stays there.

Break Old Patterns

One of the most powerful weapons against negative thinking is its counterpart, positive thinking. Just as doleful or dismal thoughts become habits, upbeat and bright thoughts and communication can become a personal style. Following are the steps for breaking the negative thinking habit:

1. Note how you react to life events and become aware of the pattern. If your psyche is on auto-pilot, your mood or expectation is somewhat arbitrarily assigned. As soon as you begin looking for patterns, you start the process of disconnecting the unhealthy ones.

"I never noticed before, but every time my son suggests an alternative solution to a problem, I automatically dismiss it."

"At that meeting this morning I kept track and found I made eight comments to those around me, and all were critical or negative."

2. Decide the specific patterns you want to change.

"I notice I automatically assume there's going to be a problem when a customer calls. I would like to start answering the phone with a more helpful attitude."

"Whenever we start pushing toward a deadline at work, everyone, including me, seems to spend as much time complaining as working. I would like to keep my thoughts clear."

3. Catch yourself and others—don't allow your spirit to be bombarded with negativity from within or without.

If you think, "I forgot my wallet. What an idiotic thing to do," catch yourself: "Oops, there I go. How could I reframe that negative view?" Correct yourself and say, "Well, that's the first time in four years I've done that. Now, where might I have left it?"

4. Practice operating as a positive self-talker. Expect and verbalize positive outcomes: Not "I'll never get the boss to notice my good work," rather, "How can I get the boss to notice my good work?"; not "Alan won't call. He's always too busy for me," rather, "I haven't heard from Alan. Maybe I should call him."

When facing the challenges and frustrations of your daily life, you may find another approach to be helpful. By redesigning your responses to reflect a positive expectation, you build confidence in yourself. David Greenberg, motivational speaker and executive coach, says, "Of course, even positive, successful people have negatives sometimes—negative thoughts or events— but they don't allow the effects to stay with them long. If the computer breaks, don't consume your thoughts with the inconvenience, focus instead on the repair person who will come and make it work again and on how nice that will be." (See Coach's Corner at the end of this chapter.)

When you speak to yourself and others in positive ways, you make the statement that you believe in yourself and in your ability to cope with whatever challenge and frustration may arise.

Creating a Positive Environment

You might notice that there are others around you who have patterns of negative talk as well. Some people who would ordinarily have a positive life view and attitude find themselves in negative environments. These environments can affect the way we feel about our work and relationships.

Once you begin approaching communication in a more empowered and effectual way, you may notice how easy it still is to be infected or influenced by negative talk around you. If your friends constantly criticize each other or you, then that is creating a negative environment. Often when they say something unkind or sarcastic, they say, "I'm just telling it like it is." Perhaps they are, or maybe they are only telling the side they see from their own negative perspective.

Several approaches are possible to deal with negative environments created by friends or coworkers.

1. Defuse the effect the negativism has on you. This is easily accomplished when you recognize the dismal talk for what it is and laugh about it to yourself: "I can't believe how negative Angela sounds today!"

2. Stay away from the "gloom and doom" people and attach yourself to more positive and upbeat individuals. You will be amazed at how your energy level and your demeanor are affected positively by surrounding yourself with people who are positive and forward looking.

3. Confront the "wet blankets" and expose their negativism. Someone may say, "Gosh Nick, where on earth did you find that jacket?" Your reply might be, "That sounds like you don't like my jacket choice for the meeting today."

Sometimes people do not realize the habit they have let themselves develop. Your approach to this may be getting the work group to agree to improve conditions for everyone by choosing to have constructive conversations.

Renee is unhappy with her job. She loves the work as an accountant, but is becoming affected by the working environment. People complain a lot, and no one seems enthusiastic or motivated to do a good job. A coworker complains that the boss is too demanding. Another says that the workers are underpaid. Renee's officemate confides that she is looking for another job because she is not appreciated for the work she does. Renee decides to talk with the boss and recommend some changes to make the office more productive.

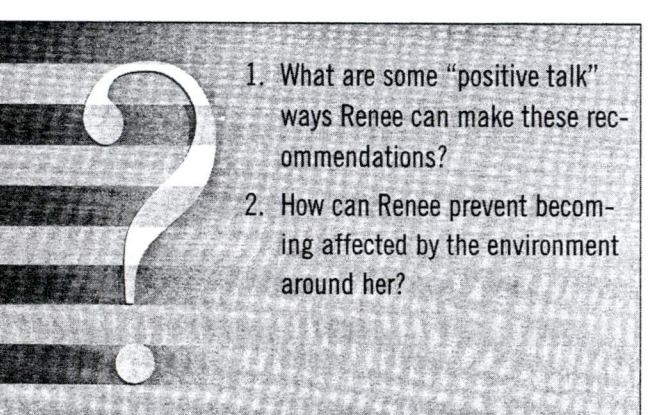

1. What are some "positive talk" ways Renee can make these recommendations?

2. How can Renee prevent becoming affected by the environment around her?

Positive thinking, demonstrated by using constructive internal and external communication patterns, is an effective tool to reverse negative directions in your life. It is your responsibility to use the tool to create the life you really want for yourself.

TRANSITION TIP
Jasyn Banks, Sales

One thing that keeps you motivated is being "hungry," wanting to go forward with making life the way you want it. As soon as you realize that choosing the easy route is not an option to get where you want to go, then you move forward with whatever it takes. Of course, there will be tasks along the way that you just don't want to do, even though you know you have to. Do those first when you're fresh, and then everything else that day is something you enjoy. Also, do something new all of the time: attend seminars, network to meet new people, learn to play golf; new stuff keeps your life interesting.

Changing old habits requires time. But, that time will be well spent and the payoff will be very rewarding. The key is to be persistent: that will bring you ever closer to the destiny you choose. Sometimes you have to engineer positive experiences to help that process along.

Activating Joy in Life

If you want to receive the most from life, you had better not wait passively for happy circumstances to come your way. You can take some positive steps that will lead you to greater satisfaction with the life you have today. Following are a few simple observations and suggestions from people who have made excellent and rewarding lives for themselves and have taught others how to do the same:

- separate fantasy from reality
- acknowledge gifts
- recognize contributions
- clean house periodically
- revel in your own experience

Separate Fantasy from Reality

Identify fantasy events and people for what they are: isolated, serendipitous events. These fantasy situations should not be the standards by which you rate the rest of your experience. The man (or woman) who is too perfect to be true, really is. Mr. or Ms. Wonderful is generally a carefully created, temporary persona designed to be appealing for a specific purpose. No one can be "perfect" over time and relationships with real people are messy and complicated.

The same holds true for events as well. The perfect dinner, weekend, gift, vacation, or even job is generally a single occurrence—a fantasy that should be enjoyed and savored. These events should be viewed as pleasant memories that accumulate over time and help nourish your spirit. Trying to plan and re-create such situations, though, nearly always fails because the synergistic element, the unexpected coming together of several exciting or pleasurable conditions, is part of the wonder of the experience.

Acknowledge Gifts

Recognize and take time to be grateful for talents, unexpected kindnesses, and interventions that come your way.

Your Own Gifts

Uncovering your own natural talents and gifts is sometimes a function of your environment. If you grew up in an athletic family, but your innate talent is music, you may not know how really gifted you are. However, trying to label talents often limits our view of what those are. Jennifer may not see her ability to organize almost any activity or space as a talent. Sunil, at age 40, took a computer basics class and discovered a natural ease with programming he never knew he had.

Your talents may be in an area to which you have not yet been exposed. Many writers published their first book after age 50. Some people who have never had children find they are good teachers of young people. Other people have the gift of making people around them feel calm and at ease (highly valued in an emergency room nurse or trauma doctor). Everyone has something important to contribute and feel good about (Gardner, 1993). Taking time to note your unique gifts helps you affirm yourself in specific ways.

5.3 ACTIVITY

Look at your life in the larger picture (not just grades or job skills) and list three categories of things that you do well and feel good about when you do them. For example, "I can get people who don't know each other to talk together in a short time." Or, "I am quick at sizing up a situation and figuring out what needs to be done, whether I would be the person to do it or not."

This might take some thought on your part because we often do not look at ourselves in this way—in terms of our gifts.

Gift 1. _____

Gift 2. _____

Gift 3. _____

Life Events

You may have heard of children being called gifts, but there are also many other delightful things that happen in life that add to our joy and satisfaction. Making a difference in someone's life in a positive way, arriving in Honolulu and discovering the full moon over Waikiki beach, or even happening on a close parking space on a rainy day can all contribute to our happiness. When

Virgaletha became bored with her job and could not figure out what to do about it, she received an unexpected phone call from her college roommate who offered her an interesting new position at her company. These events come to us, often through no particular planning or specific work on our part, yet they add significantly to our enjoyment of life.

Caution must be observed here, however. Expecting such "breaks," as many call these gift events, creates a climate for constant disappointment. You do not place an order for a gift; you accept it graciously for the addition it makes to your life. So many people live, as one retired "hustler" put it, "on the verge of a cinch." Welcome the unexpected events that bring you those moments of joy and allow them to enrich you; do not live your life waiting for the next one to occur.

Other People

People will come into and out of your life, each leaving something behind that becomes a part of your experience. Never forget to acknowledge to yourself, and to them, the important contribution they make to your happiness. Just knowing certain people, even for a brief time, can alter your life completely. A single conversation at an airport may give you an insight that opens up a whole new world of experience for you. Someone may appear just when you need help or comfort, then go out of your life just as quickly when you are no longer in need. There is no point trying to find that person to thank him. That conversation or help was a gift; be grateful for it and hope you have the chance to contribute to someone else's life in the same way you were enriched.

Recognize Contributions

Growth in understanding a task or life adds considerably to happiness. Education in the classroom is only the beginning. To profit from the instructional value of events and people, you have to pay attention. If you believe that people come into your life so you can learn something from them, then everyone you meet takes on a new importance.

Life events are the same way. You can look at an experience and say, "Glad that's over." Or, you can view the same experience for the new insight you gained from having gone through it. The more you understand, the more sense you can make of your life, and the better you can shape it. Remember, though, the person or event that has the greatest contribution to make to your growth and insight will not come with a label that says, "I am here to teach you." Life's wisdom does not come by way of ghosts in the night, as occurred in Dickens' *A Christmas Carol*.

You have to involve yourself enough in the ideas and experiences of the people who seem to purposefully cross your path to figure out what each has to contribute. This viewpoint makes you begin to treat everyone in your acquaintance with a new respect and a positive attitude. You appreciate people and events for the richness they bring to your life.

Clean House Periodically

Regularly look around you at your physical space, your responsibilities, your activities, and your beliefs. The longer you live, the more you tend to accumulate things because they had value to you at one time. You take on more and more responsibilities over time because you want other people in your life. Also, you engage in numerous activities so you have a reason to get up in the morning.

Physical Space

Have you ever moved into a new house or apartment? If you have, you remember the cleanness and simplicity of the bare walls and floors. Your field of vision was uncluttered everywhere you looked. Though there is a starkness to that visual experience, there is also a calm. Then, you acquire items through gifts, yard sales, or other purchases and clutter begins to take up the free space. Many of these items have, or had at one time, sentimental value from how or when you acquired them. Turning the acquisition clock back and clearing your physical space can be refreshing.

There are several methods for doing this:

1. Move—this forces you to move everything out and make decisions about keeping different items. Surprisingly, the value you place on some items changes when you have to pay to keep them in your life.

2. Store—choose some of the items in your house (e.g., pictures, furniture, silk plants, certainly clothing) and rent a storage place for three months. At the end of that time, if you have not really missed the items in storage, or cannot even remember what is there, a garage sale or large-scale donation is in order.

3. Donate—the sofa you are going to sell, the screens you took off when you installed the storm windows, the leftover paint, and the lumber and tools you no longer use are all valuable to charity organizations. Shelters and organizations that help homeless or abused families to start over can use most anything. If it is not usable, throw it away—you are probably never going to get around to fixing it and it just makes you feel bad that you mean to but do not. The few dollars you could get for many of these things do not compare to the tremendous good a donation will do and the great benefit you will receive.

4. Sell—take the plunge; sell everything and start over. This tactic sounds somewhat drastic, possibly, but is amazingly liberating, especially if you are making a life or career change. Purging yourself of most of your possessions this way allows you to reinvent your environment to accommodate a new lifestyle or attitude.

Responsibilities

Adults have many responsibilities in life, so many more than young people do that adults sometimes want to retreat to a younger, simpler time. They may do this by buying frivolous things on a whim, drinking too much, skipping work, and many other ways of "acting out" the need to get away from overwhelming responsibilities.

Laying down responsibilities is an excellent road to happiness, but it must be done selectively or the repercussions could be serious. Responsibilities seem to accumulate over time: housecleaning, then yard maintenance, car maintenance, financial obligations, clubs, work, maintaining friendships, looking after aging parents or grandparents, children, and something as simple as food—it does not appear unless you prepare it or go get it. Of course, you cannot avoid all of these responsibilities, but reducing the number helps.

A condo or an apartment, for example, allows you to avoid yard work; mass transit allows you to avoid having to maintain a car; paying a maid frees you from cleaning; meal services replace cooking; electronic fund drafting makes bill paying less time consuming. Choosing not to have a pet, spouse, children, or involvement with others will simplify your life dramatically. But, at some point, you must examine the value of the trade-off. A dog may be a hassle, but the unconditional love, good humor, and forgiveness may be worth the trouble.

Three tactics are useful to address the responsibility issues. First, examine the number of responsibilities to determine which you can abandon. For example, the club that you are president of will be unhappy if you step down, but you may find a new freedom in giving up that responsibility. Second, retain only those responsibilities that enrich your life. Teaching Sunday school is a responsibility, but you may gain a feeling of renewal when you do it. Third, take regular "holidays" *before* you need them. Set aside a day for relief on which you take off from work, board the dog, or arrange for the kids to stay with a friend. Treat the day as a mandatory day of no responsibilities. Do not clean, go to bed at 8:30 if you want, take pictures of flowers—do those things that you believe your responsibilities prevent you from doing.

Holidays are often most therapeutic if taken in small increments at close intervals, such as a long weekend every month instead of two weeks together. Maybe just going in late one day a week would help. Chapter 9, "Self-

Nurturing," gives you details on how to take care of yourself. Right now, the focus is on stepping off the train occasionally and reveling in the freedom of knowing that you have chosen responsibilities that enrich your life. Abandon the ones that do not contribute in some way to your joy.

Activity

Excessive activity often comes from people defining themselves by what they do, not who or what they are. Parents, particularly, fall into this. Children, even teenagers, often confess that they just want their parents to spend time with them—not plan elaborate activities or fuss over clothes or food—just be in their lives. Munira has her children, ages six and nine, fix supper one night a week while she sits in the kitchen and talks with them. The meal is often cereal or peanut butter on crackers, but everyone enjoys the time together.

Shane, a single man, gets caught up in meeting friends for tennis, basketball, drinks at the sports bar, networking lunches, and washing the car every Saturday. The fact that he has fewer responsibilities than a parent, does not mean he has fewer activities that he has to squeeze into every day or week. He has now begun relaxing alone in a bookstore coffee shop one evening a week and has noticed a great improvement in how he feels about everything.

Today's society attaches little prestige to the nonpurposive expenditure of time. We have become a population of frantic activity-mongers: "Yeah, I shot nine holes of golf after work." Or, "I spent three hours on the Internet researching investments." Rarely do you hear, "I took a walk in the woods today and watched a squirrel bury nuts," or "You know, I'm going to just stay home tonight and think for a few hours." Sometimes each of us just needs to stop. It might be uncomfortable at first because frenzy has become a way of life. But for those who need help stepping back from that way of life, fishing is excellent training. And, if you are lucky, the fish will not bother you too much.

Ideas and Beliefs

Over time, what we know and have come to understand and accept may not be valid anymore, and hanging on to those old ideas and beliefs becomes more than just burdensome. They get in the way of our ability to experience joy. The woman who was taught to clean the refrigerator every Saturday morning at 6 A.M. can probably abandon that practice with no ill effects.

Couples with both spouses working often struggle with the feeling that their life should be like their parents', but the world has changed dramatically, as has the view of family. Different does not have to be worse and clinging to an impossible-to-attain image of what *should be* is better replaced with energy used creatively to shape what *is*. Values are important; they give us a moral compass, and rituals connect us to a reassuring predictability in our lives (Fulghum, 1996). However, there are many old habits, beliefs, and practices that should be examined for their current relevance.

ACTIVITY   5.4

Look objectively at all you have around you and all of your activities with the goal of setting some aside.

1. What can you do to reduce clutter in your physical space?
2. What activity feels stressful to continue to do even though you enjoyed it at one time?

Revel in Your Own Experience

"I cried because I had no shoes, until I met a man who had no feet. . . ." This old adage speaks a simple truth of our existence. We tend to forget how well off we are because we compare our present situation to how well off we want to be instead of to how inadequate our life could be.

Your definition of life happiness is only relevant to you—you do not have to be as prestigiously employed or as educated or as smartly dressed as everyone thinks you should be. You only have to be in a good place physically, financially, spiritually, and intellectually. The term *good* means emotionally and physically *healthy*.

Sometimes an examination of your values is required to put your good fortune into proper perspective. If you do not have the life you think you want, you might do well to look at your situation differently, look at its potential for happiness. Wanting more is part of the human experience, but ambition can be as paralyzing as apathy. If being consumed with developing a better body or portfolio or power position is keeping you from finding joy where you are, then perhaps it is time to reflect on how you define joy. When each day is a celebration, upending your entire existence to get to someone else's idea of a party becomes unnecessary.

This does not mean to dismiss growth and change; they enrich everyone's life. It does mean, however, that framing your own experience is purely under your control. A list for just such an exercise was found hanging on the wall of an auto repair shop.

Today I can grumble about my health or rejoice that I am alive.

Today I can mourn my lack of friends or I can embark upon a quest to discover new relationships.

Today I can whine because I have to go to work, or I can shout for joy because I have a job to do.

Today I can complain because I have to clean the house or I can feel honored because I have shelter for my mind and body.

Any time you have difficulty finding something to love about your life, go volunteer at a homeless shelter or help build or refurbish a house for someone. When you are lost in not having enough, you can reclaim your spirit by giving of your time and energy to others. Cultivating happiness in others has the wonderful side effect of multiplying your own.

Positive thinking is not the result of a happy life, it is the method for building one. An expectation of beneficial and constructive outcomes creates a more positive and effectual you. A positive and effectual operating style attracts opportunity and upbeat, positive people: the recipe for a happy life.

TRANSITION SKILLS SUMMARY

Choose optimism

Recognize and eliminate negative patterns

Adopt a positive style

Create a positive environment

Activate joy

GOAL SETTING

Self-nurturing: I will make my emotional and relational life more positive by

_____

_____

_____

Self-advocacy: I will make my professional life more positive by

_____

_____

_____

C O A C H'S   C O R N E R

The most positive and successful people all have GAS.

Goal

Attraction

System™

GAS occurs when two elements come together: the brain's filtering system and the law of attraction.

The brain's filtering system allows you to see what you want to see. Your lover, for instance, appears wonderful to you while you think he or she is wonderful. When you begin looking for faults, however, you see negatives. You can change what you choose to see—focus on the good and tell the brain what is important to you. When you program your goal, best stated in writing as a contract with your subconscious, you will begin to see opportunities all around you to achieve that goal.

The law of attraction is simple: what you think, comes to you. You think of someone you haven't seen in years, and that person calls or contacts you in some way. You think of an old song, and suddenly it comes on the radio. This isn't something we can explain, really; it just is.

So, your subconscious draws to you whatever you have stated you want. You cannot have a negative goal, though; the subconscious draws whatever you focus on. For example, if you say to yourself in a restaurant, "I don't want this spaghetti to fall on my crisp white shirt," all your brain records is "spaghetti on crisp white shirt."

Commit your thoughts and fine tune your attention on what you want. Don't cloud the focus by worrying about how you will get there. If the *what* is clear in your mind, then the *how* will come to you, literally. The same is true of opportunity. As long as your focus is on the job you have, you cannot focus on another, more satisfying job. If you focus on the fear of not knowing exactly how you might move to another position, then you will not see an opportunity that will get you to that new place.

DAVID GREENBERG, motivational speaker, executive speaking coach.
E-mail: GreenbergSpeaks@aol.com.

CHAPTER 6

Improving Your Communication Style

One of the key factors in maintaining equilibrium in your life and in all of your relationships is good communication. Good communication helps by establishing a balanced, harmonious rightness and understanding in your day-to-day activities and exchanges. Conversely, you will hear "poor communication" named as the culprit in a large percentage of troublesome issues, personal and professional. If a couple's relationship is failing, "they just can't communicate." Or, if a team is not performing well, "we just don't communicate." When trouble brews in business, "communication is the biggest problem we have."

Good communication occurs when an individual makes the effort to get a certain, well-thought-out point across. The point may be to reflect an idea or feeling, convey information accurately, or to express a formal or casual style. Whatever the rationale or occasion, a *constructive communication* exchange takes into account the interests of both you and the other person. In addition, it must be honest and straightforward.

Communication skills become very important in the adult relationships you will have, both personal relationships and those at work. Understanding the way people relate to each other makes you more aware of the communication styles of coworkers and potential employers. This helps you to understand what is required to be successful in your job. "Financial security today depends on the ability to interact with other people," observes Suzette Elgin (1997) in her book *How to Disagree Without Being Disagreeable*.

She further suggests that a resume and a flashy interview may get you the job, but people skills allow you to thrive in the workplace. This is especially the case with short-term and contract employees that so many companies are using these days; there is not as much time to thoroughly get to know someone. You must get "up to speed" quickly in your interpersonal skills (p. 24). As your life evolves, you will find that being able to communicate with people greatly improves the possibilities for smooth and satisfying transitions.

Value of Effective Communication

In good communication, you have to be able to exchange ideas about:

- disagreeing constructively
- making decisions
- distributing responsibilities
- experiencing emotions
- asserting needs
- expressing affection

In family systems, many disagreements occur because interchanges are not handled in a healthy way. Constructive communication on the personal level is not just an exchange of information (which is often the case in work situations), but a connection to emotions. Special care must be taken with these relationships that are so necessary to our overall well-being.

In the realm of the professional world, on the other hand, you have to be a good communicator in many different media across many types of situations. You will be called on to:

- write reports, memos, proposals, e-mails, reviews
- discuss results, plans, objectives
- read body language and situations for meaning
- get your point across to explain or persuade
- give directions
- teach others
- share and gather information in teams and groups
- ask clarifying questions
- troubleshoot with other team members
- justify or persuade others of the value of project, contribution, or idea

Unless you can effectively communicate, you may not get hired for the job you really want. If you do get hired, you may wind up feeling that you are out of the loop and are being left behind because you are unable to get others to understand important ideas you have. To reduce the risks of ineffective communication in your relationships, take charge of eliminating weak skill areas.

Identifying Ineffective Communication Patterns

Guidelines for good communication are offered throughout this chapter, but, first, a quick discussion of the characteristics of ineffective communication. Bad communication can occur several ways, but two categories cover most such exchanges: (1) clumsy exchanges due to poor skill or ability and (2) purposeful attempts to mislead or hurt someone, or protect yourself.

Clumsy Exchanges

Clumsy exchanges are common, and they come in many forms:

- Unfamiliarity with the language, conventions, or priorities.
- Lack of adeptness at "reading" people and social cues.
- Misunderstanding the purpose or nature of the exchange.
- Use of excessive "communication" (talk or other media) to cover an insecurity.
- Inappropriate vocabulary, gestures, or other body language.
- Irrelevant facts.
- Badly placed or offensive humor.

Unrealistically, we expect that others will automatically know what point we are trying to get across, no matter how poorly we attempt to do that. It is possible to forget that people may not understand something in the way that we want them to. We get into communication trouble when we *assume* that:

1. Everyone is motivated at the same level to have an exchange with us.
2. We always send clear and well-expressed messages.
3. An immediate absorption and embracing of our ideas takes place in the other person.

These assumptions cause trouble when communication is imperfect, because they lead us to construe the miscommunication as a conscious act of disrespect, disregard, or hostility. In actuality, however, omissions or imperfect exchanges likely mean no disregard, disrespect, or hostility at all. The failure to connect occurs because others with whom we may communicate are operating under the same mistaken assumptions, with the same predictable effect.

In his book *How to Really Love Your Child*, Dr. Ross Campbell (1992) notes that many parents who come to him for counseling say that they love their children and show that love many different ways. The children of these caring parents say that they believe their parents do not love them. After discovering that this confusing discrepancy occurred often, he questioned the parents and children on their interpretation of what "showing love" meant. Not surprisingly, he found that what the child felt strongly to be acts or conditions of love and what the parents thought were sincere demonstrations were very different.

> Jackson, who had been to McDonald's every Saturday morning for breakfast with his dad, became very disturbed when those morning outings stopped. The dad had assumed that because his now-teenage son frequently was out late dating on Friday nights, the caring thing to do was to let him sleep. Jackson thought that because his father did not call him as usual was often gone by the time Jackson arose, the caring connection had ceased (Campbell, 1992).

After all, even in the family that we grew up in, where there was a daily familiarity with each other's wants and needs, we did not have perfect communication. Consequently, many of us have had ineffective patterns as models, lack experience in the skills of communication, and believe a myriad of potentially relationship-sabotaging assumptions.

The truth is that most people could use some improvement in their style and skill for communicating, especially because the ability to communicate effectively has become highly prized in today's world. Also, it is much easier to maintain an equilibrium in all aspects of your life if you have good skills. You are more valued as a friend, as a mate, as an employee, and as an individual if you are able to have meaningful exchanges with others.

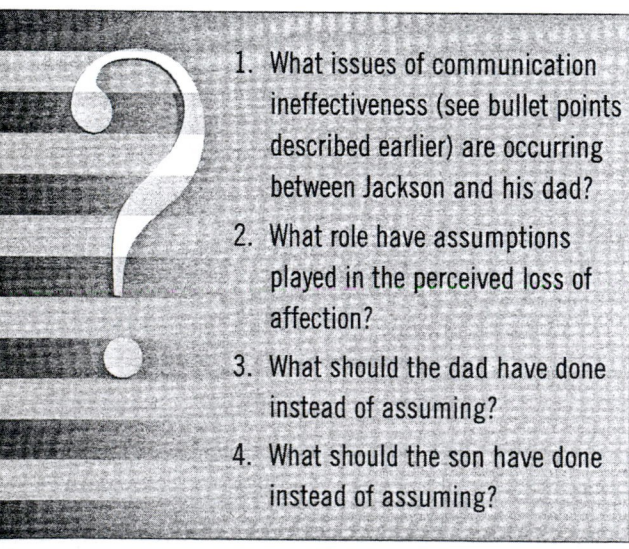

1. What issues of communication ineffectiveness (see bullet points described earlier) are occurring between Jackson and his dad?

2. What role have assumptions played in the perceived loss of affection?

3. What should the dad have done instead of assuming?

4. What should the son have done instead of assuming?

Purposeful Miscommunication

Another type of ineffective communication is the purposeful attempt to mislead or hurt others, or to protect yourself. Elements include:

- Pointless anger dumped on another person to retaliate or attack.
- Information withheld due to fear of expressing or revealing certain ideas.
- Chatter used as a smoke screen to hide someone's anxious feelings.
- False statements said to make an individual look good (or look bad).
- Facts presented in a selective, manipulative way to mislead or influence.

Most everyone has done one or more of these things. Children do them fairly often because they have not learned the value of mature exchanges or the skills to conduct them. Unfortunately, even adults cling to some of these firmly engrained patterns because they too have not recognized their own responsibility for the success of any communication.

The Process Models

In any exchange, many elements and decisions occur. Because of this, it is understandable that communication can be full of glitches—intended or otherwise. These glitches, if unnoticed, will be the undoing of the interchange and will leave the participants wondering what happened. Models of communication help to illustrate graphically some of the activities and processes that go on during an exchange. They also give us some guidelines that will help improve our understanding of others' messages and improve our precision in the messages we send.

Degrees of Engagement

A number of communication issues help in determining the degree of engagement. Some examples are:

- Are the parties motivated to engage in the interaction?
- Do they have the skill to send clear and appropriate messages?
- Are they willing to exert the energy to actively pursue understanding?
- Is a past, unconscious, ineffective pattern sabotaging good relations?
- Has a decision been made to deliberately mislead?
- Does everyone involved have the same expectation about the value and purpose of the communication?

The communication process can be described in terms of three different levels or degrees of involvement a listener might have with the sender's message: understanding, acceptance, and integration.

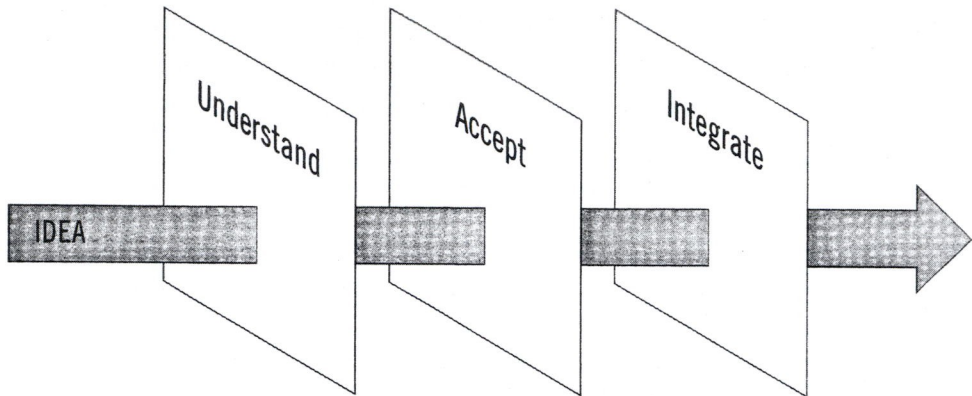

Not all communication requires the deepest levels of involvement to be effective; the situation should determine the goal. An explanation of each of these levels will demonstrate this idea.

Understanding

Understanding is the surface and basic level any exchange must have to be called communication. You and the other party must be able to process the words, gestures, syntax, symbolic representations, and certain situational elements for any kind of meaningful exchange to take place. Not a great deal of "buy-in" or commitment is necessary for this degree of internalization. A mere understanding is likely sufficient for conveying information; processing data, directions, or instructions; and describing physical objects.

You can probably see, however, that breakdowns may occur even at this level. Examples are a specialized language in some professional fields, differences in cultural communication styles, hearing impairments, and speech deficiencies. Many kinds of interference, such as internal or external distractions, can limit or prevent understanding. As long as the parties are aware of these obstacles, they can take steps to overcome them. One tool for doing this is the statement of understanding.

Some statements of understanding might be:

- "I can hear you."
- "Your hand pointing right means that I turn here."
- "Your frown tells me you are angry."
- "You say the meeting is at 6 o'clock?"

Acceptance

Acceptance is the next deepest level of exchange, where we begin to process intent, fervor, commitment to the idea, truthfulness, and credibility. Credibility is in this section because at the understanding level we do not necessarily have to make judgments about the message we are receiving. At the acceptance level we make judgments about people's sincerity, their motivations behind their message, even about the people themselves. Sadly, we may be more apt to accept information from a person who looks credible, than from someone who is more informed, if the latter person does not fit our expectation.

Body language is processed differently at this level as well. We may look for subtle signals that suggest integrity or an attempt to deceive. At the acceptance level, we do not have to make any commitment to change anything about our behavior or our thinking. We only have to acknowledge as sincere or truthful the other person's message. Statements we might hear at this level include:

- "That merits consideration."
- "I appreciate why you feel that way."
- "I believe you mean what you say."
- "We will have to agree to disagree on this one."
- "I get it, but I don't buy it."

Integration

When we commit to think, feel, or act differently, we have internalized a message and integrated it into our operating beliefs and actions. This is a higher level of involvement because it requires that we change something about what we know, what we feel, or what we do. For someone to carry out organizational goals, that person must understand what the goals are and what his or her part is in carrying out those goals. In addition, the employee must accept the validity of the goals and perhaps even the intent management has. Finally, the individual commits effort and intellect, and perhaps even enthusiasm or zeal, toward carrying out the goal activity.

As an example, the value of regular exercise must be understood on an informational level, accepted as beneficial, and finally operationalized as regular visits to a health club or workout group. Many relationships suffer not from problems at the understanding level, but from problems on the acceptance or integration levels. To tell your significant other that you believe that housework, child care, and car maintenance should be shared, then never actually take the initiative to do any of these things, sends a message. It means that you did not accept the importance of the idea or internalize it enough to commit to action. Integration statements include:

- "I see this differently now."
- "I didn't know that before and believed something else to be true."
- "I understand the procedure and the reasoning for it now and will be able to perform it correctly."
- "I realize how important this is now and I will add it to my life."
- "I will stop that habit because I accept that it is bad for me and others."
- "I can be more positive about that now."

The Transactional Model of Communication

In order for us to better understand communication patterns, let us look at a model that has endured for four decades because it is simple to understand and easy to put into practice quickly. In his Transactional Model, Eric Berne (1972, 1996) identified the three working parts of the personality as the *Parent*, the *Adult*, and the *Child*. Each one of us has all three parts, and we can use any one of the parts to communicate with others.

The Parent consists of two aspects, the critical side and the nurturing side. The critical side is supposed to keep the individual in check and on the right track. Vocabulary for the critical side includes authority words such as "should," "have to," "must," and "need to." Specific body language includes real or imagined finger pointing or other disapproving expressions. Phrases such as "Can't you ever get it right?" remind us of an exasperated parent's chastisement for some error.

The nurturing side of the Parent comforts and makes sure that we are not abused, overly stressed, or placed in harm's way. Body language for the nurturing side includes a hug to ease sadness or a reassuring look in an anxious situation. The caring Parent might say, "Take it easy, you've been working too hard." Or "Here, let me take care of that for you." "Are you sure you really need to spend that much money? Or have that second piece of pie? Or stay out so late at night?"

Next is the Adult, the strategist of the personality that collects, processes, and evaluates information to come to logical conclusions. The Adult is matter-of-fact, reasonable, and logical in nature, not responding emotionally to loaded or critical statements. The Adult strategist might say, "That comment you made sounded like you thought my department caused the problem. Is that what you meant?" Or, "No, I don't have that information now, but if you give me your e-mail address, I will send it on to you." Or, "I will meet you at the restaurant at six o'clock." All of these examples are straight forward, are nonreactive, and address information.

The Child readily expresses the variety of feelings that she may be experiencing at any time. Body language for the Child is likely very expressive, such as gesturing in surprise or glee; slumped shoulders in sadness or chagrin;

starting or recoiling in fear; fists clenched and body tight in anger. A Child might say, "Wahoo! I feel so happy I could burst." Or, "Boo hoo hoo! I lost my favorite watch at the mall." Or, "Yes! Yes! Yes! I will marry you." There is also the whiny aspect of the Child's communication style, "I can't do this; help me." Or, "I never get any breaks."

Ideally, adults operate in the Adult mode most of the time, but few of us are feeling very adult when we are sick or sad or threatened. An interesting phenomenon occurs with the use of these different styles in human relations. Parent speech often causes a Child response (likely an old family pattern playing out unconsciously). "You had better get that report to me on time or else" might elicit a response like, "I'll get it to you when I'm ready." You can almost see the child stomping her foot even though the people in the conversation are both grown-ups. As you might guess, this kind of exchange is not productive—in either personal or business situations.

Child patterns can evoke Parent responses as well. If people tend to talk down to you, you might look at your own way of expressing yourself. You might be unconsciously using some Child phrases or expressions. For example, "But I tried really hard; I just don't know what happened." This is a Child sentence; an Adult statement would include accepting responsibility for the action (or lack of it) and identifying a solution. "I know I missed the deadline, and I have asked Kenneth to show me a quicker way to generate the reports with the new software." Trying to protect yourself by shifting blame or making excuses is Child speech and generally only elicits critical Parent responses in return.

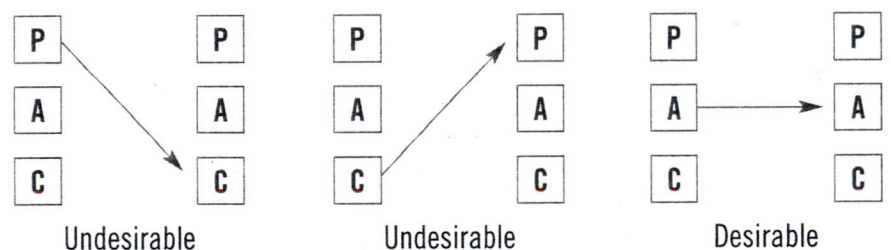

| Undesirable | Undesirable | Desirable |

When somebody comes at you in Parent and you squelch your first reaction, which will likely be in Child, and instead respond in Adult, the conversation often changes direction. The Adult response can drain the negativity out of the Child's whine and move the conversation in a more constructive problem-solving direction. The same is true with a Parent statement. "You just are not dressing very well" is a critical statement, maybe even an attack. A Child response would rise to the statement as an attack. "My clothes are just fine." An Adult return would attempt to secure useful information: "Oh, and what do you think needs improvement?"

Even if the comment was not meant in a constructive and helpful way, but as an attack, your playing it "straight" will help to defuse or redirect the comment.

Using the Adult approach, you are able to convey messages in a clear, concise way. Take the time to think out what you want to get across in any given situation, whether it is business or personal. By avoiding an impulsive response, you are more likely to get the reactions you desire from the messages you send.

Akeem is an electrical engineer with an international aircraft manufacturing company and has only been employed for six months. He has recently been summoned to his supervisor's office for his probationary review. The following exchange occurred:

"Well, Akeem, I see you have been with us just six months."

"Yes, and I'm sure I'll be even better six months from now."

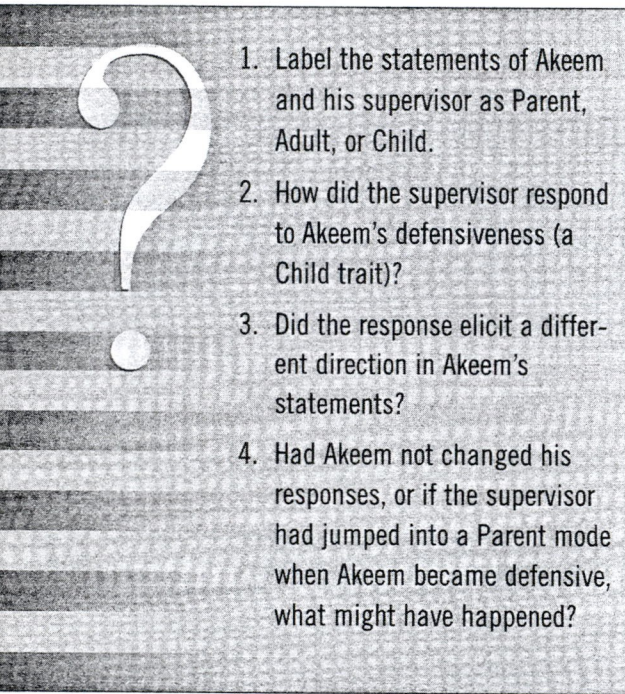

1. Label the statements of Akeem and his supervisor as Parent, Adult, or Child.

2. How did the supervisor respond to Akeem's defensiveness (a Child trait)?

3. Did the response elicit a different direction in Akeem's statements?

4. Had Akeem not changed his responses, or if the supervisor had jumped into a Parent mode when Akeem became defensive, what might have happened?

"Your troubleshooting skills seem to be consistently good, but I think you need to improve your turnaround time. We have tight deadlines around here, and I hope you will get up to speed quickly."

"That's not fair. I'm good at what I do. Am I supposed to rush and do a crappy job?"

"No, quality is important, but when you are alert to ways you can become more efficient, you may be able to cut down on your time. Sometimes, it's the way you lay your tools out that slows you down."

"Okay. Fritz seems to have a handle on all of this. I'll ask him to show me what he does."

"Good. We're pleased with your progress so far and look forward to your year-end review being very positive."

"Thanks."

You can use your strategist mode any time you want, no matter what the situation. You can note and process messages that come at you to figure out the most constructive response. Then when you begin to communicate to others, you will be centered within yourself, will have a clear picture of what you want to happen, and will have practiced in your own head ways to get the points across.

Good communication requires forethought, planning, and a willingness to make the effort.

Nonverbal Communication

Up to this point, we have been talking about verbal exchanges that occur between two or more individuals. There is another aspect of communication that has nothing to do with words. Commonly called body language, it has to do with expressions and behaviors that are acted out in such a way as to convey a message to another person. These nonverbal messages go on all the time. We seem to read them more than the verbal messages on most occasions. Often, they reflect what is secretly going on in our heads, the things that we are not willing to spell out in plain English.

If you take the time to observe others' nonverbal messages, you can tell a lot about what is going on in that person's mind. Learning to read messages in the form of body language will help you get along better as your life transitions take you into more complex and far-reaching relationships. For example, if your boss comes in with one earring missing, this might mean that today is not the best time to negotiate a day off. You tell your child more about your approval or disapproval of clothing choices with a single facial expression than with words. If you learn that the cloudy look on your lover's face means she is in need of quiet time alone, then you will be less likely to persist in trying to cheer her up, which might add to the problem. Practice observing with the intent of gaining an understanding of the nonverbal cues of those around you.

Closure Signals

An important body language to learn to read is the signal that indicates someone wants to end a conversation. Often, people are thinking of their own agenda and forget that others have an agenda also. It can be very uncomfortable for some to shut down a conversation. People often fear that the other person will feel rejected. It is up to us to become aware and read the signals quickly. That way we do not create unpleasant situations. Also, you will find that people will avoid your attempts at conversation if you persist in disrespecting their time. Some signs of a conversation being over are:

- When the other person stands up and starts moving around.
- When the other person puts paperwork away.
- When the other person states that he has enjoyed your visit.
- When the other person says she hopes to see you soon.
- When the other person says, "In conclusion . . ."
- When the other person keeps looking at his watch.
- When the other person begins to walk away.

Body Mirroring

A body language technique that you might find useful when you want to make another person feel comfortable while talking with you is *body mirroring*. You achieve this comfort and connection by replicating some of a person's gestures or postures in a subtle and inconspicuous way. Obviously, you do not want to make the other person feel like you are mimicking him in a disrespectful way or making fun of him. The behavior *must* be subtle and nonoffensive.

For example, Mary is interviewing with Mr. Katz for a sales position. If Mr. Katz is leaning forward in his chair, then Mary would lean forward. If Mr. Katz shifts positions and puts his hand on his chin, Mary would gently shift and place her hand on or near her chin. If he leans back and puts his hands in his lap, Mary would do the same. Mary would mirror as many of his gestures as was possible. If Mr. Katz feels at ease with Mary, he might be more interested in hiring her.

Whether you are operating from a business perspective or a personal perspective, this technique can win over others very quickly. It really does not matter if you like the people. If you make them feel comfortable, you get them to lower their defenses, and you have a greater opportunity to get to know their pleasant side. So, anytime you are meeting new people with whom you want to connect, try this technique. This is an excellent way to make the inroads that you need.

6.1 ACTIVITY

This week observe the body language of someone with whom you feel very comfortable and connected. Take note of any times during your conversation where you shifted posture or position and the other person did the same.

1. What mannerism did you note being mirrored first? _____

   _____

2. Did the person shift position more than once after you did? _____

   _____

Now, try the mirroring technique with someone you have not been as comfortable with in conversation.

   Did your use of the technique make any difference in the tone or feeling of the conversation? _____

   _____

Diversity and Nonverbal Communication

International commerce has become a way of life in this new millennium. You will more than likely run into people from different cultures sometime in your future business dealings, or perhaps even in your personal life. Accommodating the different, and sometimes even uncomfortable, operating styles, beliefs, customs, and language of someone from another culture can be quite interesting and might even enhance your relationships. In this chapter, however, the focus is on communication issues.

It is important to address diversity because you cannot know how to communicate with everyone if you are only using your own frame of reference—the culture you grew up in—to communicate. Although that frame of reference may be quite comfortable for you, it could be very confusing to someone from another culture.

Body language is an area where there are some particular differences that can be unsettling. If someone stands too close to the person with whom he is speaking, or too far away, offense may be taken. Not all people welcome body contact and consider an offered hand or pat on the back to be invasive.

A firm handshake, valued by Americans, is seen as aggressive behavior, and thus undesirable, by some other cultures. Eye contact, or the lack of it, may show respect in one culture and disrespect to authority in another. Tolerance for silence or loud talking varies as well. Many cultures view silence during conversation to be a good thing, while Americans tend to be less comfortable with silence. People in one culture might show respect by never arguing with someone in authority, whereas others might feel that an unwillingness to argue shows a lack of conviction for an idea or, in some cases, a lack of respect for the other person's thoughts or opinions.

Everyone from another culture brings a particular set of customs and mores to the area where they are living. These customs and mores are ingrained in the individual's personality and translate into an operating style that is at the subconscious level. It is possible that a person from another part of the world who has been living in your area for some time still may not be completely familiar with your culture's ways of doing things. After all, you could travel to Taiwan and would not expect to move seamlessly through the society of that country for many years. Another mistake is judgments based on a person's language ability—not everyone who speaks English well knows the subtleties of expression we use without thinking, especially the body language.

Some of the customs and mores others bring may be similar in nature to ours; some may be very different. It is important to expect that you do not know what the other person's customs are. If it is at all possible, ask people to clarify how their culture handles certain situations, especially ones that relate to respect, conflict, or other communication issues. That way you not only show respect to the other person, you give yourself a chance to expand your knowledge of other cultures. You also demonstrate your ability to be flexible.

Many other types of body language can be observed. For each activity, describe what you might assume from the body language you observe. Then, after each assumption, suggest a possible alternative interpretation of the nonverbal message. Keep in mind that not all cultures express things the same way.

1. Your best friend is standing in the doorway with her arms wide open. You would assume that _____

   Alternate interpretation? _____

2. Your boss is sitting with his arms folded and glaring at you. You assume that

   _____

   Alternate interpretation? _____

3. You observe someone waiting in the doctor's office with slumped shoulders and a sad look on his face. You assume that _____

   Alternate interpretation? _____

4. You are going to your car and observe a man crouched down next to your car. You assume that _____

   Alternate interpretation? _____

5. You enter a building and find a group of people clapping and laughing. You assume that _____

   Alternate interpretation? _____

6. You have just met a new person and she is looking down at the ground. You assume that _____

   Alternate interpretation? _____

7. Your neighbor comes screeching up in front of your house, slams on the brakes, jumps out of the car, and races up to you huffing and puffing. You assume that

   _____

   Alternate interpretation? _____

8. You walk into an office and a person quickly hangs up the phone. You assume that _____

   Alternate interpretation? _____

Improving Personal Communication

Up to this point, much of the information about communication has been aimed at business. There has been good reason for this because you are headed for a successful career. But, as we have emphasized in other chapters, your personal life is equally as important. Remember, a stable personal life is the springboard to success. So, let us take a look at the personal communication that occurs in relationships away from the work setting.

Barriers to Good Relational Communication

There are two common barriers to good communication in personal relationships: defensiveness and unvoiced expectations.

Defensiveness

The first barrier, defensiveness, is the instantaneous reaction that occurs when we feel that we are being psychologically threatened. A person on the defensive ceases to be receptive to messages from the other person; she ceases listening. When active listening stops, good communication stops. We do not hear what the other person is saying because we are too busy thinking of ways to defend against what we perceive is a verbal attack (or potential attack).

In truth, however, active listening is an excellent way to cope with a situation that puts you on the defensive. You want to understand the feelings of those close to you to achieve better communication and a closer and more intimate connection to your loved one. Defensive language is just that, armor or weapons garnered in the face of a psychological attack. Recognize the signs and work to get at the reason for the fear. Active listening and earnest questioning will help you to do this. If someone says to you, "You must think that you are the queen of England and are entitled to special privileges." Your first reaction is to defend yourself. A better response is to say, "You sound upset. Can you tell me what is going on?"

Unvoiced Expectations

The second barrier to personal relationship communication occurs when the parties have differing expectations of each other. Each expects the other person to know what each wants by mind reading. Without verbalizing these expectations, two people can be on different tracks and different wave lengths. That usually is a wreck waiting to happen. An unwillingness to communicate, whatever the reason, exacerbates relationship problems; it does not make them go away.

Rarely do people honestly and forthrightly tell those closest to them what their real expectations are. But, if we all shared a list of our expectations of the other person, it might lead us to find out what omission caused pain or misunderstanding. Perhaps, we might find out that our expectations are partially different. We may even find out that each wants or expects something totally different. The object is to present the expectations for discussion, negotiation, or adjustment. When this occurs, the principles of good communication have prevailed and the relationship has an edge on surviving.

Fostering Effective Communication

Confirmation

The technique of confirmation is an important communication tool, useful in the process of listening to someone. You repeat what the person has just said to you. For example, I may say, "Tomorrow we will meet at 6 A.M., pack the car for our trip, eat breakfast, gas up the car, and be ready to leave by 7." You say back to me, "What I heard you say is this, 'We will meet at six, pack up, eat breakfast, get gas, and be ready to hit the road by seven.'"

By repeating what the person has said, you are doing a number of things:

- You are acknowledging that you have heard the other person.
- You demonstrate your grasp of what was said by giving it back.
- You connect on verbal and psychological levels.
- The person who was speaking feels satisfied because she was heard.
- There is a general sense that good communication has taken place.
- You open up the channels for further positive communication.
- You give the person a chance to listen for errors or omissions in his message.

Affirmation

A second technique, affirmation, communicates more—it validates the person. Confirming the receipt of information is not the same as affirming the person. Eye contact, focused attention, and nodding or smiling as the occasion warrants all serve to convey your respect and appreciation for the contribution of what was said. Verbally, however, specific techniques send a message of affirmation. The first is the question. Asking a question shows interest: "How did you come up with that?" Another verbal approach is to offer encouraging phrases: "Tell me how that would work," or "Thank you for that. I hadn't thought of it just that way before."

Maybe the reason this does not feel natural is that somewhere in adolescence, we received the message that self-deprecation or criticizing others was acceptable. So, any affirmation or compliment from another had to be discounted. Or, we might harbor the view that a compliment to someone else diminishes us in some way. With this background, we too often carry over into adulthood the inability to accept and give compliments.

Graciousness is the guide word on compliments. If someone in your professional or personal life is kind enough to pay you a compliment, remember that person took the time to notice some achievement or quality of yours and went to the trouble to seek you out and acknowledge you. If you devalue the object of the compliment, you devalue the person who gave it to you. Learn to be grateful and affirming in the way you handle compliments—they are rare in the adult world, especially the world of work.

> "Charles, the work you did on that project saved us. It was great!"
>
> Charles' response, "Thanks for saying that, Heather; it feels good to have someone notice my hard work."

In addition, add to your communication habits regular acknowledgements of the contribution and effort of those around you. Compliments serve as both affirmation and encouragement. Your spouse, child, parents, coworkers, and even your boss occasionally could use a compliment. It is not considered appropriate, however, to comment on someone's body, physical features, or dress in the workplace. Compliments of a personal nature should be limited to personal situations. However, words acknowledging achievement, excellence, or improvement are always valuable.

Affirming the people in your life, personal or professional, costs you nothing and contributes immeasurably to your relationships. Listen to your child or spouse without offering a suggestion or critique. Be in their time, not yours, on a regular basis and you will affirm those around you in a personal and appreciated way.

Apology

No matter what type of relationship we are in, whether business or personal, we all have to know how to apologize. A certain amount of maturity is required for a sincere apology because our first reaction when we know we have erred may be to explain it away, shift the responsibility, or not acknowledge the error at all. Apologies are not substitutes for correct behavior and responsible acts, but they are important because they:

- Build bridges between people when there has been a disruption in communication.
- Send a message of responsibility and respect.
- Help to ensure that the relationship will continue in a nondefensive way.

You need to know two types of apologies to be successful. There is the formal apology, which is excellent in the business world, and the informal apology, which is more suited to your personal life. In the formal apology, you first say that you would like to apologize. Then, you state what the apology is for. It is done in a business-like manner. It could even be written in a letter. For example, "Mr. Jones, I would like to apologize for not getting this report to you yesterday. We thought it would be ready. But, due to the fact that we found new data that we felt would be helpful to your project, we delayed sending it."

In a business situation you must understand that a late delivery of any report or data creates a problem. The problem may not be limited just to the person who requested the report. It may also impact someone else in your department who needed your work to complete another project on time. Your apology in that case must extend to your responsibility for the difficulties caused as well as for being late.

An informal apology, on the other hand, is offered to people close to you. It might go like this: "Jan, I'm sorry for being late for dinner. I was delayed in traffic." In an informal apology, you can keep the language conversational. You should take responsibility for your part in the situation with words that are direct and to the point, but cover the issues. Avoid belaboring the situation or the apology, and do not expect that every time you make an apology, you will get an immediate response from the other person. You may need to give the person time to get over hurt feelings or anger. However, an apology sends a clear message that you want the relationship to continue in a positive way. That is an important start to forgiveness.

6.3 ACTIVITY

Think of a situation in which you owe someone an apology. Write several versions of an apology that would be appropriate to the person and situation.

Person: _____

_____

_____

Situation: _____

_____

_____

Apology: _____

_____

_____

Many skills, techniques, and focused efforts go into creating a harmonious life for yourself with those around you. Transitions change the way people are able to interact with one another. Diligence in pursuing open and effective communication is a necessity for moving your whole life forward. You can never reach new levels with old ways. A transition takes you to a new level; communication skills help you achieve a new equilibrium at that level.

TRANSITION SKILLS SUMMARY

Identify ineffective communication patterns

Understand nonverbal communication

Eliminate barriers

Foster effective exchanges

GOAL SETTING

Self-nurturing: In my personal and relational life, my goals for communication are:

_____

_____

_____

Self-advocacy: In my professional life, my goals for communication are:

_____

_____

_____

COACH'S CORNER

The transition to communication in the career world requires several shifts in style from other communication situations.

1. Move from listening for things important or relevant to you to listening for issues important to the other person. Be totally there for the other person; don't offer, just listen.

2. Clarify to ensure understanding.
   a. Write down what the other person is saying.
   b. Question to sort out vague ideas. Stay away from "why" questions because they put people on the defensive. Ask for examples.
   c. Use "reflective listening." Paraphrase what you think you heard to show you were listening and to ensure that information was correctly received.

3. Learn to differentiate between when people are talking through something and when they are making points for the record. Some people think by talking; your role might be to ask questions that help the person simplify or solidify his position. By doing this, you will be seen as more committed and interested in what is going on.

4. Initiate communication situations. Organizations are not set up for teaching, and waiting to be discovered by a "mentor" may be fruitless. You should approach those who have information that would be helpful to you. Seeking someone out for communication can be a compliment, so there is a good chance you will be well received.

5. Capitalize on the spontaneous event. If you find yourself unexpectedly with a power person in your organization, be certain you have something relevant or interesting to discuss. Good communication skills and pertinent questions suggest intelligence and potential to managers.

HOWARD BORCK, PH.D., National Training Manager, Habitat for Humanity International; e-mail: Hborck@HFHI.org

CHAPTER 7

Problem Solving

P roblems to be solved, decisions to be made. For some, having to make a decision is a problem. From something as common as negotiating a traffic tie-up to something as complex as finding ways to increase stockholder dividends, situations require our attention. Due to the sheer numbers of problems that can present themselves, it is not possible to address them all. Learning to make good judgments about which problems to concern yourself with and which to ignore is an important step to a balanced life.

Each transition you face brings with it rewards and the satisfaction of growing ever closer to your goals. Movement of any sort, though, brings with it the potential for problems that can be viewed as either obstacles or opportunities. When you acquire problem-solving skills, the process will be less stressful. Anything you know how to do well presents a much easier path to success. Improving your problem-solving ability will help you:

- feel stronger and more in control of your life
- experience less stress and less inclination to worry
- begin to manage your life from a base of power rather than a base of fear

Choosing Problems to Solve

Several important considerations will help guide you as you choose where to invest your problem-solving talents and energies.

Responsibility

Is the situation within your responsibility, or does it by rights belong to someone else?

To meddle in someone else's problem may not be perceived as helpful at all; rather, it may be seen as insulting or disrespectful. By not allowing others to solve their own problems, you send them the message that you think they are incompetent. In addition, you show disrespect for their boundaries by becoming involved in something uninvited. Sometimes, you are invited to "help" with a problem. But, when you "rescue" people by solving their problems for them, you deny them the chance to learn good problem-solving skills and self-sufficiency on their own. You cheat them out of a growth opportunity.

Ethics

Does your moral or ethical system require that you either address or avoid the situation?

Someone with "backyard ethics" conducts his or her affairs in a moral and just way, but views situations far removed from the immediate sphere as better left alone. This way of thinking can be summed up by the statement, "We take care of our own backyard. If everyone else would do the same, the world would be okay." Generally, this attitude reflects a self-reliance motivation. Sometimes, though, this attitude grows from threat of severe retribution if a problem is entered into uninvited, such as in violent neighborhoods.

Other ethical systems, called "we are the world ethics," require their advocates to step in when wrongdoing (by their standards) is observed—whether invited or not. This is the situation with those who work to save the rain forests, even if they do not live there, or fly to other countries to volunteer to help hungry or oppressed people.

Disagreement

Might there be disagreement regarding the perception of the severity of the problem or the need to address it at all?

Even people within the same culture have differences in values. The United States, in particular, is moving to a more culturally diverse society (especially in high-tech companies and the communities where these companies are located). Thus, value differences from other cultures are entering into the way issues are addressed. For this reason, divergent opinions may directly affect the way a situation is viewed and whether it is viewed as a problem at all.

This is not the place for a lengthy discussion of cultural differences; however, a look at the effect of "frame of reference" on a situation is appropriate. In his book *The Art of Thinking*, Vincent Ruggiero (2000) devotes a good deal of discussion to the difference between a problem and an issue. He defines a problem as a situation that knowledgeable, intelligent people agree has to be corrected or solved; for example, the still-rampant spread of AIDS throughout the world population. Most knowledgeable, intelligent people see this as a problem that requires the commitment of resources to find a solution.

He labels as issues, however, those conditions or situations over which knowledgeable, intelligent people might disagree. Examples might be an interpretation of a written piece of work or the significance of a particular event. Another obvious issue is religion, which is easily identifiable as a topic of frequent disagreement. Interestingly, though, quite a number of problems are agreed on as needing a solution by intelligent people; the difficulty comes with trying to develop and carry out solutions that are acceptable to all.

Birth control or population control is an excellent example of this kind of situation. Some primitive cultures abandoned old people who could no longer contribute to the food gathering or maintenance of the tribe or unit. In this way, they controlled population in relation to the food supply and the ability to work. Abortion has been viewed variously as a method of combatting poverty and as an ethical issue. Long hours and low pay in Third-World factories can be seen variously as a positive survival opportunity for poor people or as malicious exploitation of the rights of humans. Cultural differences can have an effect on whether a situation is viewed as a problem or an issue. But, it is unrealistic to expect complete agreement even within the same culture, much less across nationalities.

A problem should be approached as a process of seeking out a solution that will resolve the situation for all affected parties. An issue should be addressed by gathering information on all viewpoints and determining the most valid viewpoint based on merit and supportability.

Risk

What level of risk is involved with the problem?

Good problem solvers always attempt to determine the level of risk associated with a problem. They ask, "What are the chances of success and what kind of risks are involved for myself or for anyone touched directly by the problem (or solution)?" Risking your company's money, or your own, can be stressful. Risking other people's jobs is even more so. Said one CEO of a start-up company, "I couldn't sleep nights if things weren't going well; I worried about all those little mouths to feed." The consideration of risk in problem solving is a complex issue. If someone has not had much experience or training in problem solving, then placing a crucial issue in that person's hands might be a risk due to inadequate ability. Another element of risk relates more to the lack of solid information about the issue or the implications of specific outcomes. There can be a risk that the solution cannot be made to happen, or the risk might be that the outcome, if achieved, may not be as beneficial as hoped.

There are varying degrees of risk, and they can usually be reduced by gathering information. A calculated risk occurs when some likely consequences are known, but not all. Solutions can be weighed for the probability of success or failure as compared to the potential for return. When not enough information is available due to unprecedented conditions or volatile and rapidly changing situations, sometimes an "educated guess" from an expert in the area can be valuable.

Movies such as *Outbreak*, *Armageddon*, and *Space Cowboys* addressed the situation of the calculated risk. However, in each of those movies, there was at least one expert whose knowledge, skill, and experience in some similar or related situation allowed an "educated guess" that proved effective. You do not ask a landscaper to make an educated guess about your air-conditioning problems, nor do you expect that a purchasing agent would necessarily be on top of technology development. But, the risk of making a decision without extensive knowledge of potential outcomes is reduced with the educated guess.

Risking embarrassment, financial loss, or position for one's self is a wholly different issue from risk assessment in industry. A company has an accountability to shareholders, employees, customers, and the industry in which it operates. Decisions about problems that affect any or all of these must carefully consider the risks of any particular course of action.

 **ACTIVITY**

What are your feelings about risk? Can you give an example where you avoided a potentially good outcome because the possibility of a bad outcome deterred you? How do you determine what you are willing to risk and what you are not?

At its worst, risk management in business becomes a numbers game: the statistical probability that a large enough number of people will sue the company over a product defect versus the cost of a recall and retool of the product. Calculating as nearly as possible, using expert and timely information, the risk of possible negative outcomes and preparing for those outcomes at least in a cursory way can be considered responsible business practice.

Solvability

Is the problem likely unsolvable?

When faced with a world of problems and difficulties, we can easily become overwhelmed with our own inability to make a real difference. As moral human beings, we would like to help alleviate suffering, encourage and foster human rights, and facilitate the movement toward peace in war-consumed countries. But no one of us has that capability. Former President Jimmy Carter is making a good contribution, though, with his Carter Center activities. The goals of the center are stated as: "Waging Peace, Fighting Disease, Building Hope." But even he uses a large and highly skilled team.

You may run across problems within your company that may at first appear to have no good solution. This requires care in its assessment, however. Just because you or those around you have not thought of a solution yet, the problem is not necessarily unsolvable. Some things, like a serious illness, someone's addictions, a manufacturing flaw in your company's product, are not immediately solvable by you. Some guidelines might help when you are faced with what appears to be an unsolvable problem.

- Accept that you cannot solve other people's problems for them.
- You alone cannot solve the world's problems; however, you can focus on what you can do, such as gain information or offer moral support. You should not let problems outside your control cause you to shut down; accept that there are some things you cannot control.

Keep in mind also that with advances in science, technology, and knowledge bases, problems that defied solutions even last week might be laid to rest easily this week. Conditions change; changes provide new opportunities and new solutions.

Josef and Heather had started work at the same company at the same time straight out of college. They had become friends, having been through training together, and kept in touch even though they worked in different buildings. One day, Josef went over to meet Heather at her office. While he waited in the outer office, he saw Heather and several others through the glass of the conference room. While he watched, he saw one of the men gesture toward Heather as she stood at the head of the conference table. As he gestured, he laughed, as did the others in the room. Heather, however, did not laugh with them and turned away. The others continued talking and smiling among themselves and did not look up as Heather gathered her papers and left. She had a troubled look on her face as she came out, but smiled when she saw Josef. "Let's go," she said as she hurried them out the door.

Over lunch he asked, "What was that all about back there?"

"What?" Heather answered evasively.

"What was so amusing to those other guys that wasn't to you?" He pressed the issue, though it obviously was making her uncomfortable.

"Oh, nothing. Those salesmen are just off the wall with their jokes sometimes. But because I'm new to the group, I have to sort of get along."

"What was the joke?"

Heather fidgeted in her seat, silent for several seconds. Then, she blurted, "They were joking about me, saying that they were glad I was on the team because with my looks, I could make more sales. As if that wasn't bad enough, one commented on my legs and one on my hair and my clothes." She was obviously agitated at this point.

1. What is the problem for Josef?
2. Should he be involved in this problem?
3. What are the risks to the company if Josef reports what he has seen and Heather does too?
4. Could there be anything in Josef's ethical system that might make him get involved or not?
5. Is Heather's problem solvable by Josef?

Josef leaned across the table and spoke reassuringly. "Maybe they didn't mean anything by it, but you should tell them if what they say makes you uncomfortable."

"I can't say anything. I'm new and I need them to help me learn the customers. I'm on probation the first six months. I can't afford to make waves."

Josef shook his head. "Well, they still shouldn't treat you like that." They returned to their meal and ate silently for a time.

Determining whether a problem should be taken on or not should be a strategic, analytical decision. However, each person brings his or her own perspective and approach to disturbing or challenging situations. Some approaches are more effective than others, but any taken to extreme can hamper good problem solving.

Individual Responses to Problem Situations

Following are some archetypes of responses to situations perceived to be problematic. Each is portrayed in an excessive way, but each is also representative of some common difficulties people have when dealing with confusing or frustrating dilemmas.

Patty Pensive—isolates herself to really think things through. She is very thorough in gathering information about the problem, but ends up being paralyzed by the process. There is never enough information to make her secure in deciding on a solution. She appears indecisive because it takes her so long to develop a solution.

Eric Extreme—hurls himself into the first "good" solution that comes to his mind and works diligently to make the solution work. He often overlooks important information and does not adequately anticipate consequences. He appears decisive, but makes some problems worse by premature and unsubstantiated action.

Preston Procrastinator—distracts himself from the problem with other "important" tasks. Recognizing his inability to solve problems well, he becomes anxious and ignores the situation. In some cases, this works for him because some problems do solve themselves if left alone. He does not see, however, that his delay in addressing the problem sometimes makes the situation markedly worse.

Harry Hysterical—exhibits a flurry of agitated behavior, often far more dramatic than the situation warrants. He allows his emotional, panic reaction to inhibit or eliminate rational thinking about the problem. This illogical behavior persists because people may feel sorry for him and help or relieve him of the responsibility for the solution. Though a certain amount of commitment to or passion for an outcome is good, this overdone hysterical reaction prevents clear thinking.

Norma Narrow—rigidly adheres to rules or procedures even if the best solution is somewhat outside the habitual approaches and the "approved" methods are not workable. She takes only one approach to the problem, discounting anything outside the parameters she observes. Though it is good to be focused and to take rules and procedures into consideration, the path to good solutions can be blocked by unmovable boundaries. Norma is always "right," but is often ineffective.

Betty Big—generates hundreds of solutions, many of which are potentially good ones if implemented. But Betty is an "idea person" and would rather delegate the "nuts and bolts" operations to someone else. Her method is good in that she sees the larger issues and comes up with many creative possibilities. She is seen as brilliant by others, but hers is often the good idea that never gets put into action.

Caring Carl—concerns himself inordinately with the effects of problems on others' feelings. There are two basic flaws in Carl's thinking: (1) he might incorrectly guess the effect an outcome may have on someone else, and (2) when some people's solutions are not selected, they are often not "happy," even though the chosen solution makes absolutely the best sense. This approach can also be good because it takes into consideration the people element in problems rather than just the rule of "dollars and cents" approaches.

Industry expects a specific approach to problems: a solution approach. No one, not your manager, not your coworkers, not the people in other departments, wants you to be the "chicken little" of the company. Yes, you are expected to note problem and potential problem situations and tell someone about them. However, repeatedly sounding the alarm will not score you points with management. What will is surfacing problems and offering solutions along with them.

If a project is coming in late, or some vital equipment is overdue, your manager or your project team expects you to report on when it will be completed or what will be required to complete it on time. Blaming and finger-pointing only make you look bad. No one cares why the glass is half empty; the most important information is what it will take to fill it. In other words, what resources are needed to fix the problem or to prevent its future occurrence.

Using Critical Thinking to Isolate the Problem

Critical thinking, in the form of good problem-solving skills, will free you to address difficult or adverse situations. Knee-jerk reactions, like the bad examples shown earlier, can leave you stuck in ineffective patterns. A positive approach to problems using critical-thinking skills will lead you to good solutions.

The beginning of the solution to any problem is isolating exactly what the problem is. That seems easier than it is in practice and takes considerable skill.

An example is one many people have faced at some point in their lives. Marcus's phone bill and the rent are both due and his girlfriend's birthday is coming up. His income is reasonable from his CAD (computer-aided design) job, but he is paying off his student loan and trying to save for a new car because his old one is nearly unusable. He says the problem is, "I don't have enough money."

Actually, the problem is more complex than that. Until Marcus looks at the situation critically, he is not going to be able to effectively solve the problem. A detailed examination of the problem reveals that:

- His girlfriend will have her feelings hurt if the present is not nice.
- He will be evicted and have no place to live if the rent is not paid.
- His phone will be cut off and his job involves telecommuting from home.
- He worries that his girlfriend might leave him if he ignores her birthday.
- Others might think he is cheap or poor if he does not get a nice present.
- He does not want to ask his parents for extra money because that would take away from his independence.

- He has no other source of income because learning his company's software takes all of his time.

This analysis shows that Marcus's real problem is that he feels like he must live up to other people's expectations: his girlfriend's, his parents', and other people he knows. If he begins to look at the problem from this angle, he might realize that his relationships are not quite as fragile as he perceives. His girlfriend might not actually be expecting an expensive gift; she might, instead, just want some uninterrupted time with him. It also might not hurt for Marcus to have a discussion with her about money and their relationship.

So, *the first step in discovering a solution is to think critically about what the problem really is.* This is true for relationships and it is even more true on the job.

In a manufacturing plant, Rosalind, the human resources director, noted that absenteeism and turnover were especially high in one department. She concluded that employee motivation was the problem and began looking at incentive programs that would cost the company many thousands of dollars to implement.

Just before she contracted for the program, Rosalind talked with an employee in the department over coffee. When she asked about the morale in the department, the employee responded emotionally. The manager would quite often, and for no apparent reason, verbally attack employees at random. The work environment was so tense that no one wanted to come to the plant knowing they would have to be around that volatile manager.

Rosalind followed up on the situation and found out that the manager had a chemical abuse problem. He was placed on leave for six weeks and was referred to a company-sponsored rehabilitation program for addiction. In his absence, productivity immediately improved and absenteeism dropped. The problem was not the employees; it was the manager. The company almost spent many thousands of dollars solving the wrong problem.

Previously, a cursory definition of a problem was offered by Vincent Ruggiero. It said that a problem was a situation that intelligent and knowledgeable people agreed needed to be corrected. For practical purposes, this text defines a problem as *a discrepancy between what can be, should be, or is expected to be and what is.*

For example, in a relationship spouse A expects that a married person shows commitment and affection by coming home on time from work. Spouse B regularly has to close out the records for the day and ends up 30 to 60 minutes late fairly often. This is a discrepancy between what is expected and what is. Defined as a problem, this can be addressed and solved in a constructive and supportive way. Defined as a hurtful omission, this discrepancy can escalate into an emotional and damaging exchange.

In technical sales, the product representative must function as a consultant by looking into the prospective client's business operations to discover where the product might dramatically improve productivity or cut costs. The client might not recognize how much better his business could function unless the representative defines the difference between what current operations are yielding and what could be attainable with the new product or system.

An example of a "should be" discrepancy might occur in carrying out a policy. For instance, a policy in customer service might be that the representative who is talking to the customer has the authority to act to resolve customer issues. If supervisors require representatives to secure signatures or call them for approval of customer resolutions, then there is a discrepancy between what should be and what is. Once that is noted and defined, causes and solutions related to the problem can be addressed.

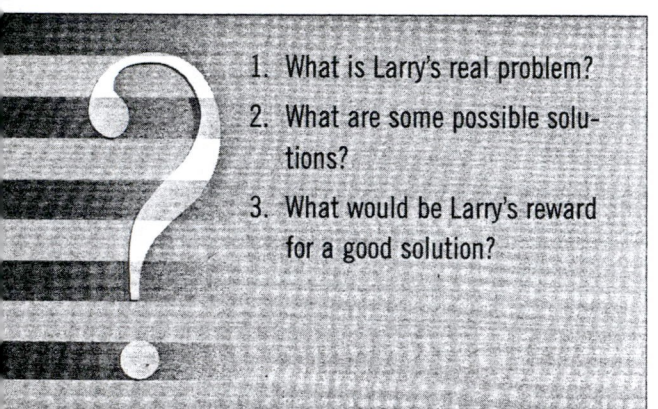

1. What is Larry's real problem?

2. What are some possible solutions?

3. What would be Larry's reward for a good solution?

Larry has been in his job with Erzone company for eight weeks. A company he had interviewed with prior to going with Erzone has called him with an offer of $4,000 more per year than what he is making at Erzone.

Consider this illustration to help you come up with a larger view of the problem.

In the diagram, you can see the problem, **P**, inside a box. If you look at the problem from all of the perspectives around the box, you will have examined a problem thoroughly.

- If I were in the middle of the problem—if it were affecting me directly—how would I define it?

- If I were behind the problem—at the place where it first began—how would I describe what happened to create the problem situation?
- If I were in front of the problem—if it were already solved satisfactorily—how would the solution situation appear?
- If I were beside the problem—able to see both the problem and all of the issues around it—how would I put it into perspective?
- If I were above the problem—if it did not affect me at all—how would I define it?

It is probably not uncommon that people look at a problem from the outside, but neglecting to look at it from all of the "outsides," as well as from the perspective of being in the middle of the dilemma, narrows the view. This narrowing immediately limits the scope of the areas in which solutions will be sought and may cause people to overlook an important aspect that could lead to a solution.

ACTIVITY 7.2

Think of a situation that is currently creating a problem for you. Write down several possible views of the problem. Then, look at alternative views and write a single, specific problem statement.

Situation:

_____

_____

_____

Alternative views of the problem:

_____

_____

_____

Specific problem statement:

_____

_____

_____

Once you have isolated the problem, you are ready to begin seeking solutions. Keep one important consideration in mind: people problems are the single greatest factor in project failure (Ghattas and McKee, 2000). However, people are not problems. Any party in a relationship or work dilemma can choose to ignore the problem or fall into the "chicken little" mode of announcing problems but offering no solutions.

If you describe the problem by saying, "You are the problem," you do two things: you cease to look for answers to the real problem, and you allow the other person to abdicate his responsibility for a mutual solution. It is easy to walk away from, "you're the problem," with a few mutterings and maybe a swear word or two. It is more difficult and more rewarding to define a problem and seek a joint, satisfactory solution.

Thinking Creatively to Generate Solutions

Here is where you have to become creative in your thinking. Concepts such as the telephone and the microwave oven did not come from conventional thinking. They arose from an inventor's ability to visualize new solutions to existing problems. *Good solutions come from those alternatives generated by the imagination, not from everyday thinking.* Also, the best solution is rarely the first or second one you come up with; more likely it will be the last one. Imaginative solutions lead to creative problem solving, which gets you out of the problem rut. The rule for coming up with solutions is that there are no rules. The more creative and outlandish the idea seems, the closer you may be to finding your answer.

Sometimes research into the problem to discover what others have done to address it can save time and energy. Be careful not to let this limit you, however. Your situation may well be different and require a more far-reaching or unique approach. Often, the usual solutions have not successfully eliminated the problem; they may just mask or put it off for a while. Complex problems require information, logic, and creativity.

7.3   ACTIVITY

Part 1. Begin to practice thinking creatively by writing down every use you can think of for old running shoes. Give yourself five minutes and work toward a list of 10 or more.

Part 2. Now, pick a problem you have isolated for yourself to work on. List at least five possible solutions. Take a break for five minutes and list five more. Don't worry if they are workable or not, just pat yourself on the back for your creativity, especially if you go over five in either set.

Problem: _____

Solution set 1:

_____

_____

_____

Solution set 2:

_____

_____

_____

Because you are now expanding your view of problems and of possible solutions, it is time to analyze what you have come up with and begin to narrow your choices.

Analyzing to Weed Out the Least Workable Options

Once options are generated, it is time to rule out the ones that have negative consequences. Remember that you want positive outcomes in your life, and problem solving should help you find new ways to make things go better for you. Of the positive options you have left, investigate what would be involved in carrying each out. The following example will guide you.

A shipping manager has to cut the budget in his department by $35,000 for the next year. He has several options:

- fire a $35,000 per year employee
- fire two part-time clerical people
- cut hours for three hourly employees
- offer reduced time or reduced pay to employees

- cut out training and incentive programs for the year
- suggest an early retirement option
- cut benefits
- eliminate achievement awards and lunches
- dock pay for sick leave
- increase productivity to offset losses
- drop dependents from the benefits plan
- eliminate the college co-op program

He sees only two positive solutions for his purposes. He investigates the number of people who have small children or live-in elderly parents to see how many might actually welcome reduced hours in order to have more time to spend on family business. Looking at the other side of the issue, he recognizes that the order to cut costs is due to productivity losses. Increases in productivity might eliminate the need for the cut altogether.

7.4   ACTIVITY

Take the solutions you developed in Activity 7.3 and eliminate the least workable. (Note: you might want to investigate the steps it would take to implement several before you decide what can work and what can't.) You can ask for information from others.

Solution alternative #1:

_____

_____

I could make this work by:

_____

_____

Solution alternative #2:

_____

_____

I could make this work by:

_____

_____

Solution alternative #3:

_____

_____

I could make this work by:

_____

_____

You see, going all around a problem, with no limits on what you can consider, may lead you to options that may create positive outcomes. Investigating the workability of more than one option might surprise you. Something you thought could never happen might actually become a reality through your efforts. The final step, then, puts your ideas and investigation to work.

Acting to Implement Your Choice

Action is the key to lowering stress in difficult situations. Problems sometimes paralyze us with their size, so we become inactive, feeling powerless to help. Positive activity becomes the great helper. The mere carrying out of options can give us a feeling of contributing to a solution instead being ground down by circumstances. Perhaps your solution requires a little more asking, planning, and researching to be effectively implemented. Don't stop. Go ahead: ask, plan, and research. You will feel more positive and will be more motivated to keep at the task of carrying out your ideas. Even if the first solution you pick proves imperfect, you have other good ones you have already thought of and investigated. Get going!

Once you begin the action phase of problem solving, you must go back to the original definition: *a discrepancy between what can be, should be, or is expected to be, and what is.* When you have implemented your choice of possible solutions, you have not finished until you have checked the solution against the original effect or situation you wanted to achieve. You have probably heard the expression, "Don't make matters worse." Of course, your goal is never to do that, but it is possible.

In business, outcomes and their potential effects can actually be computed in some situations where cause-and-effect relationships are statistically known. For example, if civil unrest has cut off the source of cocoa beans for your company's chocolate bars, then the solution to the supply problem will have certain predictable outcomes. Decisions are made in industry using this approach every day. If the cost of cocoa beans is exactly one third the price of a chocolate bar, and if the price of cocoa beans from a new source is 20 cents more per unit, then there are two choices. The result will require the price of the bar to go or the company will make less money on every bar sold.

However, the company's marketing department does consumer research to see if a higher price would cut sales. If so, then a decision has to be made. "Will we lose more if we absorb the increased cost or if we raise prices and reduce the number of sales?" Interestingly, market researchers can make very good predictions of the effects on sales of price increases or decreases. This allows the company to prepare for and work around the effects.

In the case of a company in financial trouble, a solution might be to lay off one-third of the workforce in order to stay solvent and be able to offer some security to the remaining employees. At some level, then, the logical cause-and-effect assumption is that a layoff would lead to stronger feelings of job security for the rest of the workers and would increase loyalty and possibly productivity. If a layoff is implemented, then close monitoring of the responses of the other workers would let management know if the solution was a good one. What can happen in these cases is that layoffs often lead to a detrimental exodus of other valued, possibly highly productive employees who have either become indignant over management's treatment or fearful due to loss of faith in management's ability to keep the company solvent.

In other situations, constantly changing conditions may make one solution, which appeared the best at the time, quickly become the wrong choice. Some guidelines will help in assessing the success of a solution when implemented:

1. Ask representatives of those departments (or individuals) affected by the solution to monitor conditions for improvement or deterioration.

2. Formalize an assessment process at specified intervals to evaluate whether the solution is successful or if other action is needed.

3. Though every plan for correction of a problem should be given time to work, be ready to abandon an obviously failing course of action in favor of a second plan.

4. Reassess or redefine the situation if conditions change so dramatically that the solution (or maybe even the problem) becomes irrelevant.

ACTIVITY

ACTIVITY   7.5

Look at a problem you have recently dealt with and evaluate the outcome based on what you had hoped to achieve with the action you took.

How the solution was implemented: _____

Outcome: _____

   Has this problem been resolved now or does it need another look? You can do this process as many times as needed to arrive at a lasting solution.

Congratulating Yourself

Every problem you solve is an achievement. Enjoy your success and let each success support you in your next challenge. Each successful problem solution adds to your confidence in your ability to address transitions in your life. Forward movement changes conditions, and some of those changes might create problems. Good problem solvers have a calmer view of transitions and the challenges they often spawn.

   Always remember to give yourself credit for the growth you are experiencing. Each chapter you read in this book and each activity you do puts you ahead of those who are still lost in inactivity, overcome by a life that may be out of control or stagnant. You are learning to steer your way out of storms. There will always be more storms, but you will learn from each one, and the next will be easier, as will the next, and the next.

ACTIVITY

For the problems you have worked on in this chapter, list each one you have found a solution for and describe why it is a good solution. This exercise will allow you to affirm the good you are doing for yourself by becoming a careful problem solver.

Solution #1: _____

This solution was good because

_____

_____

Solution #2: _____

This solution was good because

_____

_____

Many people think that problem-solving skills and creativity belong only to a few gifted individuals. Actually, by using the skills you have learned in this chapter, you will improve your ability to consistently work through problems toward positive solutions. Up to now you may have made decisions on "gut instinct" or intuition. From this point on, however, you can add to your intuition a good, solid approach to life's challenges and greet transitions with the power of your new skill.

TRANSITION SKILLS SUMMARY

Decide whether or not to address problem

Isolate the "real" problem

Generate solutions

Weed out the least workable

Implement the best solution

Congratulate yourself

GOAL SETTING

Self-nurturing: How are you going to improve your personal situation by applying problem-solving skills?

_____

_____

_____

Self-advocacy: What changes can you make in the way you address problems that will help you perform more effectively in the workplace?

_____

_____

_____

COACH'S CORNER

Problem-solving approaches must change as a person's personal and professional life becomes more complex. In our daily lives, we tend to deal with problems as they confront us, fix them, and get them out of our face. With business problems and more complex personal problems, a process approach is required. Through patience and dedication, a solution to the source of the problem is sought rather than a fix for the symptom or result. Through a series of questions, the problem solver pursues the situation to its origin. This requires a great deal of maturity because the road of inquiry may lead back to the questioner who must then take responsibility for a solution that will keep the situation from happening again.

Questions that are useful include:

- What actually happened?

- Where did it come from?

- In whose opinion (or perception) is this a problem?

A company's culture has a lot to do with how problems are handled, but the most progressive take a solution-oriented approach: Don't shoot the messenger, reward the solution provider. Generally, the person with whom the problem originated owns it; he is likely the one most affected by the situation. This person pursues it until it is solved or the resolution is found to lie elsewhere. That is not to say it is shifted to move it away, but it could indeed lie outside your department's control.

For example, a cash flow problem led to an investigation into policies and collections procedures and found that time limits on payments were too long, tying up excessive amounts of the company's money. The problem—cash flow— was traced to its source—time limits on payments.

Organizational thinking should take precedence over self-protective thinking. The problem should be considered with regard to how it affects the boss, the clients, the company, and the department. Solutions should be valued; self-protection is detrimental to the process because facts may be distorted or concealed, preventing discovery of the real problem.

(continued)

Decisions are choices plus action and can evolve from problems.

1. Explore problems and decisions from as many different aspects as possible.

2. Trust your instincts.

3. Take responsibility for your role in the problem or solution.

4. Do the right thing.

CAROLINE MENDEZ, Certified Professional Coach, Evolve, Inc.
E-mail: Coach@evolve-inc.com.

CHAPTER 8

Confronting Conflict

onflict is a part of everyone's life. Yet, few of us approach conflict with enthusiasm. Part of the discomfort is that growing up, we seldom get the opportunity to learn positive conflict resolution. We all remember seeing conflicts; these are natural in every family. Probably, though, you do not remember seeing conflicts resolved. In this chapter, you will learn where conflicts come from and how to recognize them at their source. You will also come to understand your own and others' reactions to conflict. Finally, you will learn a positive approach to truly resolving the difficulties in your life that result from conflict.

Once you become competent in conflict resolution, you will:

- be able to create and maintain harmony
- be able to sustain relationships over time
- lower your stress level in interpersonal interactions
- gain confidence in your own ability to create positive outcomes from difficult situations

Conflicting Needs as a Source of Interpersonal Conflict

Conflicting needs are a fundamental source of discord in relating to others. Any time my need is different from yours, we have a conflict to some degree. How we treat that conflict is subject to our learned approach to conflict, degree of need, kind of relationship, strength of emotion, and level of self-esteem. Thus, if the conflict of need is in an area where you do not have a strong emotional involvement, you may be calm and logical in your handling of the situation. If the other person involved is someone you like and respect, then you will likely be highly motivated to seek a positive solution that is acceptable to both.

On the other hand, if your feelings are hurt or if you feel that the other person's need is overbearing and unfair, then you may react with anger. Conflicts can be quite volatile under these circumstances, but they do not have to be. The following situation illustrates a simple need conflict.

Phillip is a furniture designer and works much of the time at home. Sometimes, he is up very late, especially when he has a deadline to meet, because he likes to take a break when his sons come home from school. Jorge, Phillip's neighbor, is a programmer and works the 11 to 7 shift so he can keep his young daughter while his wife works. At four in the afternoon, Phillip takes his break to be with his sons. Many of the neighborhood boys visit because Phillip has built a skating ramp in the driveway, and Phillip helps them to practice their tricks. Jorge goes to bed about 4 P.M. when his wife comes home. The sound of the skates on the ramp keeps Jorge from sleeping.

There is a need conflict. Jorge knows he sometimes has a bad temper and that if he speaks to Phillip, there is the potential for an ugly argument. So, knowing this, Jorge might act in any of several ways depending on his learned approach to conflict:

- He may not say anything in order to avoid creating bad feelings.
- He might yell and threaten Phillip, or make noise early to waken him.
- He could become depressed over his inability to control the situation.

8.1 ACTIVITY

In this situation, which of Jorge's possible reactions might most closely resemble your own approach to conflict?

Your approach is:

_____

_____

An example of this might be:

_____

_____

Conflicting Goals as a Source of Organizational Conflict

You will find the same kinds of interpersonal conflicts in the work environment as you do outside: people feeling threatened and acting out some angry behavior, people becoming frustrated and venting. But, you also will see a larger type of conflict: goal conflict. In these cases, the conflict is not with needs, but a goal-directed activity. Issues of "ownership" and territory can be present here as well.

The new employee cannot immediately know where these festering conflicts might lie and can inadvertently be pulled into them. In the movie *Office Space*, many typical organizational conflicts, as well as some typical responses, are humorously illustrated. After reading further, you might enjoy identifying the various approaches to organizational conflict shown in that movie.

When you find yourself in a turf battle or the object of a power-display conflict, it can be very disconcerting. But when you understand the dynamics of goal conflict in companies, you will see that they are very similar to interpersonal conflicts that occur in daily life. The stakes in business are high because, in many cases, achieving a goal means saving one's job. If one manager's goal conflicts with another manager's, then the conflict could reach into other departments.

A simple but pointed example is the strategic plan for product development. Companies move forward, grow, and stay profitable by making good choices about what products they bring to market and what products they retire. Jeff is involved with developing battery-charging technology for digital cameras. Tony's division has many hours and a considerable budget invested in charging controllers for cell phones. The board has met and decided that the company is not well served by trying to do both. One of the development efforts is to be discontinued, possibly resulting in the layoff of engineers and salespeople connected with the product. Neither Jeff nor Tony is likely to be laid off, and each will be allowed patent co-ownership on whatever is developed and ultimately marketed by the company. However, each manager hired the engineers reporting to him and each feels a great deal of loyalty to them.

1. What are the issues in conflict here?

2. What will happen to the company if this is not resolved quickly?

3. Why would Tony and Jeff be concerned about the conflict?

4. Remembering that profitability is an absolute necessity to keeping a company alive, what might a good resolution be to this conflict?

The individual employee performance review can also be a source of conflict when the employee and the manager have different perceptions of the performance. Conflict around you, as well as conflict in which you are involved, can cause inordinate stress. You will feel much less threatened by organizational conflict scenarios, though, when you understand reactions to conflict and effective methods of dealing with conflict.

Common Approaches to Conflict

As noted previously, people view the potentially disruptive situation of conflict differently. In the following sections, you will see individual reactions in interpersonal relationships and reactions to conflict in organizational settings.

Conflict in Interpersonal Relationships

Evasion

Some people evade altogether situations that might lead to conflict. A wife finds out her husband is cheating and keeps up appearances, pretending everything is okay. Employees keep bad news away from the boss to avoid a scene. Customers sometimes keep defective products, so they do not have to assert themselves to a customer service person. This pattern of evasion is learned very early in our lives and supported over time.

Those who grow up in troubled families learn to tread lightly around many issues to prevent a flare-up of anger in the household and the effects of that anger on others. These individuals feel that by evading conflict, they can prevent problems from erupting. Thus, they never learn how to address issues and see a conflict through to a positive resolution.

These early patterns set up an unconscious mechanism that causes a withdrawal from conflict of any kind. In adult life, then, conflict avoidance becomes a pattern that we are not even aware of. This evasion reaction becomes ingrained in us and causes us to resist, often at great cost, any entry into a disagreement or conflict.

Some people go to such great lengths to avoid these situations that they make themselves physically sick. Todd was taught all his life never to argue with authority, to just "take it." Eventually, after years of unresolved conflicts at his job, he began having stomach pains like those associated with ulcers. He sought out counseling at the suggestion of his medical doctor. His case is not an uncommon one.

At first, he was reluctant to talk about the problems causing his stress. "I don't know what you can do for me. I've just got some stuff that I have to work out." The discussions that followed did bring out some rather serious conflicts Todd was having at his job. When asked if he had discussed any of these with his manager, he responded, "When I was growing up, it was always, 'Keep your mouth shut and do what you're told.'" Consequently, Todd held inside the anger from every conflict he avoided. His learned conflict avoidance eventually showed up in the form of a potentially serious health problem.

ACTIVITY   **8.2**

Take a moment to recall the kinds of conflict in your upbringing. What do you remember about the way it was handled and how it made you feel?

_____

_____

As you work through the next two sections, try to determine the conflict style you have developed as a result of your past experience.

An evasion approach may cause us a great deal of emotional pain. *By avoiding conflict, we avoid the depth of close relationship.* As long as people in the world think differently, there will be variations and conflict to some degree. Part of the richness of a relationship is learning about the opposite views others may hold. We broaden our own thinking by exposing ourselves to alternative views.

Conflict is a method of enhancing this process. Conflict is a fact of life. It is as natural as breathing, loving, or eating. Once we understand that *conflict is an important part of emotional and intellectual growth*, we then relieve ourselves of the dread we feel when we approach and deal with it. All of the energy that used to be spent worrying about or evading conflict situations can instead be directed toward positive resolutions.

Anger

Another way of responding to conflict is anger. Our bodies respond to anger the same way they do to a life-threatening situation. Adrenaline causes the heart to frantically pump blood to the muscles. The stomach churns. All of that energy has to go somewhere, and sometimes it translates into angry blowups. This issue of the perceived threat is very individual, however.

If a man feels that his family is threatened by an undesirable tenant moving into the apartment complex, he might storm angrily into the rental manager's office. In this case, fear is translated into an angry behavior. If an engineer begins to suspect that the product he has designed will not be chosen for production, he might perceive that his job security is in danger. In this situation, there is an issue of control—not being able to control the outcome of the product assessment—and fear of the loss of employment. Anger may be the way he behaves in such a situation.

The energy resulting from an anger response allows us to defend ourselves in a threatening, hand-to-hand situation. Thus, it has a basis in the instinctual survival reaction. In the office or at home, however, the urge to respond to a conflict with a loud show of anger or with violence is unacceptable. (In those situations, there is much more to lose than the conflict.)

Another of the sources of anger is emotional hurt. When self-esteem is damaged, our mind translates that into an attack at some level and responds—sometimes with hostility. If someone criticizes your clothes, you might feel indignant and want to answer the criticism smartly with anger. You can also get angry from the hurt of embarrassment, as when you are the butt of a practical joke. Any of these situations can lead to a highly charged conflict that will be difficult to resolve because of the emotions involved.

You will be asked in Activity 8.3 to look at your own or others' responses to hurt or threat. In addition to learned behaviors, some personality elements enter into your reaction as well as learned behaviors. When hurt emotionally, some people respond in an aggressive or angry way, while others may shut down and become sad, which is a passive response. We all do both of these on occasion, but will generally show a pattern of response toward one or the other. By careful self-observation you can very likely determine your typical response pattern when hurt. When you understand your habitual pattern, then you can work to develop a more beneficial, strategic approach.

ACTIVITY 8.3

Write down a conflict situation that you can recall where anger was the response. Try not to describe the angry behavior, but identify the source of the anger for yourself or for the other person. Label the type of anger as emotional pain (or threat), physical pain (or threat), or lack of control.

Conflict situation:

_____

_____

Source of anger:

_____

_____

How could you tell what the source was?

_____

_____

What you may notice is that your anger comes out of the circumstances. If anger is your conflict style, then you are indeed experiencing a lot of stress because of the way you are approaching conflict in your life.

Sadness

Another possible reaction to conflict is sadness, or in its chronic or more intense form, depression. Some people just shut down and feel powerless in the face of a threat or pain. Instead of meeting the conflict head on and resolving it, they retreat within themselves and consistently give in when a conflict occurs. This continual denial of their own needs in the face of others' needs eventually mounts up. They begin to feel an unexplainable sadness, and may even suffer from serious depression.

Some of this sadness comes from being powerless to act as they feel they should. When a verbally abusive husband consistently screams at his wife, often the male child withdraws and becomes depressed. He feels he should protect his mother and cannot. A verbally abusive manager can create the same reaction if you feel you cannot respond. In a job situation, you might become sad when you have a conflict with a coworker or friend and you do not resolve it positively.

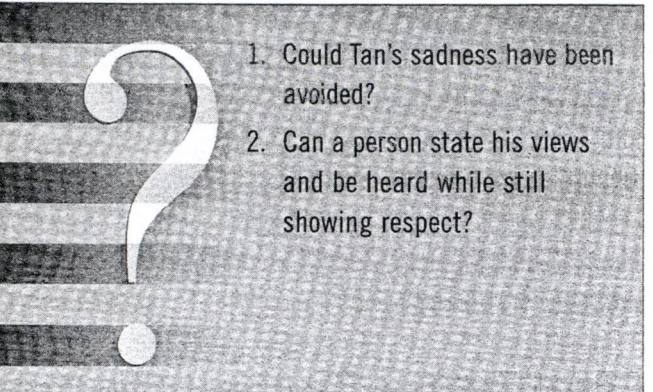

1. Could Tan's sadness have been avoided?

2. Can a person state his views and be heard while still showing respect?

Tan disagreed strongly with his father's decision to expand the family business. He felt that it would cause competition between his brothers. In addition, it would separate the family geographically because the new locations were outside the city. Having been taught that it was disrespectful to argue with the head of the family, Tan remained quiet, but became less and less enthusiastic in the discussions about the expansion and withdrew to his room each night immediately after the evening meal.

Conflict Reactions in Organizational Settings

A critical look beneath the surface of conflicts in companies reveals the same types of reactions, but the ways they are acted out in business situations may appear differently.

Territoriality

This behavior grows out of a perceived threat to an individual or a department. Generally, it is acted out by refusals to do tasks outside prescribed duties: "That's not my job." Or, it may appear as information withholding: "No, those are my accounts, you stick with your own." The latter is unfortunately common in sales environments where commissions and bonuses are awarded on the basis of individual revenue generation. Setting people in competition with each other unfortunately often fosters detrimental conflict.

Power Plays

In organizations, the coordination of effort among many people is required to achieve goals and meet objectives. Thus, when a goal conflict occurs, people tend to gather allies around them by exercising what power they have over those people. Conflict brings out the need to use power to force a win in such situations. Power and influence are discussed in more detail in Chapter 10.

Sabotage and Backbiting

When conflict is not met head-on, that does not mean it has disappeared. Often, it bubbles up in more subtle ways: people conveniently forget deadlines on projects important to others, or carefully place reports of oversights or mistakes that could hurt someone's credibility or reputation. Interestingly enough, absenteeism is often attributed to unresolved conflicts in the workplace. The attitude is, "I'll show him; I just won't show up today. That'll mess his schedule up good."

Loss of Morale, Negativity

This is often the result of the conflict that occurs when expectations are not met. Employees have certain expectations of their jobs, such as fair pay, respect, opportunity for professional fulfillment, and advancement. When the employee feels as if the company (or the manager) has not met these expectations, then there is a conflict between the expectations and the reality. If this type of conflict is not confronted in some constructive way, productivity drops and the work environment becomes unpleasant.

Retreat, Rebellion

Conflicts between management choices and employee well-being that are large and far-reaching can be resolved with open communication and a genuine desire to arrive at a mutually workable solution. An example of this type of situation is when management chooses a direction for the company that will result in layoffs or a change in location. If employees feel that broaching or challenging the issue is fruitless, or if they feel that the choice was self-serving by management, widespread departures by good employees can occur. In some cases, this type of conflict leads to covert alliances within the company that result in the deposing of one or more upper managers.

None of the responses mentioned to this point are constructive ways to handle a conflict. And, if you observe the patterns, all of these reactions assume that the conflict could not have a positive outcome for all concerned. If you believe that conflicts necessarily go badly and that you have no control over the outcome of conflict, then you may readily adopt one of those approaches.

Handle Conflict Constructively

Conflict resolution is for the person or company that genuinely cares about both self and others, and is motivated to resolve, rather than temporarily stifle, conflict. This requires a certain amount of maturity. Experience teaches that unresolved conflicts come back over and over. There are several very effective techniques for conflict resolution.

The best way to approach conflict is to do it from your own sense of inner strength, and with a positive expectation about the outcome. When you are self-assured and positive, you are less likely to react to the conflict situation in one of the ineffective ways described previously.

Handle Emotions

When you have a sense of strength about yourself, you can back off from a situation that could be volatile. By taking one step back, you initially give yourself an opportunity to detach somewhat from the intensity of the conflict. Though there are no concrete rules of interpersonal conflict, there are guidelines for communicating that can help the whole process go smoothly.

When discussing conflict, focus on the situation as the topic to be resolved. Using the "I feel" statement is key here. You might say, "I feel . . . (insert emotion) . . . when you . . . (insert the problem or issue)." This way of communicating ensures a discussion related to the issues, rather than an individual, emotional response to the character of the person.

It is easy to get lost in emotion in a conflict to the extent that emotion becomes your entire focus. Feelings, however, are not the issue. Behavior is the issue. By using "I feel . . . " statements, you begin to separate the emotions from the issues. When there is intense emotion, it might be appropriate to ask yourself, "Why am I this upset about this situation?" or "Why might this other person be upset about the situation?"

Sometimes we bring old baggage from previous, unresolved conflicts to the discussion. This baggage could be in the form of anger or hurt left over from an earlier, and maybe unrelated, situation. If this is the case, then it is even more important to separate this excess emotion from the issues at hand. Focus on the issues rather than the person. *Acknowledge the feelings, but recognize that resolution of the behavior issues will solve the conflict situation.*

The more your emotions become hooked into the scene, the less likely you are to be able to think clearly. You will also be less likely to come up with solutions that could be suitable to both parties. *So, the first step is to back off and get a handle on your own emotions.* (An effective way to do this is to ask yourself what emotions you are experiencing at the time.)

Interestingly enough, we cannot seem to be logical and emotional at the same time. Thus, if you can evoke reason and observation as a response in yourself, you will see the emotional fallout diminish.

8.4   ACTIVITY

Over the next two days take note of the times you feel emotional in a conflict. Say to yourself, "I recognize I am angry (or hurt, or embarrassed), and I need to look past my reaction to see the real problem in this conflict."

Conflict situation:

I recognize that I am _____

I think _____ might be one of the problems.

Did you notice any difference in the intensity of your feeling after you identified it? Did your ability to separate the emotions from the issues help you to think more clearly?

Listen to Details

The second step is to listen with great attention to detail. After you have taken your emotional step back, try to listen very carefully to what the other person is saying, so carefully that you can repeat exactly what that person has said without missing a word. This kind of attention allows you to enter into the other person's world. When you do this, you learn something vitally important about the other person's inner workings and needs. You may even choose to clarify what is being said: "I don't understand exactly what makes you feel so angry about this situation. Can you explain it in a different way?"

The next time you find yourself in a conflict situation, listen carefully to what is being said. Look for fact (issue) statements and feeling (emotion) statements.

Look at the following dialog and analyze it for conflict elements.

LaShonda and Venson worked together on several overlapping projects. Venson designed the wording and the strategy for presentations to be given by the marketing department. LaShonda developed the art and set it all up on the presentation software.

"LaShonda," Venson said, "why don't you have that presentation ready? Mark needs it in two hours, and he wanted to run through it first. You know it doesn't look good when things come out of our department late."

"Venson, that stuff you gave me yesterday took me most of the night to do."

"Why? I gave you the outline and the spin we wanted to put on the proposal."

"Yeah, but you didn't get it to me until 3. I hate it when you do that dump and run thing."

"What's your problem? That's your job. Did you miss a night out partying?"

"I resent the implication in that. I am a professional and I do good work."

"Yeah, but who cares, if you can't meet timetables?"

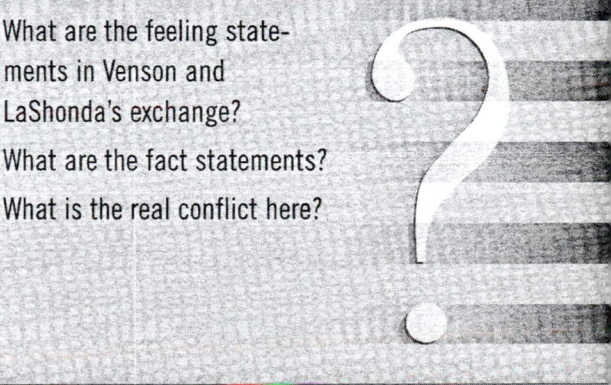

1. What are the feeling statements in Venson and LaShonda's exchange?

2. What are the fact statements?

3. What is the real conflict here?

So many of us are poor listeners. We become intent on stating our case or voicing how unhappy we are with someone else. Then we fail to really tune into what the other person is saying. When the issues are broached, listening ensures that the situation is clearly defined for both parties.

State Your Needs

Now, you can make your needs known. Keep in mind here that a person with whom you have an ongoing relationship, especially a personal one, should listen and respond appropriately to this statement of need. Most of the time, however, we are more interested in speaking our case than in listening actively to the other person's case. Assert your needs in a straightforward and nonemotional way. This conveys that your view of the situation is as valid as the other person's.

If Sharon feels that her car was not repaired properly, her first response might be to avoid a confrontation and pay her bill anyway. Instead, she could be assertive and ask the technician to explain what service was done to her car and why it was done. She is expressing her need to understand where her money is going and how her car has been repaired.

Sometimes this is the point where you begin to clarify why there is a conflict to begin with. One author, Pete Bradshaw (1985), breaks down our needs into four areas:

1. Power, control, and influence
2. Achievement, accomplishment, and mastery
3. Behavior consistent with beliefs and values
4. Security in being cared for and liked

He explains that a needy condition in any or several of these areas of a person's life makes a conflict in that area more disturbing and the response, thus, more zealous. For example, if a person feels out of control in her life, a conflict in that area creates a control issue that will not be resolved until that issue has been addressed. In the earlier example, LaShonda needed to feel that her efforts and skill were noted, and she probably would remain agitated about the situation until that part of the conflict was resolved. Her coworker, on the other hand, needed to behave consistently with his belief that work should be delivered to clients on time.

Rarely in conversation, especially in the workplace, do we receive a good reaction if we say, "In this conflict, I need to feel cared for and valued." But if we are aware of our needs and can voice them in a way others can understand them, we are more likely to get at what is important to resolve the conflict. If Harry and Estelle want to meet for lunch, and Harry suggests an Indian restaurant, Estelle, who really doesn't like Indian food, has several options:

1. Go to the restaurant because Harry wants to and sit with nothing to eat.
2. Tell Harry she doesn't want to have lunch with him.
3. Tell Harry she really doesn't like that type of food.

Option 3 is a voicing of her need or concern. Estelle needed to meet Harry somewhere she could enjoy having lunch too. When she did this, however, Harry attacked her taste, saying she probably did not know if she liked the food or not. He did not respect her need or try to find a solution that might work for both of them. He could have, instead, responded with a need of his own. "There isn't an Indian restaurant near me, so I look forward to eating there when I come to town."

With both of their needs voiced, and a respect for those needs, they might have resolved the situation constructively. Instead, Estelle chose not to meet Harry for lunch.

When someone attempts to influence you, it can be at the expense of your own needs or limits. If you meet the other person's needs without addressing your own, there is still conflict, but it stays inside you. For a conflict to be completely resolved, your needs, as well as the other person's, must be affirmed.

ACTIVITY 8.5

Recall a conflict where you felt you gave in or ended up agreeing to a solution that really was not good for you. Write an assertive statement of needs that you might have used.

Conflict situation:

_____

_____

Assertive needs statement:

_____

_____

Sometimes, we are surprised that other people's needs are different from our own. We get so stuck in our own brand of thinking that we forget that many other views can exist on any given subject. So, when differences arise, it becomes necessary for each person to begin the negotiation process.

Discern and Acknowledge Others' Needs

In a successful negotiation, both parties state their needs and the value they place on those needs. Thus, each negotiator understands the other person's viewpoint and the reasons the other person feels so strongly about that viewpoint. It serves your own needs to understand the other person's position because then a resolution is equally supported by both parties. Recognize the other person's right to have opposing needs. One difficulty is that not everyone is good at expressing needs. So, sometimes you may have to guess what the person's needs really are.

You can bet that voiced or not, each person in a conflict has an idea of what a satisfactory resolution for him is. It may not be the resolution that you end up with, but until you understand the need or expectation of the other person, the conflict will continue. This is a common difficulty in conflict resolution. It is especially helpful when you can teach others around you how to verbalize needs and goals. Look at the next two exchanges. The first is a very simple example of what happens when needs are not communicated so they can be addressed.

> Mom: "Hello, sweetie."
>
> Baby: "Waaaaaaaah."
>
> Mom: "You must be wet."
>
> Baby: "Waaaaaaaaaaaaaaaaaah."
>
> Mom: "Are you hungry?"
>
> Baby: (louder now and with a red face) "WAAAAAAaaaaaah."
>
> Mom: (becoming agitated) "What do you want?"
>
> Baby: (turning purple and wailing loudly) "WAAAAAAAAAAAAAAAH."

Before you roll your eyes at what may seem like an outrageous example, think of this: As adults we sometimes are not too far removed from the baby who cries when she is not taken care of. When this happens, the conflict turns into more of an argument and often becomes much louder. When someone with whom we are in conflict does not listen or respond appropriately, we tend to resort to stronger language. By recognizing the necessity to communicate needs, we can better manage the language of conflict.

> Customer: "I bought this suit at one of your stores and it's trash."
>
> Representative: "When did you purchase it and from which of our stores?"
>
> Customer: "Look, you, I said this thing is junk. Why don't you just do your job, or can't you do that?"
>
> Representative: "Sir, I understand this is an unpleasant problem, and we need to deal with it right away. I'm sure you purchased the suit for something important."

Customer: "You're d_____ right. I've got an interview in the morning and I need the suit!"

Representative: "We'll take care of this. If you'll tell me where and when you bought it, I'll authorize the store closest to you now to make one available for tomorrow's interview. You can leave the suit you are having a problem with, and the manager will work out a repair or replacement afterwards. But this will get you set for that interview right away."

Customer: "Well, uh, okay. That will work. It's my second interview and I have to look just right."

Representative: "Yes, I'm sure you'll do well, and thank you for choosing our company. Just bring your receipt or the tags with the suit. What store was that?"

Of course, part of the need was to have an intact and unflawed suit. That is what the customer voiced. The *real* need, however, was to be well dressed for the interview. Until that need was addressed, the situation was going to escalate.

Persist in Solving a Mutual Problem

Good conflict resolution requires time and persistence. There are quick solutions to most problems, and they are arrived at fairly easily. However, these solutions are rarely the best for either party and are seldom supported for any period of time. They are often only temporary bandages on a situation that requires major care. Sometimes, you just have to ask the question, "What will it take for you to be satisfied in this situation?" Surprisingly, the answer is often simpler than you think.

Sasha and her husband, Michael, have just had their tenth discussion, or argument, about a particularly sore spot in their marriage. Michael wants to have a baby and at this time Sasha does not. Michael has stormed out of the house, and Sasha has locked herself in the bathroom. Sasha has a career position on a senior management track at her company. Women who have children never seem to go anywhere in her company. There doesn't seem to be actual discrimination. It's more that those women don't stay late or come in on weekends like others on the management team do.

1. What emotion(s) do you think Michael is feeling?

2. What might Sasha be thinking?

3. What are the issues in this conflict?

4. What are Sasha's needs? Michael's needs?

5. What might be a mutually acceptable solution to this problem?

Michael came from a very happy family with three children and feels that a big reason he and Sasha got married was to eventually have a family.

The conflict between Michael and Sasha is not going to be resolved with any quick fix. Michael and Sasha, however, have a commitment to each other in the form of marriage, and with that comes a promise to work through issues such as these. Giving up on conflicts with family or with your work is not the way to keep your life moving forward.

A transition is by nature and definition a renegotiation for new conditions. Each conflict is an opportunity to move to a new level of understanding and interacting. When a marriage hits a wall and both parties say that they are not going to relate in the same way they have in the past, two things can happen. The people part company or they creatively look at their relationship and negotiate a new contract that is satisfying to both of them. In other words, they discard the *way* they relate, not the *desire* to continue to relate to each other. Couples who stay together and work through this renegotiation process describe a more intimate and mutually satisfying result.

Organizations work in much the same way. A little conflict forces employees and even departments into a problem-solving mode. The creativity and teamwork required to resolve complex business conflicts enrich the organization. (See Chapter 7.)

Your goal in conflict resolution is not to make the conflict go away, but to resolve the issues that created the conflict. As long as the issue is still a problem for the other person, it will continue to come up over and over and be a problem for you. Therefore, a mutual solution is the only workable option. As you can see, all parties must agree to persist to a resolution because anyone who gives in or walks away from the situation will not support the resolution. The conflict that is not fully resolved will reappear.

8.6 ACTIVITY

Select a conflict that is troublesome to you now. Describe the ideal solution for you.

Conflict description:

_____

_____

Ideal solution:

_____

_____

Now, describe what problems may develop or grow if this conflict is not resolved.

Problems for you:

_____

_____

Problems for the other person(s):

_____

_____

Come up with three possible solutions, at least one of which must be desirable to the other person.

1. _____

2. _____

3. _____

Give a good reason why you and the other person should persist to solve this mutual problem.

_____

_____

Resolution:

_____

_____

Negotiate

Some conflicts in business are so complex and far reaching that professional negotiators are brought in to help the parties involved work through to a satisfactory result. The following guidelines for negotiating may be applicable to other conflict situations as well.

1. Confirm from the start that the conflict outcome is negotiable and that all affected parties have input in some way.

2. Ensure that the person (or people) you are negotiating with have the authority to commit to the solution agreed on.

3. Ask questions to learn what the other party wants and needs and why she feels what she seeks is a reasonable request. (Whether you think it is reasonable or not is irrelevant at this stage. You must gain an understanding of why *she* thinks she is entitled to what is being sought.)

4. Seek to ascertain the emotional value of each issue under discussion. Beginning with less emotionally charged issues may lay the groundwork for later agreements on tougher topics.

5. Remove time as a parameter in the process. If you allow as much time as necessary, the other side may become pressed for a resolution to meet a timetable of its own. If a timely resolution is a necessity, secure an agreement from the other party for a "time's up" point.

6. Couch the wording of proposed resolutions in terms of the mutual benefits from each course of action. No one will agree to something that is not beneficial, but your creativity and understanding of the situation might be required to clarify the benefits.

7. Write down immediately all points of agreement, no matter how small or insignificant they may seem. As you proceed, you will need to remind each other of any common ground.

8. When an agreement is reached, attempt to elicit the plans the other party intends to put into effect to support the solution. Be prepared to do the same for your commitments.

9. Congratulate the other party on the intelligence and integrity shown by the resolution. It takes a lot to get to the point of agreement in the case of volatile or complex conflicts. Recognition of the effort and creativity required by all parties is a respectful way to leave the situation.

Conflict resolution is a healthy way of solving problems when our needs or goals differ. There will always be alternative ways of looking at any issue, and alternative values placed on these issues. *Conflict is not detrimental unless we let it cripple our relationships and damage our sense of self.* Businesses know that a little conflict is healthy to stimulate creativity, ensure good critical thinking on important issues, and prevent stagnation. A healthy session where important issues are brought forward in a caring and resolution committed way can keep any relationship moving to ever higher levels of adaptation and intimacy. *Transitions are necessary because new conditions conflict with old conditions.* Following good conflict management guidelines can ensure positive results, including increased satisfaction with new levels of your life.

TRANSITION SKILLS SUMMARY

Recognize symptoms of conflicts not addressed

Back off and handle your own emotions

Listen with great attention to detail

Assert your own needs

Acknowledge the other person's needs

Focus on the issues rather than the person

Persist in resolving a mutual problem

GOAL SETTING

My self-nurturing goal for managing conflicts in new ways in my personal life is:

_____

_____

_____

My self-advocacy goal for managing conflict in new ways in my professional life is:

_____

_____

_____

COACH'S CORNER

Mediation is usually ordered by a judge in cases where lengthy hashing out of issues would take up inordinate amounts of court time. Usually in divorce or property disputes where resolution is difficult, the parties involved agree to use a court-recommended mediator to help them reach an agreement. In situations with attorneys in a court, each attorney sees a "win" only if his client gets what the client wants. In mediation, the goal

(continued)

is an agreement—not necessarily one or the other getting what she wants. Successful mediation requires the surfacing of two major points:

1. Each party has to separate what is wanted from what is truly needed.
2. The mediator must establish what each party fears losing because that issue will likely be nonnegotiable. Deference to that issue may, however, be used to barter for a concession on another point later.

Sometimes in a company a conflict stops forward movement or production. Mediation in these situations must consider time as one of the issues. Sometimes, both parties have to acknowledge the bad effects they will share if the resolution process takes too long.

DONALD "SKIP" HALL, court-licensed mediator, e-mail: halls@yca.net.

CHAPTER 9

Self-Nurturing for Survival

T ake care of yourself!" we say to our friends. We enthusiastically and sincerely wish this for others, but we all too often neglect to do this for ourselves. Taking care of ourselves is necessary for a mentally and emotionally fit life. Ironically, many of us grow up with the mistaken idea that someone else should take care of us. As children, we were, of course, taken care of by our parents.

For most of us, though, there is no clear-cut time when the controls are handed over formally, and we take responsibility for creating our own happiness. In education, we take courses and progress toward a formal graduation. This graduation is a transition to a new level of education or work. But in life, there is no official "graduation" from being cared for in the sense that a parent cares for a child.

We would probably all like the ease of a life where someone provides for us: fun or interesting activities; tasty, nutritious meals to preserve bodily health; finances for fiscal security; a clean living area; and social or work contacts that are positive and satisfying. It is hard for the child in each of us to resist the urge to expect (or at least to hope for) others to pick up where our parents left off.

There must be a time, however, when we drop the expectation that others will do our work for us—the work of seeing to our well-being.

Maybe the adults in your childhood understood balance between giving to others and giving to themselves. However, some of us grew up in a family of self-styled martyrs who wore themselves out meeting everyone's needs, then resenting that they never received anything back. These people create a cycle of dependence and guilt that can be very damaging. Regardless of what patterns were demonstrated by the adult figures in your past, you can take charge of your own life in this area by developing and following a plan that includes physical, emotional, intellectual, and spiritual self-nurturing.

You must begin to act with empowerment and maturity and learn effective ways to care for yourself. However difficult this may seem at first, it is an important step toward happiness.

Understanding the Value of Self-Nurturing

The benefits of self-nurturing include:

- Recharging our personal "power supply."
- Growing through understanding and acting to fill our own needs and not depending on others for our care.
- Demonstrating we value ourselves and our well-being. That sends a message to others that we respect ourselves.
- Avoiding burnout. By maintaining the balance in our lives, we keep ourselves from spending all of our energy in one area.
- Providing emotional and spiritual reserves when we need them. When the spirit is at a low ebb, coping with trials and emergencies is much more difficult.

Most of us do an excellent job of surviving, and a pretty good job of self-care. We avoid the risks of too much drinking, drug usage, overeating, overspending, or unprotected sex. Self-nurturing goes beyond mere survival, though.

In truth, self-nurturing is the hallmark of a well-balanced person who understands the value in helping to create an overall successful life. Those who practice self-nurturing are more resistant to becoming ill, are more resilient under stress, are less likely to miss work days, and are able to manage conflict when it arises.

Those who do not invest in self-nurturing tend to be overly stressed, are more prone to burnout, are more susceptible to depression and illness, and are likely to make more mistakes, which could be costly in jobs and relationships. Though there are many values to self-nurturing in a general sense, there are specific areas of life where it provides a notable benefit.

Alleviating Fear

Self-nurturing offers an antidote to fear. We have all experienced fear in our lives. Most of us find ways to get through the fear, especially if it is at a moderate to low level. But, there are times when we are overcome by intense fear and are unable to conquer it. Eventually, the fear either dissipates, we find a way through it, or we run away from it as fast as we can.

Behaviors that contribute to a sense of well-being and calmness counteract a chronically fearful or worrisome mindset. Reasonable precautions can ensure safety. Most police departments give safe-living seminars in many convenient locations. Self-nurturing includes knowing how to stay safe and acting accordingly.

Reasonable health care and an awareness of the warning signs of major diseases can help you to a long life free of serious illness. Self-nurturing keeps you focused on the positive; there is no room for excessive fear and worry in a positive lifestyle.

Reducing Stress

Stress is another barrier to a healthy life. Here, we are talking about the type of stress that emotionally and physically drains and often comes from excesses: work, commitments, or activities.

Though some stress keeps us stimulated and on our toes, the negative force of stress wreaks havoc. We have to do more than merely recognize a stressed condition (and we all know what this feels like); we must take steps to actively deal with and decrease harmful levels.

The solution may be as simple as looking for a stress-management article or course. Most hospitals sponsor workshops, and many companies will sponsor workshops free for employees. However, merely reading or hearing about methods of alleviating stress is not enough. Self-nurturing requires putting these methods into practice Whatever approach you choose is an act of self-nurturing that demonstrates taking responsibility for your well-being.

Diminishing Anger

Anger is another one of those inevitable feelings, and there is nothing wrong with feeling angry. What you want to avoid, though, is getting stuck in anger and allowing it to consume your every thought. When embarrassment, hurt, disappointment, or powerlessness hit, often anger boils up as a result.

Self-nurturing activity in this case is choosing to address the anger, rather than becoming consumed by it. Anger, like stress, is physically unhealthy.

When anger strikes, using the techniques that have been presented in this book will help you to resolve the feelings as quickly as possible.

You may not see the act of resolving anger as self-nurturing, but it is; it frees your thoughts, so you can move on to new and more productive areas in your life.

Carter was a young professional working as an adjuster for a major insurance company. Though his life was good overall, he was plagued by a generally disquieting and edgy feeling. He could hardly remember a day when he was free of those feelings. His childhood had been fraught with his alcoholic father's constant disruptions in the household with his drunken behavior. All Carter and his mother ever thought about was how to survive. When he moved out on his own, he thought he had escaped, but fear, anger, and stress continued to trouble him even though there was nothing immediately threatening in his life. After seeking professional counseling, and considering many different approaches, Carter chose to address his anger through a series of forgiveness activities. By accepting responsibility for his own emotional and relational health, he freed himself to move forward.

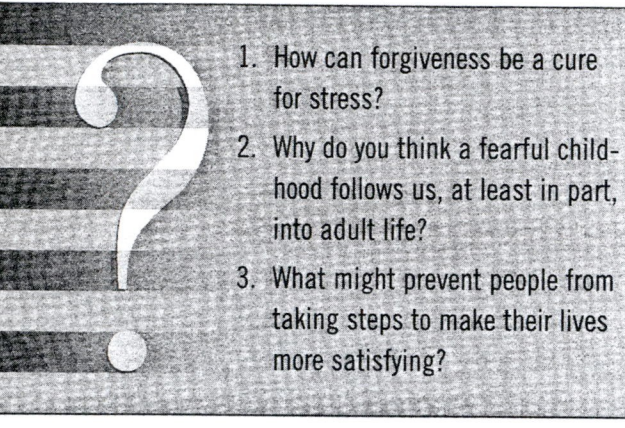

1. How can forgiveness be a cure for stress?
2. Why do you think a fearful childhood follows us, at least in part, into adult life?
3. What might prevent people from taking steps to make their lives more satisfying?

Improving Self-Esteem

If our self-esteem is low and we do not think well of ourselves, we are not as likely to take good care of ourselves and be self-nurturing. Self-esteem is a legacy of our past, and we, as adults, are responsible for changing that part of us that we do not like.

Self-respect is a self-nurturing frame of mind. People with high self-esteem set limits on the needs and choices of others; others' needs should stop when they violate spirit or worth. Self-nurturing celebrates your unique and valuable contribution to the world. When you take charge and demonstrate self-nurturing behavior, you automatically increase your self-esteem. Therefore, you begin a positive cycle that stops only when you no longer make the effort to be in charge of yourself.

Preventing Depression

Depression can make us feel so overwhelmed that we wind up doing only what is necessary to survive. It can be a very destructive force in our lives if left unchecked. Clinical levels of depression rob us of the ability to see our life in a positive way, and it thwarts our energy so that we feel like we cannot get ahead. It can cause individuals to be angry and argumentative, to feel unvalued, or to overeat or not be hungry at all. It can also cause major disruptions in sleep patterns, which inevitably contribute to increased depression.

Sadly, it is very difficult to think of being self-nurturing when we are depressed. More than at any other time, we need self-nurturing, but the stamina to be self-nurturing just is not there. There are direct links between exercise and mood, diet and mood, allergies and mood, and vitamin or endocrine deficiencies and mood. Simply taking a walk each day in the outdoors and taking a vitamin supplement can ward off many forms of mild depression. A regular self-nurturing activity can eliminate many of the causes of depression that are nonchemical in origin.

However, if you find yourself becoming more and more unable to take care of yourself and your responsibilities because of a depressed state, consider seeking professional help. Many suicides are committed because the individual did not realize the level of depression being experienced.

Moderating Excessive Need for Achievement

Many of us are driven by a need to succeed. There is nothing wrong with that; our survival depends on a certain amount of drive. It becomes excessive, however, when we make ourselves crazy trying to achieve just for the sake of achieving. Some people seem to relish the excitement of the high-speed, constant pursuit of "more." Yet, that kind of life excludes other meaningful activity and relationships. If we live our lives invested in these types of excesses, we will definitely be putting ourselves in a stressful position.

If this driven lifestyle is the case with you, you have probably forgotten the definition of yourself as *who you are*, and have fallen into seeing yourself as *what you do*. This is a self-damaging behavior because it robs you of the joy of accomplishment; there is, and never will be, enough. Setting a value on self-nurturing allows you to stop the behavior long enough to assess the situation and regain sight of the need to have a balanced life and be at peace with that life.

ACTIVITY   **9.1**

Identify one or two conditions that may have kept you from a sense of well-being over the past six months.

_____

_____

Developing a Self-Nurturing Repertoire

We can concentrate our self-nurturing efforts in several areas. They are:

- emotional self-nurturing
- physical self-nurturing
- intellectual self-nurturing
- spiritual self-nurturing
- fiscal self-nurturing

When we are able to divide up self-nurturing tasks into categories, it is easier to define our goals and take the action needed to fulfill those goals. Some actions could fall into several categories, depending on how you perceive them. An example of this might be sex. Some might experience sex as purely physical, others might feel it at the emotional level, and still others might feel it is a spiritual experience. For some, it could be all three. It is sometimes very hard to determine which area of our well-being is in need of support. For this reason, each of the areas should be addressed with some kind of self-nurturing activity.

Emotional Self-Nurturing

Nurturing ourselves at the emotional level is a vital part of maturing. We cannot expect that others will be consistently there to do the job for us. It is not the job of our family, friends, coworkers, or mate to do this for us. We are responsible for handling the job ourselves. If others are emotionally nurturing to us, it should be considered as extra, a gift, but our emotional reservoir should already have been partially filled by our own doing.

What follows is a list of self-nurturing behaviors that you can learn.

Take a Break

It is important to work hard, but crossing over into compulsive work habits is very dangerous. Self-nurturing means that you allow yourself a break from the daily routines of personal and professional life by taking time out to relax and recharge. This can serve both emotional and other needs. Sometimes just a shifting of gears is in order:

- Take five minutes to listen to classical music.
- Have lunch outside.

- Walk around the building or your neighborhood.
- Pick up your child at school early.
- Meditate.
- Have a massage or take an aromatherapy bath.
- Do something tactile: mold, draw, plant, or build something.

Clean Up Old Hurts

This could mean offering an apology or extracting one from someone who has hurt you. Walking around feeling upset is a distraction that can take you off your success path. Carrying around old hurts is like carrying a bag of rocks with you 24 hours a day. It is heavy and serves no purpose. Your pain, if you are the injured party, or your guilt, if you were the transgressor, are both damaging. Self-nurturing includes dealing with these.

- Make the apology you know you should make no matter how long it has been. The Internet makes it possible to find all sorts of people now. You have no idea the effect you will have. The person may not have seen what you did as badly as you do, or the long overdue apology may put someone's pain to rest.
- If your own hurt is from a close family member or friend, arrange a calm and neutral place to discuss how what they did made you feel. Do this without expecting any reaction from them—they may be hearing or seeing this situation clearly for the first time.
- If the hurt is from someone you cannot speak with for some reason, write a lengthy letter saying all the things you wish you had thought of to say at the time and telling the person how the hurt has affected your life. Then, burn the letter, saying out loud, "I forgive you because I have grown and can now move on."

Resolve Anger

Anger, like old hurts, takes up a lot of emotional room in our heads. The quicker you can address the situation that has made you angry, the better it will be for all concerned. You can directly state your feelings about what has happened to make you angry and can ask for a change in the situation that will be more palatable to you. You might not get exactly what you want, but voicing your feelings will help take the edge off.

- Stop the accumulation of anger. Use assertive talk to prevent the types of abuses or overstepping that others may direct toward you.

- Defuse the physical effects. Anger makes us release adrenalin, so we can do battle if needed. Working with weights, pressing or pulling the weight, is a healthy method of using that adrenalin. Kickboxing and boxing are other good ways to release energy.

- Investigate possible physical sources: certain kinds of emotional disorders and health conditions, or even medications taken for everyday problems, such as sinus or hay fever, can cause feelings of anger in some people.

- Seek counseling if you cannot determine the source of the anger. You can disconnect only what you can consciously address. Sometimes, a therapist can help detect a hidden stimulus.

Surround Yourself with Kind and Loving People

Sometimes, we find ourselves in deep water surrounded by sharks and we want to escape. If we have a few loving people in our lives, we will have a place to go where we can ask for support or comfort. There is nothing like knowing that we do not have to face every challenge alone. It gives us a refuge in the storm and a place to rest when we are weary from life's assaults.

- Remind yourself that you are loved. Whether you are "in love" or physically close to family or even old friends, there are people who would genuinely be delighted to hear from you. Anyone who has ever loved you still does in some small way; cherish that. If you are a person of faith, remember that a larger love is available to you. Also, if you are ever in doubt about being loved, go home and greet your dog—uncompromising, all-forgiving love is epitomized by the pets in our lives.

- Spend time with kind and accepting people. It is not enough just to avoid critical and negative people who are damaging to emotional health. Observe the people you know, even casually, and make the effort to get to know people who approach life in a kind way.

Engage in Social Activities and Hobbies

When we are able to get out of our routine and escape to fun activities, we give our minds a chance to rest. Think about this like you think about your car. You would not let your motor run all day and all night. So, why would you make your brain work all the time? Play is necessary for balance and renewal. Interacting with people who do not need anything from you—expertise or care—can be dramatically rejuvenating. Going out with friends, taking in a movie, or involving yourself in a hobby is a great form of relaxation and emotional nourishment.

- Choose one social event or activity you have never done before, even if it involves dance lessons, flying in a balloon, or fund-raising for a charity event.
- If your phone rings with an invitation, don't say "no." Whether the event sounds fun or not initially or whether it fits into your tight schedule, occasionally you are enriched by the spontaneous choice.
- Attend shows or events that involve your hobbies; maybe even participate in a classic car show, pet day activities, or an arts and crafts festival.

Ann-li was in her second year as a tech support troubleshooter for a telecommunication equipment company. As the only woman on her team, she sometimes felt overstressed trying to prove herself. Her aging father lived alone, and since her mother died, he called her many times a day with one problem or another. Her supervisor gently, but firmly, told her that as an in-house customer support person, she was expected to keep the phone free for customers. She wanted to care for her father, but she certainly needed to limit his constant calls. She was beginning to have difficulty concentrating at work.

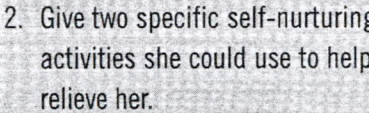

1. What are Ann-li's main stressors?
2. Give two specific self-nurturing activities she could use to help relieve her.
3. Could self-nurturing benefit her father?

Use Affirmations and Positive Thinking

Affirmations and positive thinking can help you maintain your emotions at a stable level. If we put worry into our thoughts, what we get out is tension and a stressed-out feeling. If we put hope and positive thoughts in, we get back a sense of calmness. It is like fertilizing your garden. The blooms become strong and an abundance of flowers can be anticipated.

- Pay compliments to others.
- Take time to enjoy how well your children are turning out.
- Send yourself flowers and have the florist put on the card, "For all you do so well."
- Plan a trip you will take to reward yourself for an accomplishment—or just for a fun fantasy.
- Read over notes you have received from customers or the good review you got from your manager.
- Look in the mirror and acknowledge how really good you look.
- Remind yourself how far you have come and how much potential you have.

Set Psychological Limits with Others

It is important not to allow others to take up "free rent" in our heads. If you have the feeling of being invaded psychologically, this means that someone has stepped over the boundaries. It is our responsibility to set limits and let others know where those limits are. Avoid making others play the guessing game with you about limits. Nothing good can come from that.

- Tell your children that you will not respond to "orders," only courteous requests.
- Remove consistently critical or disrespectful physical or psychological treatment from your life; either state matter-of-factly that it must stop, or distance yourself physically from the unhealthy bombardment.
- When someone does not respect your time or personal space, expose the behavior and explain why you think it is disrespectful.

9.2 ACTIVITY

Describe a situation where you think someone might be manipulating you or violating your boundaries. Write what you could say to this person to expose the behavior and clarify the type of behavior you expect.

_____

_____

_____

Physical Self-Nurturing

Physical self-nurturing is not just taking care of our basic needs like food, shelter, and water. It goes a step further and involves maintaining our health in an active way by developing routines that enhance our well-being.

Exercise

The news media are full of reports about the value of physical activities, but millions of people in our society are overweight, out of shape, and unwilling to do much about it. That could be because the task seems so large or difficult.

The solution is the "no-exercise" exercise program. Insurance actuarial tables (the recordings of factors that seem to be correlated with long life and health and those that statistically suggest the potential for damage) give us a few hints on how to get around the exercise time and effort dilemma. People who live in houses with stairs often live longer than ones who do not. Just that one exertion element makes a difference. Any exercise you do will help.

What works better for many of us is the "do a little bit" approach. If you like the atmosphere of a health club, get an orientation on the safe use of the equipment, then design your own "program." Do as many repetitions as you feel like with as little weight as you want as often as you like. Even a short "play" workout can be beneficial because it is more than you are doing now.

Start with five minutes on the treadmill at 2.8 m.p.h. (just above average walking speed) and move up to more time or up to a higher speed, but do not overdo. Start light and work easy, and you will still derive some benefit. Four sit-ups will eventually seem so easy that you will want to do five or six, later more. Exercise you do not do, no matter how good the program, will not help you. Exercise should make you feel good, and feel good about yourself, not be another source of stress in your life.

You could turn on the radio and dance for 15 to 30 minutes several times a week. Park your car at the end of the row or lot, walk faster any time you move around the building or store, do leg lifts while you are on the phone, and keep light handweights by the sofa to do arm exercises while you watch TV. Anything helps. Do not let an unwillingness to commit to a major exercise program interfere with your desire to feel good.

Take a Vacation

Allowing ourselves to rest our bodies for extended periods of time is a self-nurturing experience. Vacations refresh us, give us opportunities to see different places, allow us to detach from daily stresses, and give us something to look forward to. They give us the opportunity to escape the daily grind and give us a new perspective on life.

You do not have to go very far to get the benefits of a vacation. Several nights at a nearby bed and breakfast might be enough. Sometimes a day trip to another city with some sightseeing will also fill the bill. Try to have something to do: play in the water, golf, ride a horse, hit baseballs at an arcade, play putt-putt.

Build Healthy Eating Habits

Proper nutrition is important both physically and mentally. Eating to keep yourself healthy extends your life, prevents disease, and promotes a steady flow of energy. Although many theories and diets bombard us, most nutrition experts agree that a healthy diet does not contain burgers and fries, pizza, or other high-fat or high-sugar foods.

If you do not know what to eat, consult with a good nutritionist who is knowledgeable on the effects of diets. Being informed cannot hurt and may save you from some expensive medical bills down the road. Also, your doctor can tell you if your weight is healthy—the mirror can lie. Anorexics think they look fat, a belly can merely be sagging muscle or it could be dangerous fat. If you decide you need to lose weight, remember two things:

1. You only need to lose one pound. Each time you lose one, you can make the decision to lose another one. One at a time should be the focus—not the 30 you want to lose or the amount of time it will take you overall. One pound.

2. Weight loss is a one-year minimum commitment. Short-term ups and downs are maddening and often discouraging. Give it a try. One year out of a long life is not a huge sacrifice; it is a gift.

Secure Privacy

The need for our own private space is an issue that few people discuss openly. We are often afraid that someone's feelings will be hurt if we want to seclude ourselves in a quiet place for a while. When we ask for private space, we can make it clear to those around us that we will be using the space to revive our tired selves and not to hide from our families or our problems.

1. If you are sensitive to noise, you will find quiet very soothing. Libraries are excellent for this. Turn off the radio in the car and the TV in the house. If you work in a cubicle and cannot escape noise, purchase headphones for noise control (people will think you are listening to music).

2. Use music to "remove" yourself. Whale sounds, relaxation tapes that walk you through creative visualization exercises, new age music, classical music, and "oldies" that bring back fond memories can take you away for a time.

3. Take a stress-management day. Many workplaces no longer require you to justify why you want a day off—the term "personal day" is used to cover illness, family issues, etc. A day at home when everyone is at work, a drive in the country, even a movie alone in the daytime, all allow you to be in complete command of your personal space for just long enough to refuel.

Foster Appropriate Physical Closeness

Just as we need distance, sometimes we need closeness. Babies that are held and handled a lot fare better physically, especially premature infants that are struggling to live. When we are afraid or feeling lost, a reassuring touch or squeeze of the hand can remind us that we are not alone. People who are emotionally close feel better when they can touch the person they are close to.

It is nice if you have family and friends whom you can be physically close to, but you do not have to be in an intimate relationship to enjoy physical closeness. It does not even have to come from another human. Many people who live alone enjoy the closeness of their favorite pet. It is that connecting with another living being that helps us to feel comfortable and grounded. If we ignore these needs, we leave out of our lives a large piece of self-nurturing.

There are lines or boundaries we have to be aware of, though; not all people like to be hugged or touched except by intimate partners. Some cultures view touching, even handshakes, as invasive. Your need to be physically close should still respect the other person's need for space or boundaries.

Sex has become an artificial closeness for some: physical intimacy without connection at any other level. Sexual touching and physical affection are experienced very differently at the emotional level. Try to be very clear in your own mind and in the signals you send what you are inviting on the physical level. Confusion can be disastrous.

Make Rest a Priority

Without rest, we cannot function in a normal way. Lack of rest can cause us to deteriorate not only physically but mentally as well. We wind up making mistakes, we do not think clearly, and therefore, the decisions we make may not be good ones. We could fall asleep at the wheel of our car and kill ourselves or others around us. We could become emotionally distraught, even depressed. It is all right to stay up late sometimes, but doing so on a regular basis will wear you down and burn you out.

If you are sleeping fewer than eight hours a night (or day, depending on your work schedule), you are likely not sleeping enough for complete refueling. Naps cannot make up for the loss completely because a sleep cycle is about an hour and a half and a nap less than that offers no real contribution. However, meditative states, where the brain waves go into the alpha pattern of relaxation and concentration, can provide a certain amount of renewal in a short period of time. This is especially true if reaching this state is practiced enough to be arrived at quickly.

Sleep deprivation is damaging on many levels, and sleep disorders can plague the psyche. If you have difficulties with sleep, such as trouble falling asleep, waking up during the night, waking up too early, or falling asleep during the day, you should check with a sleep disorder clinic. Artificially induced sleep from medications or alcohol does not provide the benefits of a good night's rest.

Intellectual Self-Nurturing

There must be, if we are to truly lead an enriched life, a time where we give ourselves the gift of intellectual nurturing. Because we are in the information age, we can get bogged down and over-saturated with information. There will be a time when we will need to determine how to take care of our mind. What follows are a few suggestions that may be helpful.

Free Your Thinking

By challenging yourself with new ideas, you stimulate creativity. It has often been said that there are at least 10 options to every problem. Imagine that you could identify those 10 options every time you had a problem. Don't worry if every option is not the perfect answer. The idea is to begin to stretch your thinking to include nontraditional ideas as well as traditional ideas.

1. Make up "wonder what" scenarios—conversations between strangers in restaurants, possible solutions to world hunger, or new technologies to solve problems. Particularly freeing is the "what if" type that looks at the familiar and plays with it. "What if bananas were round and green?" "What if cars could hook together like train cars?" These are playful and can sometimes lead to some startling realizations of solutions to complex problems.
2. Experiment with creative movement as in interpretive dance or yoga.
3. Guide meditative visualization exercises in creative directions.

Gather New Ideas from Others

Ask others for opinions and expertise, take the information that is helpful, do not rule out any plausible sounding ideas, and take some sort of action on what seems most interesting. You might be the one to recognize a really good idea and implement it. Welcome different viewpoints from others.

1. Seek out people of different backgrounds and cultures and ask them about their family, lifestyle, or views.
2. See each person as a teacher and a person with an important story to tell. There is an amazing wealth of experience in the world that you can find if you seek it out.

3. Read about creative thinkers and inventors; explore different religions and philosophies; read books on creativity (Julia Cameron's *The Artist's Way*, Vincent R. Ruggiero's *The Art of Thinking*, and Langer's *Mindfulness* are all excellent).

Practice Meditation or a Visualization or Relaxation Technique

Meditation is the "time out" for the mind. If you keep your brain racing day and night, you will only wear yourself out by becoming stressed and exhausted. Meditation is simply quieting the mind so that it can rest. Many great ideas have been summoned from the depths of the unconscious during meditation. It is as if you have a guru inside yourself and meditation is the gatekeeper. When you are perplexed by something, meditation gives the mind a chance to find a path. It helps you access parts of your intelligence that may be outside of your conscious awareness.

1. Explore meditation techniques and approaches.
2. Take a class in creative visualization.
3. Learn about self-hypnosis. You can learn the techniques yourself, as there are many sources of information on the subject.
4. Consider yoga as a combination of mental and physical meditation.
5. If you are religious, use prayer time for focused thought.

Keep Learning a Priority

If you actively seek to learn new things on a regular basis, you will always be challenging and stretching your mental capacity. You will be stimulating new areas of thought and allowing yourself to evaluate old ideas in a new light. Learning is a gift that we give ourselves.

1. Take a class in a continuing education program or community special interests courses. The subject matter is really of no concern. Actually, the less you know about the topic, the better. The purpose is to challenge your mind, not get a grade.
2. Teach yourself new equipment, software, or procedures at your place of work.
3. Do research on your city, your community, or other places.
4. Join a travel or book club; even a cooking club can be very educational.
5. Learn a foreign language.
6. Read—everything.

Spiritual Self-Nurturing

In order to truly have a balanced life, we must think of nurturing our spiritual self also. This does not mean that you have to go to church every Saturday or Sunday. What it does mean is that you find a higher power, a connection to something greater than yourself, to count on, to believe in, and to turn to for help.

Some feel more comfortable looking within themselves for this. Others look to organized religions for help. It does not matter which way you go. What matters is that you consider it part of how you balance your life. Here are some suggestions that may be helpful in developing your spiritual self.

Use Prayer to Enrich Your Life

Prayer can be done anywhere anytime. It can be informal or formal depending on your preference. Many people find that prayer gives them a sense of comfort that they cannot find anywhere else. It brings a sense of enrichment and gives us a connection to something more powerful when we feel like we are powerless.

Do Spiritual Reading

The more we learn about the spiritual side of ourselves, the better we will be at balancing our lives. We can grow to understand spirituality and learn how it can help us in our professional and personal life. We can use spiritual reading to keep us on the right track and to help us maintain an ethical and moral value system that is of the highest standard.

Attend Spiritual Services or Gatherings

Organized religion is not for everyone, but it certainly has a place in our lives if we choose it. For many, the very act of going to church is a ritual that brings a connection to other believers and gives them a sense that they belong. They use the church as a way of guiding their children in moral principles. They also experience rejuvenation in their own faith and are reminded of their own need to prepare for the final moments of their lives where they will cross into another dimension.

Do for Others

So often, we get caught up in our own lives and forget that we have special gifts to give others. Acts of kindness do not have to be big. Sometimes, the little ones are the best. You may not want, or even have the time, to dedicate hours and hours each week to volunteer work. You may only have that moment where you give a smile to someone who looks sad or where you help someone by holding the door open for them. No matter what the act of kindness is, it will ultimately benefit you as much as it benefits others. It will give you a sense of self-worth and it will spread a positive attitude all around.

1. Volunteer at a shelter.
2. Visit someone who you know is alone a lot.
3. Pay someone's power bill anonymously. (Power companies have the people who need this on file.)
4. Take a bag of dog food to the county animal shelter or humane society.
5. Offer to babysit or chauffeur children for a working mom.
6. Mow an elderly neighbor's lawn.

Fiscal Self-Nurturing

Managing the flow of money into and out of a household can be a very taxing endeavor. But when you think about it as an act of taking care of yourself, it can become a different issue. Money is not at the forefront of all concerns or stresses in a person's life, but the lack of enough to maintain a reasonable standard of living and offer security against debt can be a major source of concern. A few guidelines for approaching the issue, along with some hints for sound fiscal responsibility, might help to bring this area of your life into line.

Needs Versus Wants

Many things we think we need, upon close scrutiny, become unnecessary. The car or clothes we had to have, the house or furniture, the private school or the club membership, even the way we entertain ourselves can have a specific value. When the responsibility of debt outweighs freedom, then the pursuit of happiness has gone down the wrong road.

If buying things made a person happy, the person with the most things would be the happiest. However, the thing-centered person can never have enough. In addition, the more things a person owns, the more he becomes a slave to them. If money is freedom, the things you may buy with it can become a prison. Separating your "wants" from the things that truly support your life is a tough task, but a sane balance between the two only occurs if you begin to approach your life with that as a goal.

Keeping Down Debt

Rich people often pay cash for things for two reasons: because they can and because they know that financing sucks money into a black hole and out of your reach. If a car costs $22,000 and you finance it, you could probably buy the car twice, depending on the rate and time allotted. With credit cards, you may end up paying interest on interest and never catch up. Bankruptcy ruins your credit for seven years.

If you have just gotten your first career position or have just moved into that higher-paying job you have sacrificed for, stop for just a minute. If you can maintain your current lifestyle for one more year, while making considerably more money (maybe $20,000 per year more), you can put thousands of dollars in an investment account.

With $10,000–$20,000 in this account, you can borrow money from yourself if you need to finance a car. Pay yourself back with interest and reap the profits of the financial game. Also, a buffer of $5,000 to $10,000 in the bank goes a long way toward allowing you to sleep at night. Save every month, pay off credit cards every month (or throw them away entirely). If you want to establish credit, borrow a relatively small amount of money from a bank, put it in savings, and pay the loan off early with the money.

Know how much you spend every month. One reason people get into money trouble is that they honestly do not realize how much they spend each month. Do not forget student loans. There are people in their 30s and 40s who cannot buy a house because they defaulted on student loans decades before.

Long-Term Financial Planning

Depending on your age, you will have different needs for financial planning, but experts suggest two points: Save every month and move money to an investment account as soon as you reach the minimum amount. Second, the earlier you can pay off debts to free up your money for saving and investing, the earlier you will be able to realize financial security on a large scale.

If you are 22 years old, a retirement account may seem unnecessary, so call it an investment account and leave it alone, except to put money in. If you are 40 with no retirement account (like 17 percent of U.S. workers), saving $20 per week (even at a 5 percent annual return) will add up to $50,000 in 25 years (*Fortune*, 2000). Only a few people in their 30s are retired, but some are. For those in their 60s, the figures say that 35 percent are still working. Some build resumes or gain skills so they can do the job or run the business of their dreams by age 40, not really retired, just off the corporate treadmill. If this is your goal, a good investment plan is an excellent idea.

TRANSITION SKILLS SUMMARY

Recognize the value of self-nurturing

Meet your body's basic needs

Take a break when needed

Challenge your intellect

Secure privacy when needed

Form meaningful relationships

Manage finances responsibly

GOAL SETTING

My self-nurturing goals for my personal and relational well-being:

_____

_____

_____

My self-advocacy goals for my professional well-being:

_____

_____

_____

COACH'S CORNER

The business of life, especially for the person going into a new career, can be stressful. We see it at our center: people tired, feeling stressed, unhappy with their weight, illnesses. A lot of this comes from an improper focus. When people focus outside, on the materialistic, they are always looking for more. Wanting more keeps people attached outside and feeling stressed.

Another way people become out of focus is that they keep looking for knowledge to guide them, for information. This is not the way to feel good. Knowledge can control how you see your life—what you know is what you use to define your

(continued)

world. Our knowledge can be incorrect, because much of what we know, we learned as children, and children cannot discern and protect themselves from negative messages.

Knowledge gained without experience is only information. When we gain experience, it helps us become grown-up: able to develop our inner strength to keep negative ideas and experiences from affecting and draining us. Thus, experience creates wisdom. Wisdom is not information, but how to use it. Our knowledge and regrets of the past, along with worries about the future, keep us from savoring life as it is. When you drink a cup of tea, can you enjoy the tea, or are you worrying about your next meeting or appointment?

Where we direct our energy affects the way we feel. If our mind energy is centered outside, we become weak. But, if the mind energy is focused inside, we are strong. People need to learn to focus their energy to cultivate joy and appreciation.

1. Look at the meaning of your life as a whole, not just at what is happening or what you know now.

2. Investigate and study what is inside; this is where you can become focused and where you will find joy.

3. Pursue spirituality.

4. Work for the spiritual development of the world. Individual alignment and growth are meaningless if others around the world are having difficulties.

You can start by working on your body, developing energy and strength. Something as simple as deep breathing or stretching can help to move energy around and make you feel better. Then you can begin to develop your mind and direct energy there. Finally, you will integrate body, mind, and spirit. When you direct your focus properly, you feel connected and filled with health and well-being.

MASTER CHO OF THE DAHN CENTER (reflecting the teachings of Dr. Seung Heun Lee, Grand Master of Dahn Hak and author of *Healing Society: A Prescription for Global Enlightenment*. 2000. Charlottesville: Hampton Roads Publishing Co., www.healingsociety.com.)

CHAPTER 10

Self-Advocacy

Self-advocacy means accepting responsibility for your professional development and success. Many elements contribute to your ability to gain control of your professional destiny:

- creating visibility
- demonstrating expertise
- cultivating reciprocal power bases
- tying contribution to revenue stream

Each of these elements is within your control. Some elements, such as chance, economic conditions or shifts, and changes in markets or competitive position, are not within your control. However, the presence of all of the bullet elements will give you a measure of command over the effects these conditions will ultimately have on your ability to meet your goals.

Managers have neither the time nor the freedom from their own responsibilities to observe you at length, document your strengths and successes, or take you aside for regular coaching and support sessions. They do, however, want you to be successful, if for no other reason than the fact that your successes reflect well on them. Though there is always the chance that a manager may try to take credit for your accomplishments, some time, diligence, and achievement will make your own competence known.

Creating Visibility

Typically, raises and promotions go to those who are highly visible, not necessarily to the most competent. This is not to say that those who are promoted are not competent; most are, but some rise at least a few tiers in the company based on their ability to create the impression of competence. As you might guess, the converse occurs when talented, hard-working employees are not recognized. Thus, your challenge as a self-advocate is to make your good work known. This is called self-promotion or visibility enhancement.

First, a clarification. Leftover from adolescence is the idea that we can never speak of our accomplishments for fear of attack, often by those who do not have many accomplishments themselves. Throw that idea away and look at the "now" situation: you are responsible for letting decision makers and power holders in the organization know how important your contribution is. If you do not "toot your own horn," no one else will. Keep in mind, however, the following caveats:

- *DON'T attempt to create the impression that you have an inside track to a superior or that you are chummy with certain strategic managers.* They may not appreciate your contrived familiarity and confront you about it, maybe even in front of others. This is especially true in the case of male–female status differences. That game is tiresome and more than potentially damaging.

- *DON'T constantly regale others in the coffee room or in casual conversation with your latest achievements.* This is a sure way to create in coworkers an aversion to your presence. Offering, when asked, information learned from your experiences is welcome and respected. It will help to establish you as a good source when problems or questions arise.

- *DON'T relate experiences at other companies where you were considered competent and perhaps even "heroic."* What happened yesterday or elsewhere is perceived as irrelevant (at least until you have some pretty dramatic achievements in your profile). "What have you done lately?" is the natural question to follow such reporting. If you are new to the company or the industry, that question will leave you open for possible embarrassment.

- *DON'T embarrass yourself or your company by a lack of knowledge in social graces.* If you do not know the ins and outs of social decorum, you should learn. Just the example of smoking is notable. The trend is toward nonsmoking buildings, events, and so forth. If you smoke, you may not make as good an impression as you would like. Know how to dress for various occasions; many magazines or image consultants can help you there. Understanding what not to talk about with clients or in polite company will prevent awkward situations. Excessive drinking at company or client functions or the inappropriate behavior that often accompanies it can put you on the "do not invite" list pretty quickly. Politeness and courtesy suggest class, an important quality in valued employees and managers.

Any one of the DON'Ts by itself will probably not give you too much of the wrong visibility. However, if you are unsure of yourself in a new position, you might be inclined to try to justify your worth with some overbearing talk or behavior. Instead, relax about how people feel about you at first and build the right impression. Remember, you will eventually generate some kind of impression within your company. That impression may well determine how you are treated. You should be the author of that impression, not the occasional chance encounters others in your company may have with you or your work. The following guidelines will help you craft the perception others will have of you in your company.

- *DO seek out opportunities to showcase your work.* You can do this by volunteering your expertise in giving presentations for your manager, your department, or someone in your department who needs that. You can also use reporting methods to bring attention to your work. Status reports to your manager that describe your accomplishments each week should be the very minimum of self-promotion activity. Polished proposals you have written and professional-looking visuals for reporting at meetings with higher-ups will show decision makers, as well as your colleagues, how competent you are. Also, many companies have an internal newsletter that would likely appreciate news of an award or particular achievement by you or your team.

- *DO seek out projects that upper management values.* Your manager ultimately has the say over what projects or committees you do or do not work on, but whenever you hear about something big that would have an element from your department, you can volunteer to your manager. Try to find out which project upper management feels especially strongly about and build a good case to your manager for why you should have that particular assignment. You may not always have your request honored, but by doing this, you send a message to your manager that you want to make a contribution to the important business of the company.

- *DO send notes.* This includes thank-you notes for a favor or a lunch, as well as a short note attached to an article that might be of interest to a colleague or a higher-up. If you know what the person's interests are outside work, such as racing power boats or collecting wines, then an occasional note that says, "Thought you might find this interesting," might be well received. Says Renee Walkup, a consultant and trainer in self-promotion, "Consider our society. Nobody sends thank-you notes anymore, or much of any other kind of handwritten communication for that matter. Think how you will stand out if you take the time to do that." Of course, be certain your handwriting is legible and neat, or the effect will not be positive.

The next suggestion requires some daring and some careful handling, but the new employee can use this more easily, probably, than someone who has been with the company longer.

- *DO make an appointment to see a senior manager in your division, or even the president of your company.* Two obvious visibility results can come from this: the high-level decision maker can know your face, name, and potential to contribute, and you will be able to find out what the manager likes to talk about. You might ask about the person's history with the company, what company successes he or she is most proud of and what led him or her to the company originally. This last question is innocent enough; it shows interest in the background of a senior manager in the company you work for. But its real value is that the answer generally elicits various stories of past accomplishments of that person and also how he or she rose to power in your company. A lot can be learned about what performance is valued by your company.

Another helpful question (helpful for you) is to inquire about what role this person sees your department (or group or division) playing in the company's strategic plans for the future. Remember to mention that your manager has given you some of this information, but that you are interested in this person's viewpoint. You may happily discover that your department is where this manager came from or that your group will be a major contributor to a project that is very important to the manager; a real plus for your future visibility.

After the meeting send a handwritten thank-you note that includes one important piece of information that made a particular impression on you.

- *DO join and attend meetings of civic and professional organizations in your area.* You will be representing your company to the larger community and making yourself visible to others outside. Make certain the impression is a positive one. Also, you may run into powerful people in your field at civic or charity projects, professional meetings, and conferences.

Creating visibility is a process; it is not a single act. The accumulation of positive impressions of you and your work forms the perception of you as a professional in your field and as a valuable contributor to the success of your organization.

Sharon, an intern during her last semester at college, had been asked to analyze and critique some software that the very large company she worked for was developing. Having gained expertise at presentations in her classes, she was not uncomfortable about putting together and presenting a formal and fairly elaborate report, though her manager was the only one who was to review it. She dressed in business attire and brought her new briefcase with everything she needed. When she arrived at the meeting room, her manager greeted her, "Oh, by the way, the regional vice president is in today and wants to sit in on your presentation. Okay?" Sharon swallowed hard and squeaked out, "Sure," as she eased into the closest chair.

Creating a positive image within your field or company mostly requires paying attention to what behavior is valued. If copyrighted art or awards of merit or service are valued, involve yourself with these activities. Joining a national organization in your field and serving on a committee will help with exposure. Within your company, though, a few simple suggestions might help.

1. What kind of impression do you think Sharon probably made just by her appearance?

2. If the presentation goes well, what might the long-term benefits be to Sharon? To her manager?

3. What if Sharon had not prepared for this meeting as she did because it was to be just with her manager and she was only an intern?

- Walk faster—important people have places to go.
- Observe and approximate the dress and hairstyles of higher-ups. If they feel comfortable with you, if you look like one of them, then they are more likely to include you in activities or consider you for their team.
- Develop a good vocabulary; people in upper management tend to have a larger vocabulary than lower-level employees.
- Find out what books and industry periodicals senior management is reading and add these to your own list.

ACTIVITY 10.1

Describe the hair style and dress of the three most powerful people in your company. (If you are not currently employed in the type of company you want to work with, visit one and observe.)

_____

_____

_____

Demonstrating Expertise

You generally are hired for one or both of two reasons. One is that your skills, experience, or knowledge would seem to ensure competence at the task required by the company. The other is that someone likes you: the human resources interviewer, a manager, a personal or professional friend. The implications of "someone likes you" will be discussed later in this chapter. Demonstrating expertise that the organization needs can take you many places in your career journey. More immediately, expertise that your manager needs can make you valuable in your own department or area.

What most people overlook in building a skill base is that *technical skills* (this term is used to refer to skills specific to your career area) are only part of the picture. The other skills set, called personal-operating competencies, will be discussed later in this chapter.

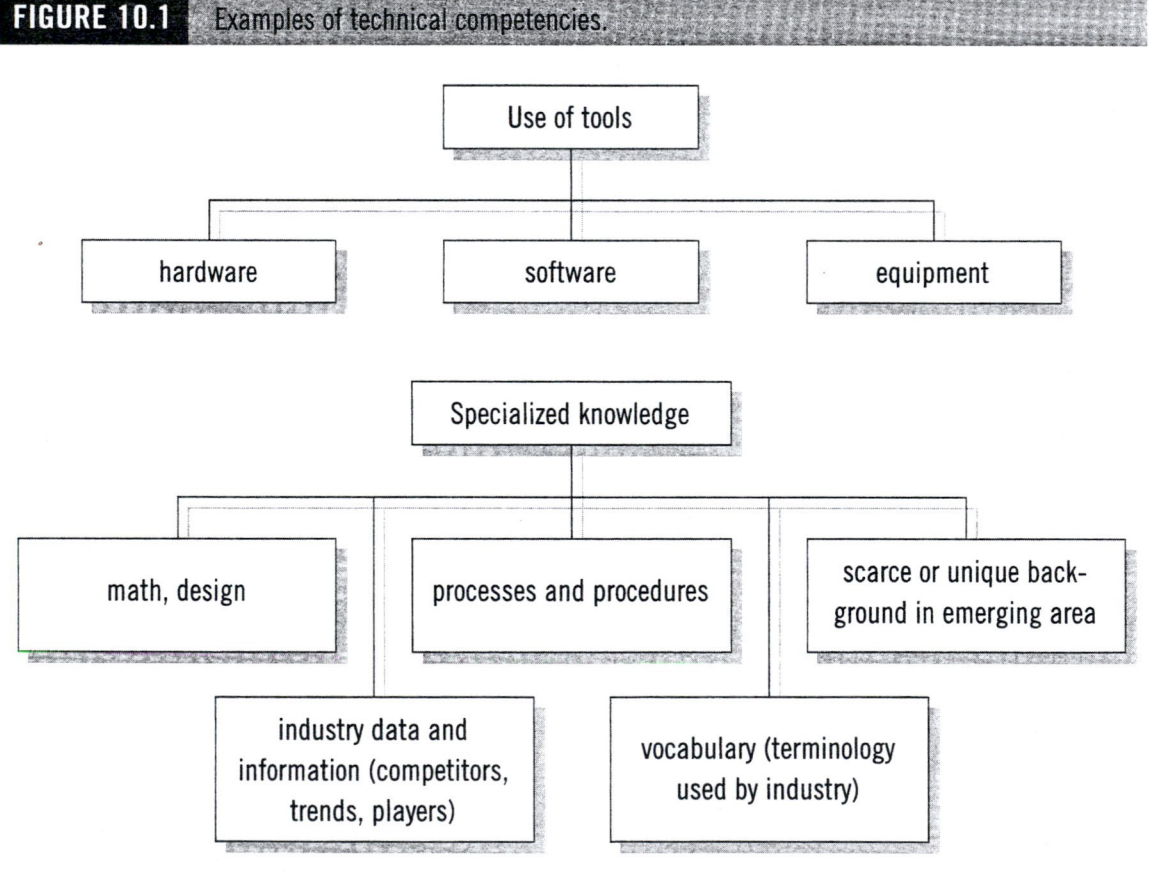

FIGURE 10.1 Examples of technical competencies.

Technical Expertise

As noted in the discussion on visibility earlier in this chapter, it is possible to create the illusion of expertise to your advantage for a time. But, at some point you will have to support that image with competent work. Visibility activities, of course, are important to establishing your technical credibility. But consistent performance of high quality work, in sometimes difficult situations, will earn you a great deal of respect.

The icing on the cake, though, would be to develop expertise in a complex, desperately needed and little understood area of your company's business.

TRANSITION TIP *Alicia Necaise, Respiratory Therapist*

In my field, we get advancements in pay and position by learning new equipment or procedures. We can also work toward new certifications. A lot of what we learn is by our own interest—volunteering for specialized teams or assignments, environments, or situations that are different from what we generally do. I would say that learning things on your own is the best way to control where you work and what you do.

Being skilled in a technical area that your manager may be rusty or only marginally knowledgeable in will help ensure your connection with the manager. Often, this will encourage your inclusion at some functions or meetings that you ordinarily might not be invited, or even allowed, to attend. Statistical analysis, presentation software or equipment expertise, the ability to find obscure or difficult-to-locate information, maybe even just in-depth involvement in the technical operations and processes of the company can create a desire or need for your particular knowledge or talent by managers and higher-ups.

Alexi, a marketing manager in a high-tech company, took as her area of focus competitive analysis and trends for the technical aspects of the industry. Though her academic background was not engineering, with diligent study she soon developed a good understanding of the finer points of her company's technology field. Eventually, she became the liaison between engineering and marketing, more or less the "translator" for the two departments. She also was sought after from both departments for her highly specialized knowledge that, in some cases, was more in-depth than some of the professionals in either department. She created a niche or role for herself by developing and demonstrating expertise the organization needed.

Nontypical combinations, such as tech or artistic people who can communicate convincingly with business decision-makers, are highly valued and can translate that into bonuses or connections.

In the workplace, you gain credibility not by telling how skilled or clever you are, but by showing it. You will know you have demonstrated expertise at a level that is to your benefit by two signals:

1. Your coworkers and manager (perhaps even from other departments) will ask you for your input or assistance, and ultimately take your advice.

2. Headhunters call you—these are employment recruiters who are hired by companies to locate and hire away the most skilled people in their industry. The acknowledged experts receive calls from these people weekly.

You are expected to have a certain level of competence in your job area, a working knowledge of processes or systems relating to your area, and a growing repertoire of skill—in other words, constantly increasing expertise.

Personal-Operating Competencies

The other skill sets, called personal-operating competencies, include organization, communication (specifically network or presentation skills), problem solving, information gathering (analysis and processing), and interpersonal.

Leadership is not included in Figure 10.2 because the combination of all of the skills or attributes in this group makes for excellent leadership potential. However, each is in and of itself a valuable expertise when the situation warrants.

FIGURE 10.2   Personal-operational skill areas valued by organizations.

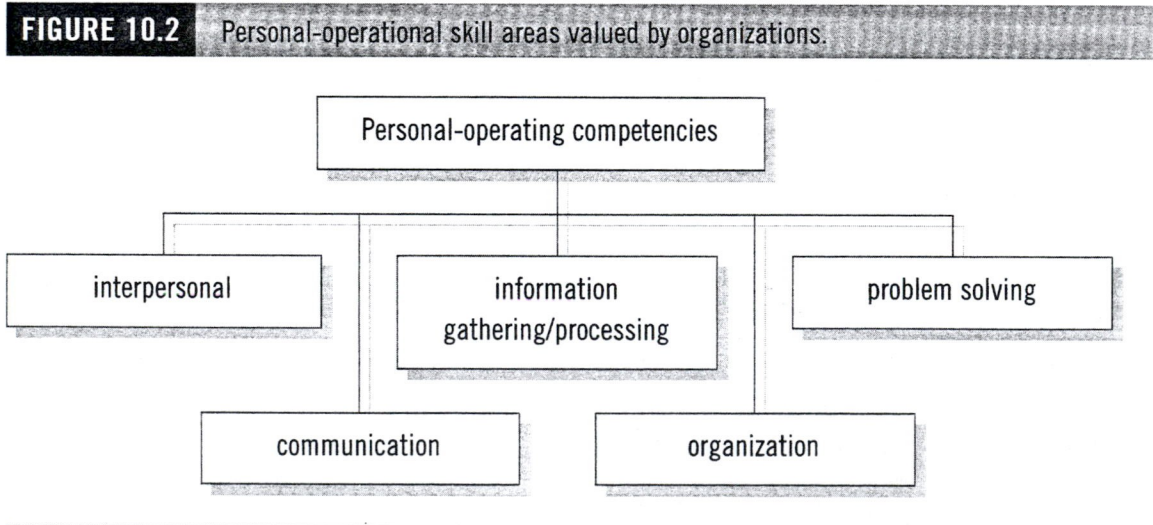

How many of these do you already know you have? Can you document examples? Though there are those born with a predisposition to be good at each (we will call that "talent"), they can all be learned. Certainly, improvement and competence can be developed in each. You will note that this book has chapters on each of these areas because they are perceived to be important by business.

1. *Communication* includes written, oral, and electronic methods (including presentation technology and skills), report writing, e-mail management and group communication systems, as well as marketing communication. In *Executive Edge*, Richard Brislen (1996) adds the ability to communicate with the community—to speak at professional and civic organizations on behalf of your company.

2. *Interpersonal* has under its umbrella conflict management, perception (ability to "read" people and respond or advise appropriately), team interaction, and hiring/training/coaching. Sometimes it is intangible, such as the ability to bring out the best in people in their performance or in negotiations.

3. *Problem solving* takes in adjusting to change, organizational troubleshooting, creative analysis, noting and resolving discrepancies, assessing risk, quality and process improvements, resource supply issues, and customer complaints.

4. *Organization* covers managing budgets as well as time, keeping track of multiple tasks and responsibilities, and recognizing specific operational needs in carrying out objectives, such as project management or coordination of a large customer order.

5. *Information gathering and processing* can be an all-consuming area because the need in business today is so great. This consists of reconnaissance information on competitors, changes that affect the industry, statistical trends, or cause-and-effect relationships both inside and outside the company.

Demonstrating expertise in these areas can be as simple as just doing them. When a project is being discussed, you can ask organization-type questions and volunteer to keep track of work assignments that result from meeting decisions. Taking on the presentation of your department's business plan or the proposal to a new client can show you to excellent advantage; even presenting project status reports on a regular basis can show your competence, as long as they are done well. Trying, but performing poorly, will not earn you any prestige points.

When you go to a manager with a problem for which you have already come up with a suggested solution, this shows your ability in that area. In fields where change is common and rapid, just keeping up with the periodi-

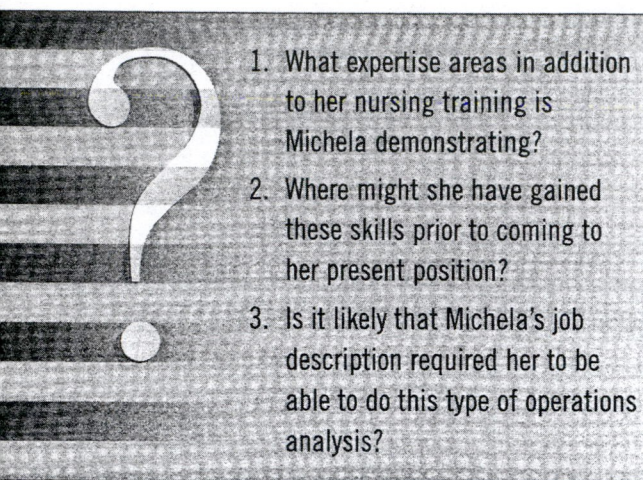

1. What expertise areas in addition to her nursing training is Michela demonstrating?

2. Where might she have gained these skills prior to coming to her present position?

3. Is it likely that Michela's job description required her to be able to do this type of operations analysis?

cals in your industry, forwarding e-mails or articles to interested parties, attending conferences and presenting the information to others when you return can label you as having the kind of expertise industry values.

Michela, after only six months in her nursing position, discovered some redundant procedures that took extra and unnecessary time away from the nurses' duties. She documented the situations where they occurred, developed a proposal for changes that would save time, and discussed it at the department meeting.

Cultivating Reciprocal Power Bases

Gaining and using power is a delicate enterprise that must be carefully orchestrated and is done well only by a very few. The reason this section addresses reciprocal power bases is that in complex organizations that operate in even more complex competitive environments, no one individual can gain enough far-reaching power to cover all situations. Thus, many times the gaining of power for yourself involves gaining the support of others, who can in some ways temporarily lend you their own deference relationships.

Power is granted or deferred. Individuals or groups agree to be directed or influenced by someone. In this way, that person has power over the group. Rarely in business is it taken in a strong-handed or abusive way and kept for long. Of course, abuses and excesses of power-wielding do exist, but those people are not effective over time. Then, because of their eventual ineffectiveness, power is taken away. Reciprocal power relationships have much more far-reaching and long-lived effects.

For example, one of the more powerful people in your professional life may be the purchasing agent for your company, especially if your ability to do your job depends on the timely delivery of equipment or materials. If you develop a good working relationship with this person, you will be more effective and thus gain more influence opportunities. Without opportunities for influence you have no power. Gaining those opportunities is the core of what the new employee needs to know about power.

You are not going to start out with 15 managers reporting to you, nor will you have colleagues so enthralled with your abilities that they will automatically follow you. For that reason your focus should be to gain some level of control over your own position and to accomplish what you need to in order to do your job well and to advance.

Gain Control Over Your Position

First, understand that you may have no real control over your position. Your company could be bought; your manager could be transferred or leave the company; corporate restructuring could eliminate your position altogether; the higher-up that you were friends with and that brought you in could be ousted (this even applies to the chairman of the board).

This is not to say that you have no control at all, just that the control comes from you, not from outside sources. Your ability to create value for yourself and to read conditions within the industry, and within your own company, will give you a degree of power over your professional fate. You can create value by your expertise, surely, but value can also take on a different face.

Make People Feel Good

On a practical level sometimes the person that everyone just feels good being around is promoted, when others are passed over. The knack of making people around you feel good has some intangibles to it. Some people are just like that. But some behavioral aspects can be learned. To make people around you feel good, you can:

- be positive in perilous or difficult situations
- stay even-tempered and consistent no matter what is happening
- offer assistance occasionally to another department
- mediate conflicts to satisfying resolutions

All these actions can contribute to the "feel good" element you can create with your presence and have nothing to do with any sort of magical charisma.

Meet Deadlines Consistently

Another aspect of value beyond job skill competence is the ability to bring in your projects on time, every time. A dependable person is considered a gem in the fast-paced, "I need that yesterday" environment. The upside to gaining this reputation is that you will be assigned duties and projects that are critical to the organization, thus putting you in the middle of everything important the company is doing. There is a downside to this kind of value, however. Good people are handed the most work. This may have already happened to you in other situations. Use your manager to help regulate and prioritize assignments that come your way. Remember, your value is task completion; overload severely inhibits your ability to complete individual tasks.

As a new employee you may or may not have a lot of control over the objectives that you must reach in your particular responsibility area. Ideally, both you and the person to whom you are accountable will set goals based on the needs of the company and your abilities. Having control over your objectives goes a long way toward your being able to meet those objectives and thus be successful. Sometimes, all you have to do is ask your manager to set goals with you (instead of for you).

Demonstrate Good Judgment

Finally, you can cultivate value through your judgment. Your ability to intelligently and correctly size up a situation or a person and offer insight or advice that leads to a positive outcome can be a boost to your career. This is hard for the new employee—nobody asks you much. But, if you develop an in-depth understanding of the company's needs and challenges, you will be in a position occasionally to voice your conviction or comment. "Occasionally" is an important word here. Keeping your mouth shut most of the time in fast-paced verbal exchanges can prevent your speaking without knowledge or out of turn. Listening and offering the occasional question that may point the discussion in a direction not already explored will create an impression of quiet competence, an impression much to your advantage.

Another important bonus from your consistent demonstration of good judgment will be more autonomy in your own position. When you have shown that the decisions and recommendations you make, as well as the ways you direct your time and energy, are always in the best interest of the organization, you gain professional respect . . . and freedom. Freedom to manage your own time and duties is an important affirmation from a manager.

Recognize Intuition

One additional comment here must include intuition, gut feeling. Some very famous and very good decisions have been made based on an intuitive notion, a "feeling." Some very bad ones have destroyed careers and companies. Do not depend on your gut feeling until you are sure you have a good "gut." When you demonstrate good judgment over and over, eventually the value of that will be recognized.

This comment from a CEO is a good example: "I always consult Renee when I am hiring someone for a critical position. Her way of sizing up a candidate has proven to be consistently correct. When she says they will likely fit and be successful, they always are. Maybe it's experience, but I think it's just that she sees important things the rest of us completely miss."

The way this value gives you control over your position is that it is transferable across departments and projects. Technical skill is valuable; being able to bring in a project on time and in budget is even more so. You can preserve your future within the company outside your immediate position. In this way, no matter what direction the company goes, even if your position is eliminated, a place will be found for you.

Invest in Exchanges with Others

It is in your best interests to develop reciprocal power relationships with the people around you. Colleagues fall into this category as well. These are other professionals either in your industry or even outside who can offer ideas, contacts, information, maybe even resources.

Trading favors is a good way to establish a positive relationship with these people, but there are guidelines for this. First, you have to have something to offer, the same as in networking. Maybe it is only a supportive ear or a ride to the airport, but the willingness to help sends a message that rarely goes unappreciated. Sometimes, though, you might supply job information, news about something that might affect the colleague's industry, or even outside help, such as stock tips or advice about dog obedience problems.

TRANSITION TIP   *Russell Walters, Environmental Specialist*

Get to know as many people in your field as you can, higher and lower in position, and help anyone whenever you can. Don't be afraid to do extra work that will make a project go better or that might solve a problem for someone. Specific contributions to your career can come from someone you did a favor for in years past. Some time ago, I helped an intern on several occasions with some research he was doing, and he eventually was the one who opened a door for me where I work now. In my company, and typically in my industry, people are hired based on someone else's referral.

Second, welcome the opportunity to invest in people. You are starting out brand new with nothing on your slate to call in if you need a favor. Be careful to not allow yourself to be drained by going overboard on this and do not always expect a return. The world, however, seems to be a reciprocal place: you get out what you put in. Service to one person, who may never be able to pay you back, may lead to some help being given to you down the road that you will not be able to repay.

Another way to gain the ability to "make things happen" (an indicator of power) is to take the time to engineer beneficial relationships. Introducing a software designer to a manufacturer or bringing a service provider into contact with someone else who very much needs the service costs you little or nothing. The net effect, though, might create a relationship that will give you resources or a power base with all parties that will be useful.

Finally, sometimes people give you power just because they like you. This is fragile, however, and if you treat these people badly, their hurt can become your trouble. But more importantly, you could lose an emotional connection with another human being who cares about you—a much greater loss than a favor. A sure indicator of power and relationships, or the lack of either, is the number of people who will return your calls. If you lose your job for whatever reason, you will bounce back more quickly if many people are willing to put effort toward helping you to re-establish in a new position.

Manage Others' Power Over You

Power is given. That includes power you give to others also. You will allow the organization a certain amount of power over your time and talents in exchange for benefits you expect to receive. When expectations from either side are not communicated and consequently not met, power relationships get out of balance. Though managers may try to exercise a great deal of power over your time and your life, you choose how much control they have.

If you expect to go home by 5:30, to be able to take a long lunch occasionally if you want, and to dress pretty much as you feel comfortable, that is not a problem. That is unless the company expects its people to work through lunch and stay late and dress in a more corporate look. Your real power is your own doing, the power to say no or yes to any request or opportunity. If you say no to the long hours, and that is the company's expectation, you may lose your job or your promotability, but that is your choice; you are exercising power over your life.

You will find, however, that many things are negotiable, but there are two very critical times: when you are discussing the terms of hire and after you have a track record of success at meeting deadlines and reaching goals. Without a lot of solid experience or accomplishments in your background, it is unlikely that you will have much input for changes in the terms of hire offered by the company. However, a polite question may uncover a policy already in place that suits your situation. Many companies allow telecommuting several days a week or flexible hours, but you have to ask for this. This situation does not require a power or influence element.

However, as discussed in the conflict chapter, negotiating anything requires a healthy respect for the power of each of the participants. Your manager can rightfully dictate certain aspects of how you spend your time and where you direct your energies. Once you become valuable, though, two-way influence can emerge, allowing you more freedom to define areas that might have been strictly under the manager's sphere of control before, such as assignments to important and highly visible projects.

As you cultivate your power bases in the company, remember that those same people who are willing to take you into their inner circle and help you also expect a favorable response to their own requests. When someone attempts to direct your efforts or career in a way that you honestly believe is detrimental to you, then you will need to use your own influence techniques to turn that in your favor.

Learn Influence Tactics

Whatever your station in a company or power milieu, you may use certain techniques and tactics to help your situation.

Chemistry

In the case of chemistry, the "boss" just likes you—there is a rapport or attraction of some sort. When this occurs, it can be a good thing, in that you may very quickly find yourself on the inside of decisions and information. However, just as in school days, the "pet" is not always popular with the outsiders. The manager often will give you more time (lunches, chats, etc.), but also will assign you work to do that falls under the manager's responsibilities, meaning longer hours and more to manage on your part. From these extra duties, though, you will have the opportunity to build a more impressive resume based on the breadth of what you were allowed to do.

A note of caution here: If you are an insider because of this "like" relationship with your manager, you have a good chance of securing the best projects and the most favorable positions. If you are not in the manager's inner circle, you likely should try to engineer a move to another area if you want to achieve promotability. Rarely does anyone move from the outside to the closer circle.

Benefits-Oriented Requests

This is a technique called the "three-cornered hat." It is useful with anyone under most any circumstances where you want to influence an outcome, such as to gain someone's support for your idea or to get someone to perform a task that you need. The method is based on three premises:

- *Premise 1:* People are for the most part self-serving. No one has a lot of time to spare on your need for action on their part; they must take care of their own responsibilities. Doing something for you takes time and energy away from those pursuits.

- *Premise 2:* People are not motivated to use creativity to meet your needs. Even people who might be inclined to do things you need are not devoting creative thought to figuring out how they can help you. Thus, they are not likely to think ahead and anticipate your needs.

- *Premise 3:* You can choose to be "right" or you can choose to be effective.

Especially in team situations, people who work in mutually dependent task relationships should do what they are supposed to do and provide the support their position requires. (Such as, finish their part of a process on time because your part cannot begin until you receive their part.) However, they become lost in their own obligations and stressors. You can be "right" all day long about what they *should* do, and you can go to your manager in indignation about why your part of the project is late, but that kind of exchange is what managers feel they should not have to deal with. So, instead of worrying about being right, use techniques that will move to action those from whom you need services or equipment or assistance.

Look at the model for an explanation of the technique.

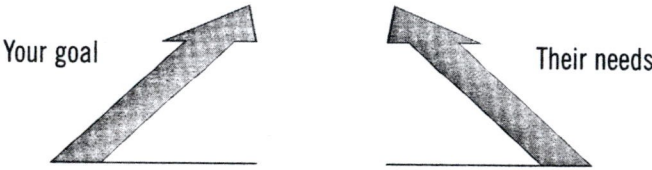

Your goal   Their needs

Their needs have nothing to do with your goal, so acting on your behalf does not occur to them.

Action occurs at the point of intersection.

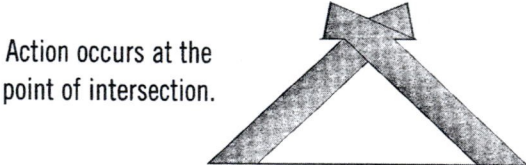

When their needs and your goal fit together, they act to your benefit.

If you can be creative enough to explain to the person you are attempting to influence how fulfilling your request will help serve that purpose, then you can expect action. By all rights, you cannot expect everyone to do your work for you, but sometimes people get lost in their own activities and lose sight of the need for their contribution to the whole effort. And your influence for an activity that contributes to a winning situation for all parties concerned should be considered a good thing.

You will have to use your own creativity and ability to see the larger picture of your needs and others' to make this work. That particular pair of abilities is very much a part of what makes a good manager or project leader. Thus, learning this technique as a new employee will help you as you seek to gain more control over your career path.

If, for example, Donald wants to encourage Phil to get a data analysis to him early, and he knows that Phil really wants to have his work recognized, then Donald could say, "Phil, I know your analysis isn't due until Friday, but my report to the operations VP needs that information. I'll be glad to include a copy of your complete report in the package I give to the VP if you can have it to me by Thursday morning."

It costs Donald nothing to include the analysis with his report, and now Phil has a reason to prepare it early. Donald gains important information he needs to prepare his report in a thorough way, and Phil gains visibility he might not otherwise have had.

Other examples might show someone how performing a task one way can save time or expense later, or why exchanging information regularly via e-mail will help individual team members be able to plan better and not lose so much time duplicating effort.

ACTIVITY 10.2

Think of someone you would like to do something for you in your professional area. Write down two beliefs or priorities he or she feels strongly about. Explain why honoring your request could help that person advance his own priorities.

1. Action you need to have:

   _____

2. Person: _____

   Priorities/beliefs:

   _____

   _____

3. Benefit-oriented request:

   _____

   _____

Tying Contribution to Revenue Stream

This is a frequently overlooked area of potential power gain by new employees as they scramble to assimilate into the day-to-day operations of the company. The ability to connect to the money influx of the company ensures some control over your position and stability. Two elements comprise your ability to do this:

- Discover and track the sources of revenue that sustain your company
- Cultivate connections to those areas

This process starts at your hiring interview with questions about customers, markets, and processes that support those areas. (You particularly need to know if the position you are being hired for is connected to those areas, although that information is gained with subtle probing rather than direct questioning. More detail is given on this type of questioning in Chapter 13.)

Know Revenue Sources

Either prior to the hiring interview or after you arrive on the job, you can find a great deal of information on the company's revenue sources just by some diligent research. If the company is public, then many sources are easily accessible on the Internet. Two of these are companysleuth.com and freeedgar.com. An excellent "industry gossip" source is the *Wall Street Journal*. For information on privately held companies, fee-paid or subscription services include Dun & Bradstreet and the site nerac.com. Several newsletter services are available for free if you give your company name and title for their database. One of these is ceoexpress.com. You are best served by finding out which publications insiders in your industry read and report their activity in. When you find which these are, make it a point to subscribe or find the copies that come to your company and read them cover to cover.

Be aware that, sadly, your own manager may not maintain detailed information on the industry or on the direction the company is headed strategically, unless he is tied into the inner circle of the decision makers. This has been said previously, but deserves reiteration: your manager may or may not be an excellent manager in all that encompasses, and even if he is excellent, your professional future is not that manager's responsibility. Your productivity in your department, not your interest in gaining power, is the major concern of your manager.

You may already be muttering, "I'm just a systems analyst" (or "a nurse" or "a field engineer" or "production supervisor" or "customer service representative"). "Why should I have to do all this extra work monitoring my company? Doesn't upper management do that?" Of course the answer is yes, but upper management has no obligation to tell you that information or notify you in advance of strategic direction changes that will affect your job. For example, a respiratory therapist's job likely will be affected if the industry trend toward managed health care means his hospital will be bought by one of these companies. Hospital administrators probably will not consult the respiratory therapists in order to make their decision.

If you work in a high-tech company, you must stay aware that these companies are constantly growing, or withering, based on the newest entrant into the technology market. For example, a new battery development might make hand-held computers last longer. If your company adds this right away to one of its products, then that might be the big seller. But if you are the product manager or support team for a fading product, you are in trouble. By securing movement to the new and "hot" area for the company, you can help ensure your future.

Connect to Revenue

Some areas of companies are considered revenue generators and some are cost centers. Sales, customer service, product support, and some areas of engineering are all considered connected to revenue. Anyone who daily adds to the company's ability to stay solvent and profitable is valuable. Any time there is an economic crunch, those who are directly connected to the company's ability to do business are retained. In the cases where they are laid off, many are hired back as contractors at a higher salary (this is because companies do not pay benefits for contractors).

Of course, there will always be industries that are known for making money: telecommunications, software, pharmaceuticals, etc. Every industry, though, has companies that are profitable and thriving; you should recognize which these are and try to associate yourself with them. In industries like advertising where your career may hinge on your securing (or supporting) a large client, you have to be prepared for the precariousness of those positions.

Whether you are in health care, information systems and services, graphic design, technology development, or engineering, the rule of survival is the same: if you cannot show how you are supporting the overall fiscal health of the organization, then you may be considered more expendable than you might think. Conversely, an excellent service provider who is recognized by customers outside or inside the company may have considerable security. Even with diligence, though, you will likely be subjected to surprise buyouts, management change, market shifts, and any number of unexpected and disruptive conditions.

The only job security you have is your own ability to gain power over your career. This comes from:

- a knowledge of, and a way to gain a connection to, the source of the sustaining financial life of your company
- a reputation for excellence and dependability in what you do
- connections to people who can make or find places for you that will benefit your career

Yes, this process of self-advocacy is a lot of work. However, finding a new job when yours has disappeared due to a shift in priorities in your industry or company is even harder.

No one is ultimately responsible for your professional future but you. This book is about transition management. This chapter is about managing transitions (or the need for them) in your work. The term *managing* suggests that you take an active part in the process. Words such as *reacting* or *muddling through* or *surviving* imply a more passive role in when and how those transitions occur.

Executive Path

Though the focus of this chapter has been the situation of the newer employee, here is a brief overview of what is required for a path to an executive chair.

Qualifications

Executives come from many quarters in a company, but most track either through sales and marketing or through operations or the financial area. Several things these individuals have in common include:

Communication skill. Executives are superior communicators. But, more important than communication is listening. "I think" and "I know" are two phrases that can get a decision-maker in trouble very quickly. No one can know everything, even if the exec's track record in the past position or company was excellent. Listening for information, listening to learn, listening to understand a problem or market challenge, listening for realistic goal-setting, all these situations require decisions, and the smart executive makes decisions based on information, not ego.

Understanding of the business of business. Executives read accounting reports, financial reports, market analyses. They see clearly the relationships between operations cost and revenue; they know what it takes to be profitable.

Decision-making ability. Most of senior management's job is decision-making. The decisions made at that level directly drive the company—in a positive or negative direction. Problem-solving challenges are global: what direction will the company take in the market; what needs to be done with operations accountabilities; what resources does the company need to reach goals?

Energy management. An executive never works 40 hours, but more often 60 hour weeks with semi-regular Saturday stop-overs at the office or work at home. Anyone who has not learned to prioritize when and how energy is spent and replenished will burn out long before reaching the board rooms. The smart senior manager has generally figured out by that level what the important concerns are: your work is not your life, it is your livelihood to support your life.

Risk tolerance and assessment. All decisions at the executive level have some risk attached to them. The big money and big growth are not made without risk. A track record in leveraging risk against need to win in the profit game is an absolute necessity for upper-level managers. Gaining experience for this must, by rights, include some failures. Pulling success out of failure is an important accomplishment to have on the record of anyone who aspires to run the show.

Flexibility and tolerance of differences. The best executives are not "one-trick ponies." They have learned that a method that worked in one situation, might not be as successful in another. Different approaches and ideas help to ensure success because there are more options to choose from, especially if a Plan B is needed quickly. Change is a given in business today, and no manager whose goal it is to remain the same can last.

Self-knowledge. Knowing what his or her individual strengths and weaknesses are guides the strategic level manager to play to strengths and find support for the weaknesses. Trying to force situations by sheer will is pointless; it usually means something is wrong with the direction or resources. Executives will be strong in many areas, but their real strength is in knowing where to find resources or information quickly.

The Path

Accumulate successes in areas that relate to the company's profitability. Of course, these successes must be current; you will be expected to show, "what have you done *lately?*"

Acquire knowledge of accounting within the company. This includes such things as what it costs to do your job, to do major projects, to add employees.

Be able to demonstrate understanding of budget processes as they relate to the business. Can you write a business plan for your department?

Under promise, over deliver. Establish yourself as one who can take whatever is thrown at you, analyze it, secure resources, then accomplish it with high quality and preferably early and under budget. If you are given a three-year timeline, complete the task in two, or one and a half, because time is money. You have to have credibility that you will do what you say you will do—every time. This holds true for meetings, also. Do not waste your people's time. Keep meetings under the time allotted; this will keep people coming to your meetings, when they might not go to others.

Make yourself indispensable. Find out your immediate manager's (and that person's manager's) goals and values, performance expectations, and budget parameters, and *make them yours*. By enabling your manager to meet his or her manager's goals, you become valuable. By taking on as much of your manager's job as you can get delegated to you, you prepare your manager for promotion and yourself to take the manager's place.

Learn to make those who report to you or are on your projects accountable. If you do not pay attention to what the people for whom you have responsibility are doing, then your accountability is affected. Knowing your people is key: know the qualifications and track record of subordinates, peers and managers. Knowledge of the resources within a company is an absolute necessity for anyone who wants to be upwardly mobile. But you must treat people well; no one will go to the wall for someone they don't respect.

Finally, be clear about your own priorities and limits. Know what you value in your personal life and how that relates to your professional life. You may have to make some tough choices on both of those fronts over the years, and wavering in your values will make you appear indecisive about what you want and are willing to do. Contrary to what is portrayed in the movies, ethics are respected in industry. That does not mean that if your manager is stupid, you tell her so. It does mean that you take responsibility for your behavior and that that behavior should have a clear ethical base (Hall, 2001).

Whether you aspire to run an international corporation or merely to maintain your own career security, career-related transitions can be the most stressful you will have, if they are not driven by you. Having some idea, plan, or control connected with work-related transitions will help you guide both your personal and your professional life in an evolution toward ever greater satisfaction. You can avoid the frantic scrambling to survive in the face of unexpected and disturbing career changes imposed from the outside.

TRANSITION SKILLS SUMMARY

Create visibility

Demonstrate expertise

Cultivate reciprocal power bases

Tie contribution to revenue stream

GOAL SETTING

My goals for my personal and relational life using self-nurturing skills:

_____

_____

_____

My goals for my professional life using self-advocacy skills:

_____

_____

_____

C O A C H'S   C O R N E R

New people to an organization are freshmen in the strictest sense of the word: they are not brought in as the CEO; they do not know company rituals or processes; they generally have no impression established with higher-ups or colleagues. Thus, following a few guidelines might help to shorten the socialization or indoctrination time and help the new employee to get off on the right foot.

1. Whatever task you are assigned, no matter how trivial or demeaning you think it might be, put your heart and soul into making it high quality, do it on time and do it with a smile.

   The reasoning behind this is the establishment of your professional character. Whatever *you* think of the task or project, it means something to someone in the

(continued)

organization, and your treatment of this first offering determines what else you may have the opportunity to do later. Your conduct shows the organization (superiors and peers) your willingness to follow instructions, to embrace whatever task the organization requires, and the integrity with which you approach your work. If you perform badly—either quality-wise or attitude-wise—on this first, possibly-junk project, you won't get the opportunity to handle the good ones.

2. The first months (maybe even the first year), keep quiet and observe. Though you are pumped with your new ideas and desire to contribute right away, no one wants to hear what you have to say, until you have proven you can listen. Study the way things happen, the way people relate to each other, the way information is passed, the way people dress and the way projects are parceled out. Get to know the customers, the products, the challenges your company deals with daily, all these before you attempt to suggest anything that you think would be in the company's interest.

Every organization has its informal power bases that never show up on the organizational chart, and it also has procedures, rituals, etc. that everyone else knows but are likely not written down or given to you in formalized training. The company also has certain values you need to recognize.

a. Power bases—the CEO, COO, VPs, etc. are easy to spot because they have their rank on the door, the preferential parking spot, the perfectly appointed office and a gatekeeper (disguised as a secretary or administrative assistant), whose job it is to control who gets an appointment and who doesn't. However, there are likely one or more informal leaders or power people who carry a lot of weight, either with management or with the employees.

You can spot this person if you observe whom everyone goes to for information, advice, or solutions. For whatever reason, this person has the ear of enough people to be central to what goes on. Discovering this person, and why he or she is deferred to, is a necessary part of understanding how things work in your company. You want to be on committees with that person, work on projects with or for that person, and, in the most ideal of situations, be mentored by that person. First, though, you have to figure out who it is by careful observation.

(continued)

b. Rituals—these can be actual rituals, generally accepted behavior patterns within the company or can be ritual behavior of important people who are higher-ups. Do's and don'ts, such as coming to work early or going home at a certain time, socializing after work, starting meetings exactly on time or 15 minutes late, calling people by first or last names, all qualify as understood procedures.

   Knowing certain rituals or patterns of a particular manager or officer is helpful for you as well. If you know a manager has breakfast or coffee at a particular restaurant on a regular day and hour, you can once in awhile just happen to be there before that person arrives. It might entitle you to a private audience or may merely just give you recognition points in a subtle way.

c. Values—what is important to the company should become your values as well. If you read in the company's mission statement that social responsibility is a value, then you should be involved in some form of community service. Ideally, you choose one avenue of this on behalf of the company, the other because it meets a personal desire on your own part. If your company is big into supporting the schools, you should volunteer to teach a class or mentor a student at the local high school.

4. Develop an entrepreneurial eye. If your job is to haul the carpet scraps out of the manufacturing plant, try to figure out a way to utilize the scrap for profit or lessen the amount of waste that ends up as scrap. If you work in a process, focus on ways to improve the efficiency of the process, first in the area of your own job, then in the larger process. Some companies have procedures for submitting improvement suggestions and may even pay bonuses for the good ones.

   Don't start making suggestions to your boss or colleagues at meetings right away. Spend time getting to know the processes thoroughly before you suggest anything. Your first suggestion will be the one they judge you on; make sure it is a REALLY good one, and one that you know will be well-received because of your understanding of the company values and goals.

TOM RAMSEY, former state legislator, now corporate training consultant.
E-mail: tpramsey@alltel.net

CHAPTER 11

Developing a Support Network

You have been learning new ways to take care of yourself and the many needs you will have in the future. Learning how to develop good relationships is very much a part of what you do to take care of yourself. Developing relationships that are sustaining to your emotional reservoir extends the concept of self-care to a new degree.

The relationships you will develop in the future will play a major role in your business life and your personal life. Knowing how to improve on what you already know about developing relationships will give you that extra edge. You will be channeling your energy into productivity and creativity.

We will be discussing two different types of relationships: draining and sustaining. As we discuss these types, keep in mind the fact that you have to create for yourself a network of people who can give you the support you need in your life, whether it is personal or career oriented. It is important to understand some general rules of relationships so that you do not get trapped in unhealthy situations. By understanding the kinds of relationships that you need, you can then discern which ones to invest in and which ones to stay away from.

The supportive sustaining relationships that you invest in should provide a richness that one simply cannot afford to live without. In actuality, these relationships become cushions that buffer our spirits from adversity. This is not to say that they take away or protect us from all trouble, but they do shore us up at times and help us to maintain balance. These relationships also act as mirrors and let us know what we are presenting to the world.

203

Finding and maintaining these relationships is not always easy. A large portion of the people seen in psychotherapists' offices may have difficulty with developing close affiliations outside the family, and some don't even have good ones there. By understanding what to watch out for, it will be easier to weed out relationships that do not work.

Draining Relationships

Draining relationships are all around us. There is probably no one in our society that hasn't at some point in life experienced a draining relationship. Perhaps some have even been the ones to do the draining. These relationships take many forms and can be very destructive. They slowly siphon off our energy, frustrate us, and generally make for an unhealthy negative environment. To further help in understanding what these relationships look like, take a look at some of the different types of people who contribute to draining relationships:

- People who dump all of their problems on others.
- People who are volatile and explode without warning.
- People who manipulate others to get their needs met.
- People who complain about things and never do anything to change their situation.
- People who feel entitled to special attention and consideration.
- People who don't communicate well and feel that you should already know what they want.
- People who criticize all the time, but never tell you what you do right.
- People who are intrusive and ignore the rights of others.
- People who are possessive or jealous.
- People who do not tell the truth.

More than likely the people who behave in a draining manner may have a number of these characteristics and may use more than one to get what they want. There is, however, a reason these people become draining individuals in the first place. It is that they, somewhere in their past, have felt unable to manage certain aspects of their lives. They developed dysfunctional ways to cope with this powerlessness, and unfortunately the dysfunctional ways worked for them at the time. Thus, the behavior was reinforced.

Because the individuals were perhaps too young to realize the effects their behavior had on their relationships, they continued the pattern. The hope was that they would be able to continue to get their needs met. The pattern, having been positively reinforced by success, became an unconscious one. This meant that the behavior would continue in an automatic fashion and require no conscious thought.

Unfortunately, draining people come in all shapes, sizes, and levels of authority. The level of draining also comes in different intensities. Some people may only drain occasionally. Others may use it on a daily basis. By learning to watch out for such behavior, you build a buffer zone for yourself that acts as a protection for your valuable psychic energy. Consider the following situation.

Syd, a 26-year-old female, entered the management ranks of a large chemical company, managing the Web research department. Even though she is newly graduated from college, she has been working in the field since high school and gained hands-on experience during her senior internship. The few other researchers in her department are older and do not have college degrees. Syd feels a little intimidated by the difference in age, but she knows she can do a good job running the department of the company. She also knows that she will have to make some changes in the department that will be unpopular. Several weeks into the job, Syd begins to feel the icy stares of one of her research assistants. Every time she asks the woman to do something, she gets cold and abrupt answers.

1. How is this situation draining to Syd?

2. What might the long-term effects be on Syd if she does not find a way to alter the situation?

3. Is it possible that the other woman experiences Syd's way of defining their relationship as draining?

Personal Relationships

One of the most frequently found types of draining relationships in our personal life is *the dump-and-run*. These people come in two types: those that use others to vent their problems, and those that drop work or responsibilities on others.

When the dumper-drainers are finished unloading their problems, fears, or anger on someone else, they depart feeling relieved. The receiver of such behavior winds up pressed by the weight of that person's problem because all of the negativity was left behind. The receiver may even feel some responsibility for the feelings of the dumper. This dump-and-run type often does not want to resolve personal situations or becomes stuck in the problems, unable to move into the solution. It is as if their emotions flood their brain and there is no room for adult thinking. So, the only escape from this overload is to deposit it on someone else.

Leah was a quiet young woman who enjoyed having her own apartment and her own life. Her mother was a woman who always had a crisis happening. Turmoil was a familiar emotional state to her. Fairly regularly, Leah's mother would call to tell her how awful some situation was, either with her condominium owners group or with one of her friends. When Leah would make suggestions to her mother as to how she could cope with the situation, she would find fault with every suggestion, but would always assure Leah that she felt much better after "sharing" her problems with Leah.

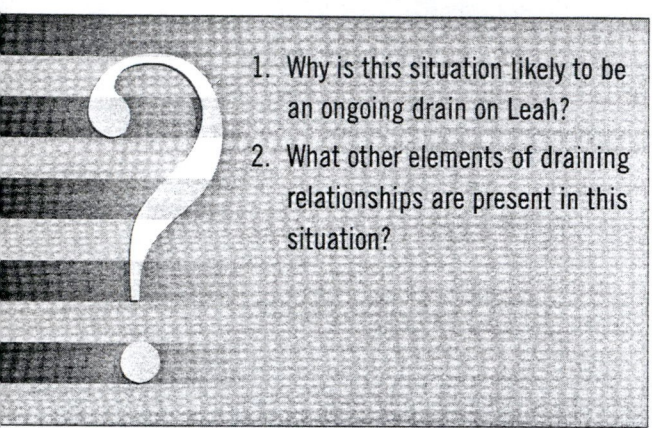

1. Why is this situation likely to be an ongoing drain on Leah?
2. What other elements of draining relationships are present in this situation?

The second type of dump-and-run drainer, when overwhelmed with responsibility or work, sheds the weight by dropping duties or commitments into the laps of friends or family. This is the working parent who too frequently drops children at Grandma's, leaving Grandma unable to make plans of her own. It is also the spouse who, because he finds a family job—bill paying or maybe house maintenance—cumbersome or offensive, simply leaves such responsibility to the other spouse. These cases often come with numerous apologies and many good "reasons" for the need—denying the needs of the recipient "dumpee."

Another common category of draining person we find in our personal life is *the criticizer*. This person feels that it is her duty to inform you of what you have done wrong and what you *should* do to fix the situation. This type is the consummate advisor and authority on everything.

Lester was married, had two children, worked an eight-hour day, and attended classes in the evening. When the weekend came around, his wife's father would come over to visit and comment on all of the unrepaired items around the house. He told Lester that he needed to organize his time better so that he could take care of the yard and home repairs. To Lester, this was not the most important priority for the little time he had at home with his family. He saw his father-in-law as intrusive and offensive and dreaded the weekly visits because they drained him.

An additional draining relationship that we see in both our personal and professional life is the *incompetent-person type*. This is a person who cannot do anything independently. He is always making mistakes, asking others to take over, and generally acting unable to figure anything out without help. The spouse who will not pay the bills because she is not a "numbers person" fits this, as well as the neighbor who constantly borrows tools and asks for yard care help.

Jermaine married Liz, rescuing her from a difficult family situation when he found out she was pregnant. But after about a year of handling baby responsibilities every time Liz fell apart (which was frequently), he was fed up with it. He saw the relationship as very draining.

A final type of draining relationship is the *bully*. This is someone who uses intimidation to coerce others into giving him his way. He often uses anger to manipulate others and is willing to make a scene at the drop of a hat just to guarantee success. This person has little concern for others' needs because he is so needy himself. Men and women can be equally guilty of this draining approach. Sometimes, even children fall into this category. If, to get her own way, a child "beats up" a parent with guilt over a divorce or throws a tantrum in a store, this is also bullying.

ACTIVITY 11.1

After looking at the descriptions and examples, describe some present or past relationships that have been draining for you and tell how they are draining.

1. Name: _____

This person(s) drains me in the following way:

_____

_____

_____

2. Name: _____

This person(s) drains me in the following way:

_____

_____

_____

Draining People in Industry Situations

It is especially unfortunate when the draining person is your manager. It would be nice if all managers were trained in managing their subordinates, but that is not reality. Situations where managers are difficult to cope with are going to happen to most of us at some point in our lives, so we may as well be prepared. Association with a manager is an important relationship, and effective handling of it must be a priority for a healthy work environment.

A draining manager can make each work day very uncomfortable. She can cause great anxiety, contribute to physical illness in the employee, and generally make the work environment an unhappy and unhealthy place to be. The situation often leaves the employee feeling hopeless and helpless, with little or no control over what happens to him. It is one of the most difficult environments to be in for employees.

Dean worked in a small manufacturing company. He was the head of marketing. He reported to Jenny, the vice president of the company, a very determined woman dedicated to the success of the business. She would grill Dean regularly about what he was doing to promote sales and would often nitpick everything he did. Once, she even threatened to withhold his bonus if he did not land a specific client's business. Dean felt constantly under attack by this scrutiny and had been thinking of quitting his job.

In this example, the vice president felt a need to scrutinize because she wanted the company to be successful. Dean felt it was overkill. He wanted to be trusted and left alone to do the job he knew he could do. He felt his monthly sales figures would be a correct indicator of his efforts.

In looking at this relationship, we can see that many of the common characteristics of draining relationships are present. These characteristics are:

- lacking direct, honest, and open communication
- ignoring the needs of others
- leaving others feeling unvalued or disrespected
- creating anxiety
- often leaving others angry or disgusted

Dean was not honest with his boss about the problems her behavior was causing. Jenny was disrespectful of Dean by not acknowledging his successes. Dean felt his work was not being valued. Jenny's behavior created a lot of anxiety for Dean, and the situation left Dean feeling angry and disgusted.

As you can see, the draining types that might exist in personal relationships exist in ample numbers in the workplace also. Coworkers or team members can dump and run, the head of operations can be a bully, and your inept supervisor can plead "I'm new" for an entire year. Sadly, many never outgrow the dependent, overbearing, or thoughtless patterns of their childhood. The maturity required to be involved in respectful, sustaining connections with others does not necessarily come with age.

Sustaining Relationships

Sustaining relationships contribute to your overall well-being and sense of feeling valued and cared for. They offer support without crossing your boundaries. They fortify you emotionally. They provide a place from which you can view the world in safety. They offer you the opportunity to be yourself without criticism. They vibrantly light up your environment with their unqualified acceptance. They offer strength to your spirit. They lighten the burdens of life and enable you to move forward with hope.

All sustaining relationships have certain characteristics in common:

- Comfort and consistency allow for the free flow of emotions.
- Both the person and the feelings are valued.
- Needs are met in a reciprocal fashion.
- Listening is two-way and responsive.
- Personal limits and boundaries are respected.
- Reasonable expectations are met with reasonable support.

Because there is comfort and safety in this type of relationship, a variety of emotions can be expressed freely and with no consequence. Happiness, sadness, or anger are tolerated as indications of what the person is experiencing. Each person is accepting of where the other is in life, yet supports personal growth without fear of losing that person. Each sees the other as fundamentally good and being able to share that goodness in a healthy way.

Corrine and Mel were friends despite an age difference. They spent many hours doing things together. Corrine came to the hospital with Mel's wife when Mel's son wrecked his car. Mel encouraged Corinne to send in a manuscript she had been working on for years. Corinne visited Mel's folk-dance class to take pictures, and Mel and his wife sent flowers to mark Corinne's promotion. There was a bond between the two of them that provided sustaining elements in each of their lives.

In sustaining relationships, people genuinely like and admire many of the qualities the other has. In addition, they are very accepting of each other's imperfections. A value in these types of relationships, whether spoken or not, is to do what it takes to maintain and enhance the relationship. Self, while not being forgotten or ignored, is secondary to the relationship. Ironically, the solidarity of the relationship enhances self.

After looking at the descriptions of sustaining relationships, write down the names of people with whom you have this kind of relationship and the way they sustain you.

1. Name: _____

This person sustains me in the following ways:

_____

_____

_____

2. Name: _____

This person sustains me in the following ways:

_____

_____

_____

Sustaining Business Relationships

Sustaining relationships can also be quite valuable in business. Although one might not have the kind of closeness that exists in a personal relationship, sustaining business relationships can provide just as much quality. They can offer support, knowledge, connections, and direction. They can support you when things get tough and they can provide relief when the stress gets too high.

One element of sustaining relationships is especially important in business: boundaries for self and for others. It is important to note that, in business, the boundaries are set in a different place. They are somewhat more rigid and defined, whereas in personal relationships, the boundaries can be looser and more relaxed. This is needed for several reasons.

1. In business, all relationships have an impact on the company.
2. Personal relationships have both an emotional and an intellectual basis, while in business, the relationships should be primarily on an intellectual level.
3. Certain protocols exist in business to ensure the recognition of power relationships and accountabilities, whereas friends should always be on equal footing.

4. Fairness of treatment among employees can be jeopardized if boundaries and limits of relationships are not observed.

In a personal situation, a close friend may confide something to you that is possibly too personal and makes you think, "I wish he hadn't told me that. It's more than I want to know." You might feel some embarrassment, but the relationship will probably bear up anyway. On the other hand, in a corporate environment, the stakes are different. If you have taken a client out for dinner, and she has a few extra drinks, she may become inappropriately friendly or may confide information about her company that you really should not know. In this situation, you should immediately invoke boundaries. Instead of creating a closer bond with the client, you may experience the *morning-after syndrome:* the client may avoid contact with you and your company as she remembers with chagrin her behavior of the night before.

Boundaries in business settings should be clearly defined.

In addition, your view of a sustaining relationship may be misconstrued if the boundary was ill-defined and your behavior was perceived to be too intrusive. This could easily fall into the realm of sexual harassment in a male–female situation. It could also distract from the need for a degree of formality to make work interactions go smoothly and operate fairly.

You can find, however, many sustaining relationships within your work community: project team members, older employees who will show you the ropes, other single mothers or dads, people from your ethnic or cultural group. You will even find yourself in very satisfying networking relationships with other professionals who share your career interests and the trials of your field of work. Sometimes, these develop into personal and lifelong attachments that cross time and distance. Again, though, boundaries are important; too much familiarity can create the wrong impression and sabotage productivity.

Nicole and Alice had gone to a Women in Management seminar and had hit it off over lunch. Alice was a high-level manager at a large firm; Nicole had just passed entry level in her company. The two women exchanged cards at the seminar and promised to meet again. Alice's company created a new position in accounting that fit Nicole's background and

1. Describe the boundary problems in the Nicole and Alice example.

2. Why do you think Alice behaved the way she did?

3. Why do you think Nicole left the company?

experience, so at Alice's request, Nicole went to work there. Alice often stopped by to talk to Nicole and even invited her and her male friend to join her at the theater. Eventually, Nicole took a job with another company in the city. Alice, who had invested a great deal of time in developing Nicole for a promotion, was upset by this. (Interestingly, Nicole and Alice eventually grew to be good friends after Nicole no longer worked in Alice's company.)

Some of the closest friends you may ever have, you will find through your job. Be careful, however, that not all of your affiliations are work related.

Professional Networking Relationships

Formal and informal groups are found in every profession. Unions, service organizations, and civic groups, as well as career specific organizations, all provide the potential for relationships and for professional support. You can meet people in your field or people who can help you in your career at Rotary Clubs, the Society for Black Engineers, Women in Management, Toastmasters, or any such group. Networking in this manner is not structured, but can be very valuable to help you move to new jobs or advance in your profession. The career advancement elements of networking are covered in more detail in the chapters on self-advocacy and career management.

TRANSITION TIP   *Bryan Jackson, Product Marketing Manager*

When I came out of school, I had the advantage of coming from a business family, so I knew the value of networking. I volunteered to coach soccer in the most affluent section of the town where I was living. Doing that, I met parents who were in the kinds of positions that could help me get started. Your job, though, is a good place to network. Don't overlook an opportunity just because you may have to start at the bottom, if you can meet a mentor or even a customer who might take an interest in your career.

Networking groups, or acquaintances who are specifically for the purpose of mutual career support, are a bit different in focus and rules. Relationships formed in these groups are primarily for sustaining professional connections and surfacing mutually beneficial opportunities. Occasionally, other types of personal or professional relationships can grow out of these, but the rule is most often barter. Relationships are for specific purposes and require a reciprocal exchange of value. People who come to a networking group looking to "take" and offer nothing in return will not be asked back. (The Coach's Corner at the end of this chapter offers advice on developing a network.)

Before you become excited about the opportunities attending a networking function can provide, you should limit your expectations from a relationship perspective. Everyone is in the room to either sell services or gain valuable information or leads from each other. The most successful people attending may offer you business or assistance that they can pass along without any real loss to themselves. You may meet someone whose company you enjoy, or with whom you have much in common and want to pursue conversation. However, in general, expect an all-business, though congenial, situation.

Building Better Relationships

Now that you have looked at your relationships, past and present, to decide whether they are draining or sustaining, you are ready to move to the next stage. This will be your work in building better relationships: turning around or abandoning draining ones, and enhancing and strengthening sustaining ones.

Several skills are involved in building relationships that are satisfying and nurturing. The term *building* is a correct description of what you will be doing because solid, sustaining relationships do not happen without care and attention. You must be prepared to make some effort to keep them going. Think of them as you would a houseplant. The plant cannot live without certain nourishing elements. It needs water and proper light and occasionally a shot of nutrients that will boost the root system to help the plant to grow. Relationships, in order to be sustaining, must also have certain elements like honesty, loyalty, trust, and understanding.

One essential requirement for this process is learning to understand the needs of others and to realize and assert your own needs within the relationship. Understandably, the boundaries of these needs will have to be adjusted depending on the nature of the association. For instance, families often meet certain needs for each other without even having to be asked. But, in the workplace, you might have to assert your needs for privacy, or for training, or for a raise, and let these be known in specific, perhaps written, ways to receive the support you need.

Supportive Listening

One way to learn about another person's need is with supportive listening. This is an attentive, nonjudgmental activity where you invite another to express his or her needs in a clear-cut fashion. Obviously, this activity is only helpful if you sincerely desire to understand the person's wants and wishes. It is only after you know what the other person wants that you can move to meet those needs. Otherwise, you are just guessing and may choose the wrong need, thus diminishing the relationship. The adage *knowledge is power* is quite true in this instance. An understanding of the other person's thoughts and feelings gives you the power to communicate successfully. The following is an example of supportive listening:

Glenn: "I am so frustrated with my job. I can't stand this place anymore. I'm just about ready to quit."

Janice: "You seem really upset. Can you tell me exactly what is disturbing you?"

Glenn: "We are having constant problems with materials arriving on time so we can complete our work orders. Those purchasing people just don't care about us!"

Janice: "This sounds like something you really need to get resolved. Let's see how we can look at this to solve the problem."

In this exchange, Janice is not taking on Glenn's problem, but she is acknowledging that Glenn feels strongly about what is happening. This supports Glenn because she has taken him seriously. She has helped Glenn look at what he is feeling and has offered to engage in the problem-solving activity with him.

Judy and Lara are talking on the phone. Lara says, "Since the baby was born, I am having a great deal of difficulty keeping up with everything around the house."

Explain why each of the responses that Judy might give is supportive listening or not. *Remember, supportive listening is designed to promote understanding and empathy, not to be an advice-giving session.*

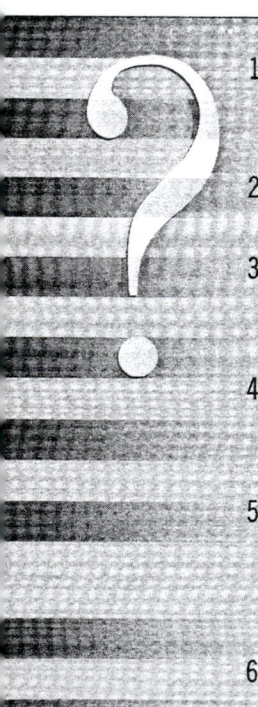

1. "If you would make a schedule for yourself, you could manage better."
2. "Why can't you get your mother to help you?"
3. "It sounds like you are feeling overwhelmed. Is there anything I can do to help?"
4. "If I go to the office earlier, I can get home a little earlier and help you."
5. "Perhaps you are suffering from postpartum depression. Why don't you see the doctor and get some help?"
6. "It sounds like you are feeling swamped with work. Would you like to sit down and take a look at what could be done?"

Voicing Needs

Few, if any, of us will receive all we could ever want in a lifetime, and certainly only some of what we ask for. If this is true, we had better get busy and start letting the world know what we want. If we do not, we greatly reduce the percentage of times we get our needs met.

Often, people confess that they have difficulty asking for what they need. They feel guilty, or they negatively assume that they will not get their needs met anyway. So, why bother to ask? If you are one of those people, think about this: Everyone who is speaking up has the same odds for getting their needs met as you, so why not jump in and be direct with people? The unasked question or the withheld request has undone many relationships. What you need matters; not voicing your needs will ensure they are not met.

Another important aspect of voicing needs is that even if you are told "no," that does not necessarily mean "no" forever. You have the right to ask if a situation is negotiable or if your need could be met at a later date. You might only have to wait a while in order to have your need met. It is easier to live with delayed gratification, if you know you will get what you want at a later date.

> Lane: "Every time I come to your office to discuss our business plans, our conversations are constantly interrupted by the telephone ringing. By the time I leave, I feel like I have wasted my time. We never seem to get anything solved. Would you be willing to forward your phone to voice mail when we schedule a meeting?"
>
> Robert: "I didn't realize that it bothered you."

Lane can tell Robert how he feels without sounding insulting or critical. He simply states the problem and offers a solution.

ACTIVITY 11.3

Identify two needs that you are willing to voice in the next 24 hours. One of these needs should be related to professional life and one should be related to personal life. Identify the people to whom you will voice them and write down what you will say. Make sure that you are stating the problem clearly and, if possible, suggest a solution. You can also ask the other person to help come up with a solution.

1. I will voice my need to _____. I will say

_____

_____

2. I will voice my need to _____. I will say

_____

_____

Handling Conflicting Needs

As you grow more comfortable with voicing and listening to needs, conflicting needs will naturally arise. Because we are not clones of each other, we have differing views, sometimes, of what is important. These conflicts help us learn more about each other.

When these occasions occur, these conflicts must be addressed immediately so that frustration does not build up. A child often has a need to play rather than do assigned chores around the house. Parents may feel strongly about children doing assigned chores. This conflict of needs can escalate quickly into a power struggle if not handled correctly. Using conflict-management and problem-solving skills, the parents and child can arrive at a solution suitable to both and consistent with the values of both. To resolve needs in opposition, you must find some common ground.

When conflicts occur, you can use the skills you learned in Chapter 8 on conflict management. Sometimes surfacing a conflict helps to get it out in the open for discussion.

Caring confrontation about a problem and determining a resolution that will work for all are necessary to sustaining relationships. They are important parts of the development of good professional relationships, as well as very much a part of improving and keeping our personal relationships. The words *caring* and *confrontation* might seem contradictory. The most damaging conflict to a relationship, however, can be the one not broached. Chemical dependency problems, the drain of a long-term illness, conflicting views on a relationship's future, and value differences, if not addressed and resolved, can destroy even the deepest connections over time.

If the goal is to preserve the relationship, then surfacing issues is important. Ignoring the anxiety and growing dissatisfaction produced by conflicting needs is not a caring or supportive act. How many times have you inquired about a stormy look on a friend's face and received the response, "I'm fine"? That expression can have as many different meanings as the human voice and body language can add inflection to it. Asking earnestly about someone's needs may bring out possible need conflicts at an early stage, when they can still be addressed and resolved.

Look at the continuation of the conversation between Lane and Robert. See if you can find a workable solution to the conflicting needs.

> Lane: "Yes, the phone does bother me. I feel we can't get any work done and then I don't know what to follow through on for the next day."
>
> *[At this point Lane has voiced his need. Robert, to be supportive, must address Lane's statement in a caring way.]*
>
> Robert: "Well, Lane, I understand your concerns and I will try to limit the conversations. But, there is a production shut down in the plant because of a problem with

our new machine. I have to be advised of the progress being made so that I can sign off on the cost of repair."

[The need conflict surfaces in what could be a potential problem in the relationship between the two men. Lane, having heard Robert's need statement, should also use supportive communication and go into a problem-solving mode.]

1. Suggest three approaches that might yield a workable solution to the conflict.

2. Was Lane wrong to voice his concern, especially because Robert may be his boss?

3. Did Robert do a good job of responding positively to Lane's need statement even though it was in conflict with his own take on the situation?

One difficulty that enters into relationship conflict, and in some cases actually contributes to an unwillingness to address need conflicts, is the fear of rejection. This fear may be the result of excess baggage brought into adulthood from a nonnurturing, negative childhood. Children who feel as if their parents did not really care for their needs grow up to be adults who worry that the ones they love won't love them back. This may be especially true if any statements of need conflict, even if tactfully offered, were squashed or belittled.

Rethinking Rejection

Everyone has fears of rejection. *The truth is, not everyone has to like you for you to have satisfying relationships.* Work acquaintances don't necessarily have to become your best friends, nor do others with whom you have built a relationship. Remember also that what may seem at first like rejection may not actually be that at all.

When the "friend" you have coffee with every day at work cancels that standing meeting, he might have a big project due. By noting that person's need to be left alone, you can be a supportive friend instead of putting yourself in a situation that could lead to feelings of rejection.

Sometimes, though, you will come across people who just do not wish to be in a relationship with you as badly as you wish to be involved with them. This situation requires you to re-examine the definition you have of rejection. In childhood, rejection meant a loss; it created sadness. So, we take that old definition into adult life when, actually, we should redefine the concept of rejection.

If someone chooses not to have a relationship with you, this could be the result of incompatible goals, differing relationship needs, or even non-meshing life schedules—some people are work oriented rather than people or relationship oriented. Other people could be so preoccupied with their own problems that they don't even think in terms of "like" or "dislike."

So, rejection involves a dropping back to the level where your feeling of self-esteem and acceptance were dependent on others. At this point in your life, though, you are no longer dependent on others for your nurturing. You can do that for yourself by treating yourself just the way you want others to treat you.

11.4 ACTIVITY

You have just joined a new company and this is your third day there. So far, no one has taken the time to introduce you around. You are beginning to feel like you are not welcome at the company and are wondering if you made a mistake taking the job.

1. How could you rethink the situation so that you do not feel rejected?

   _____

   _____

2. Identify what steps you could initiate in order to feel more a part of the organization.

   _____

   _____

Establishing Relationships in a New City

So often our careers require a move to new areas where there is no family or friends. You have worked long and hard to get that great job and now must face the challenges of a new job with support from only the organization that hired you. Additionally, you have the task of building a new social life. These new challenges can be quite an adventure. Because the need for sustaining relationships in business is addressed elsewhere in this chapter, here the discussion focuses on sustaining relationships at a personal or social level.

The types of personal and social relationships are:

- Acquaintances, those people we casually know.
- Friendships, those people whom we allow to know us in more depth.

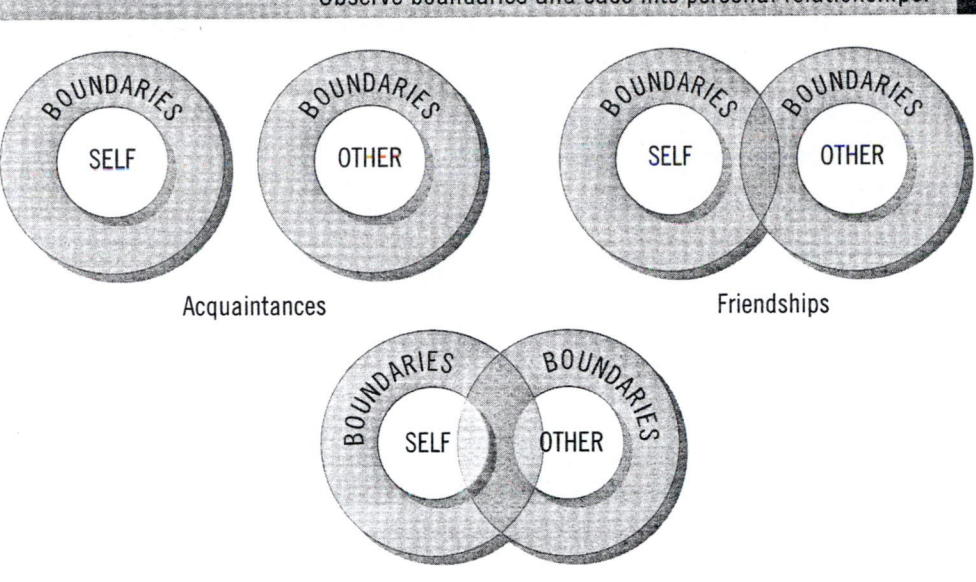

Observe boundaries and ease into personal relationships. **FIGURE 11.1**

Acquaintances

Friendships

Intimate relationships

- Intimate relationships, those whom we allow to know us at the deepest and most personal physical and emotional levels.

Obviously, you cannot jump immediately into friendship or intimate relationships. You may make lots of acquaintances before you make one friend. It is important to know what kind of friendships you would like to have in your life, as well as the kind of people you feel most comfortable with. Once you have made those choices, that leaves only the question of where to find these individuals.

Searching Out Social Connections

Let us start with where not to look for friends. The worst place to meet people with whom you wish to have a sustaining relationship is a bar. You might think it very imprudent if someone asked you to pick your friends when your mind is working only at half speed. Well, that is pretty close to what happens when you go to a bar, have a few drinks, and try to meet people. Your judgment is hampered significantly when you are intoxicated even to the slightest degree. So, how do you expect to make lasting relationships that are sustaining in that condition?

Another caution is that meeting people in bars can present a danger. If you do not have your clear senses working, you may misinterpret a situation and put yourself in harm's way. Where then does one go to meet the right people? The answer to the question can be as varied as the individual. The most important issues to consider are:

1. What kinds of interests do you have?
2. What kinds of people do you want to meet?
3. What kinds of relationships do you want to form?

Some examples of actions one might take to meet people are:

- getting involved in hobbies
- joining clubs and organizations that you have some interest in
- joining a civic organization
- taking a class in something that you enjoy
- getting to know your neighbors
- joining a church
- participating in an amateur sports league
- visiting bookstores
- volunteering at something that will help others

There are many other ways to meet people. You can ask your peers at work, who might be transplants themselves, how they made friends in the community. On the other hand, one of the things that you want to avoid is making a connection with one person and depending on that person to meet all of your needs. Expecting your officemate or the one neighbor whose name you remember to be your "welcome wagon" is unfair.

Avoiding Isolation

A more serious threat to your emotional health than a social blunder is isolation: staying home, watching TV, and substituting Internet "friends" for the warmth of face-to-face relationships. The Internet can, however, be an important way to connect in a new city. Many articles have been written about communities on the Web. Chat rooms are virtual meeting places, much like coffee shops, where you can find others who are interested in the same things you are. Ethnic, political, religious, and social contacts can be made through Internet sites. These contacts should lead to introductions to real people, though, not be a substitute for venturing out.

Keep in mind too, though, that being alone does not necessarily mean being lonely. Many civic clubs are enthusiastic about welcoming new members as are churches. A good way to make the transition to a new place is to move back into your regular activities as quickly as possible: playing basketball at the park, attending church, joining professional organizations. Also, the company of a pet is a wonderful and nurturing experience. A dog gets you out of the house for walks, and there are many places where pet owners can get together—obedience classes, parks, humane society events. Many apartments allow cats, and those that don't usually will accept fish tanks.

Sustaining relationships are those that give us a sense of belonging. They help us when we need help and they are reciprocal. They give us the opportunity to "be there" for others in a nurturing way. They are a source of new energy when we are drained by the rigors of life. Knowing how to identify draining relationships and replace them with sustaining ones keeps us from bottoming out in our life. It keeps us more centered and less likely to get overly stressed by situations and people.

The presence of sustaining relationships in our lives makes us better equipped to handle life transitions effectively. Knowing we have people supporting us in many different kinds of relationships can also make us less afraid to walk through thresholds to new and satisfying levels.

TRANSITION SKILLS SUMMARY

Use supportive listening

Voice needs

Handle conflicting needs

Rethink rejection

GOAL SETTING

Self-nurturing goals: To develop and support my personal relationships, I will:

_____

_____

_____

Self-advocacy goals: To develop and support my professional relationships, I will:

_____

_____

_____

COACH'S CORNER

Networking events become as valuable as you want to make them. They can occur at leisure groups, such as tennis clubs, or at business interest organizations. Following are some suggestions on how to make the most of such an event.

1. Seating: Avoid sitting with people you know.

2. Introductions: Make good eye contact, shake hands firmly, smile as you say your name, and remember to say the other person's name. Offer some piece of information about yourself to help the other person remember you. Name and company may soon be forgotten, but interests can create a memorable connection.

   To meet others, pretend you are the host or hostess of the event and your job is to meet attendees and make them feel comfortable. Introduce others that might have interests or challenges in common. Say the honored person's name last, introduce the younger person to the older person, and a fellow business person to the customer. Offer a sentence or two that will give them a basis for conversation after you move on. An advantageous pairing makes both parties appreciate you for bringing them together.

3. Conversation: Keep it light—no negatives, not too personal (hobbies and current events make good topics); use open-ended questions and active listening. Avoid health problems, jokes (not everyone thinks the same things are funny), prejudices, gossip, and insincere compliments. Be sure to get at least one business card.

4. Follow up: Immediately after the occasion, go to your database and record the name, event where you met, and anything else you remember about each person. This will give you multiple ways to look them up—you may forget the name, but remember they liked exotic wines. Send a note if you hear the person has received an award or if you see an article that fits his or her interests. Be sure to contact at least two people from your database each week.

RENEE WALKUP, Salespeak; e-mail rwalkup@salespeak.com.

CHAPTER 12

Maintaining Personal Relationships

As noted in Chapter 1, professional success can be lonely without the joy of sharing that success with those closest to you. Connecting on the most personal level, the level of deepest affection, respect, and unguarded sharing, affirms us in our humanity and defines our need for intimacy. It is indeed possible, and most desirable, to reach professional goals in a balanced way, a way that includes loved ones.

People who are in intimate relationships—and this does not refer solely to lifelong or sexual relationships—get many benefits from them:

- a sense of calmness and security, confidence in a continuing connection
- mental and emotional support, ideas and feelings shared
- affirmation and validation, acceptance and approval of who you are
- personal growth, a nurturing place to learn about yourself and to develop maturity

As individuals, we have the right to love and be loved, just the same as we have the right to other personal freedoms. But like personal freedom, responsible behavior in intimate relationships begins with some guidelines. Many changes in the ways we relate to each other have occurred in our evolving society, creating confusion about what those guidelines really are.

Is living together better or worse for maintaining closeness over time? Can we begin to include those we have worked with for many years as members of our extended family? How do we define a family? All labels and categories aside, each of us should be a part of the life of someone else. The closest of these relationships, for the purpose of this discussion, will be called intimate. This type of connection invites a great amount of openness about our deepest feelings. In intimate relationships, the other person can view the very core, the very essence of the loved one.

Ultimately, intimacy supports making transitions in your professional life. Unless you have stability in your close personal relationships to back you up, you may not feel secure enough to take a risk that might be an opportunity. Instability in intimate relationships may make you unable to focus and be successful in your work, or to share the joy of success.

Think of your intimate relationships as a springboard from which you jump into your career life and return to recharge your batteries. It is not absolutely necessary for you to have intimate relationships with others to be successful. But without these, you have no one to lean on when you have worked yourself to the bone, no one to give you a boost when your emotional fuel tank is empty. Who would hold your hand when you are struggling with the fallout from painful mistakes?

You see, intimate relationships are so very important, whether they are with a lover or a best friend or an understanding parent. Humans need many different kinds of close connections because these are the sources of emotional well-being. Determining what a true and healthy intimate relationship is, however, requires some discussion. A definition from a dictionary is inadequate to describe something as complex as intimate relationships. Sometimes the best way to tell what something is, is to describe what it is not. Perhaps a look at what an ineffective relationship is will lead to a better understanding.

Ineffective Relationships

One rather well-to-do 28-year-old, who became one of the "quick rich" as a software designer, talks frequently about all of the "close friends" he has among famous or influential people. He mentions places they have all flown to on a weekend just to party or go to the beach. He even shows pictures taken with some of these people at an exotic bar on some island. This same man, though, has confided on more than one occasion that he sometimes feels an emptiness or aloneness in his life that he doesn't understand.

"I don't think I have anyone that I can call a real friend." When asked what he means by a "real friend," he responds, "I don't know exactly, but I don't feel like I have one." He has tried to create intimacy by having parties and taking people places. Even with his many "girlfriends," the relationships never seem to last any length of time.

Somewhere in earlier years he failed to understand the need to cultivate and maintain intimate relationships on his way to professional success. Thus, this lack of understanding followed him and finally became visible in the shallowness of the associations in his life.

Misidentification can contribute to this lack of understanding. An ineffective relationship can sometimes be misidentified as "intimate." That is, there are certain types of associations that we expect to be intimate, such as those with parents, children, spouses, or lovers. When these are ineffective or toxic, the experience distorts our view of what true and healthy intimacy really is. The way to transform ineffective relationships into solid, intimate ones is first to identify problem relationships.

COMMON CHARACTERISTICS OF INEFFECTIVE RELATIONSHIPS

1. Lack of communication—feelings and ideas are not exchanged freely.
2. Lack of commitment—indecision and distance prevent intimacy.
3. Unresolved anger—resentment exists from past and present hurts.
4. Conflicting goals—differences appear in what each needs and is willing to give.
5. Conflicting values—disagreement occurs over what is important.
6. Thoughtlessness—disregard emerges for the feelings of the other.
7. Irresponsibility—carelessness causes mishandling of possessions or duties.
8. Self-centeredness—demands for self-satisfaction become constant.

Look at the list. You might begin to see some of your relationships a bit more clearly and to define them in ways other than healthy intimate attachments.

Even one or two of these characteristics can block growth and development in a relationship. Granted, there are very few perfect relationships. But a failure to acknowledge and deal with any of these problems can lead to the breakdown of the connection between two people.

Couples' relationships are not the only places where intimacy problems can occur. In many families, the very base from which most of us draw our support, there can be withheld love, distance, and coldness. Anyone who has grown up in one of these families can attest that they feel confused over what love really is. If the family, the first exposure to what love should be, does not offer that warm, intimate relationship, then where does a person learn about what healthy love or intimacy is?

Intimacy is not forced or bought or contrived. It is not created with hidden agendas. You cannot get intimacy by tricking people or making them owe you or depend on you. In the example mentioned earlier, the man attempted to win friends by showing them a good time. Intimate friends are willing to share the bad times too. This is what he was missing. Healthy relationships, on the other hand, can support us through major life-changing events, or even just the needs of the day, and ensure transitions that are positive. They also give us the opportunity to support others as they pass through thresholds to growth and change in their own lives.

Healthy Intimate Relationships

Healthy relationships can take many forms. Some examples are:

- the way a coach puts a bit of himself or herself into the development of the players on a team
- the way old friends who have not seen each other in years pick right up with conversation and sharing
- the way neighbors can sometimes step in and know what needs to be done in a crisis

All of these in their own way are forms of intimate relationships, but they all look different. Maybe our closest relationships should be with those *people who are willing to be our "fans," who will cheer for us in our attempts and stand with us in our failures.*

Following are some guidelines that will help you identify healthy relationships. You may find that your relationships already have some of these characteristics, but you may not have acknowledged them as signs of the level of closeness you might call intimate. Look at the list and apply it to your idea of what intimate relationships are like.

CHARACTERISTICS OF INTIMATE RELATIONSHIPS

1. Respect for each other's needs—mutual willingness to negotiate some needs for the best interests of the relationship.
2. Acceptance—both feel that weaknesses and strengths are understood.
3. Safety—physical and emotional trust that goes both ways.
4. Affirmation—validation and support that goes beyond tolerance.
5. Listening—value on both sides for what the other has to say.
6. Openness—ability to express guilt, anger, dreams, and disappointments, and know they will be handled in a kind way.
7. Closeness—physical (not necessarily sexual) closeness with an emotional level of comfort comparable to your favorite shirt or childhood toy.

One key word characterizes these relationships: reciprocal. The parties involved value and support each other in mutual ways—though perhaps not always at the same level at the same time.

> Todd and Paul are half brothers who recently discovered each other through an adoption records search. They have spent the last two years getting to know each other and have visited back and forth several times. Todd's wife was the one who conducted the search because she knew of Todd's desire to find out about his natural parentage. He had confessed to her that, though his adoptive family was loving and supportive, he still wanted to see what other blood relatives he could find.

1. Would this example suggest that Todd's relationship with his wife is a healthy intimate relationship? Explain.
2. What can Todd do to establish a closer connection with his new brother?

Types of Intimate Exchanges

People relate to those close to them in many different ways and on different levels. These are called intimate exchanges. The four basic types of intimate exchanges are: intellectual, emotional, sexual, and physical. In some relationships, we have all of these types. In others, we have one or two types.

Intellectual Intimacy

Intellectual intimacy is characterized by sharing the most private thoughts, needs, and desires. A deep level of trust must exist for this type of sharing. In addition, each individual must be personally able to communicate these thoughts, needs, and desires. An interesting (though potentially unhealthy) avenue for this intellectual intimacy is the Internet: chats, message boards, e-mail. In this electronic medium it is not uncommon for people to divulge their innermost thoughts to people they have never met (and perhaps never will). This depth of involvement is unhealthy because it is an artificial intimacy that substitutes for human contact and relationship building.

Carlton and Cokie had been best friends all of their lives, through college and the start of their careers in the world of finance. Over dinner one night, they shared with each other their deepest and most profound hopes for the future. Carlton talked about his ambition to work on Wall Street, and Cokie felt free to confess his dreams of entrepreneurship because each knew his friend would not criticize. The relationship provided a safe place to bounce ideas off each other. Trust created a comfort level that allowed each to synthesize ideas and create a plan of action for attaining those hopes and dreams. Carlton and Cokie were expressing intellectual intimacy.

In professional environments, often a coworker or mentor becomes an intellectually intimate partner. These relationships can be very important, especially when the work you do may not be easily grasped or understood by people outside your field. Concerns about the strategic direction of the company or ideas for process improvements that would fall on deaf ears outside your job can be met with enthusiasm and affirmation from these professional close friends. The term "colleague" or "associate," maybe even "partner," might be applied to these professional connections, but most fall into the realm of sustaining relationships. Long-time team members or work group associations, though, can become more than just professionally congenial; they can meet many of the guidelines for intimate relationships on the intellectual level. Some even extend to the emotional level.

Emotional Intimacy

Emotional intimacy is created from connecting on a level of feelings rather than thoughts. Communications between emotionally intimate people often cover concepts such as love, fear, anger, happiness, loneliness, and sadness. Sustaining relationships can have moments of emotional intimacy, but relationships of many years, like those with best friends, marital partners, and family members, people with whom you have a history, have longer periods of emotional intimacy.

Lauria and Candy, sisters-in-law and best friends, shared everything with each other. Lauria had confessed to Candy her fears about her health due to a family history of illnesses. Candy called Lauria first when she sold the painting she had been secretly working on.

In emotionally intimate relationships, each feels free to say in an unguarded way what emotions each is experiencing. Even the occasional negative feeling can be expressed and received constructively. Trust exists because the bond of friendship is strong enough to handle such things. People in this kind of relationship are committed to maintaining the emotional closeness and intimacy they share. An important aspect of these relationships is the willingness to persist in preserving the closeness, even when conflict, serious health matters, or dramatic life transitions occur.

Physical Intimacy

Physical intimacy is another kind of closeness we can share with others. Physical intimacy does not denote sexual intimacy, although that could be one of the outcomes. We can be physically close to our children, parents, and people that we live with, and this does not mean we are going to be sexual. The willingness to provide a hug or touch that is needed or desired supports physical intimacy. Respect for a person's boundaries of physical contact, though, should be maintained. A hug or a kiss on the cheek that you intend as a show of affection may be considered an invasion by the recipient.

Rodney's brother was killed in a car accident leaving behind a wife and two children. Rodney and his wife moved into the neighborhood where his brother's family lived. Every day after work, he picked the kids up from school and took them to his house to play. He and his wife gave the kids lots of hugs, kisses, and special attention. Though he could not replace their father, the physical affection was important to the kids, and it did help them to cope with their loss.

Sexual Intimacy

Sexual intimacy is the final area of closeness. When this is casual in nature, sex for the sake of sex, it is not intimacy. As an intimate act, sex wells up as an expression of deep love for the other person. Obviously, we do not have sex with everyone we love. And sadly, there are those who are not intimate in other ways but still share sex.

Sexual intimacy is reserved for those people who are consenting adults, willing to share that bodily experience with each other. The only two requirements for sexual intimacy are mutual consent and the use of parts of the bodies that are connected with the sexual self as defined by the people involved. Any act that is perceived as sexual in nature should be consented to by both parties. Forced sexual closeness is not sexual intimacy. It is rape and should always be reported to proper authorities.

ACTIVITY   12.1

Using the list of the types of intimacy, identify which characteristics belong to your present close relationships.

1. My relationship with _____ has characteristics of this (these) expression(s) of intimacy:

_____

_____

_____

I believe this to be an effective/ineffective intimate relationship (underline your choice).

2. My relationship with _____ has characteristics of this (these) expression(s) of intimacy:

_____

_____

_____

I believe this to be an effective/ineffective intimate relationship (underline your choice).

Stress and Intimacy

Transitions of all kinds affect intimate relationships. There is no doubt that transitions create stress and anxiety in our lives. Even if it is an exciting time in our lives, like graduating from college, getting married, buying a new car, getting a new job, or having a baby, we still feel the stress. The only difference between this kind of positive stress and negative stress is that we usually experience the positive stress with a smile on our face and happiness in our hearts.

The body experiences stress from both positive and negative life events much the same way. A lack of sleep from happily remodeling the old home you just bought creates stress on the body the same as a lack of sleep from worry. Stress may make you drowsy, hyper, angry, euphoric, or physically ill. For most of us, when we do not consciously address that stress, we tend to take it out on those loved ones that are around us. If we are to be effective in our relationships, we must be prepared to deal with the stress that these transitions create, so that our loved ones do not have to pay a price for our feelings. What is the most effective way to approach an impending transition? The best answers lie in our ability to:

1. Predict how intensely we will react to transitions.
2. Communicate to our loved ones how we may react and that we will need some support.
3. Approach the transition positively and know the stressful situation is temporary.
4. Ask clearly for what we want from the other people.

By doing these things, we are able to weather the rough spots without hurting the ones we love. Realizing that we are under stress and understanding how we act that stress out with those around us may require a hard look at ourselves. Being able to explain your stress to loved ones will prevent both you and them from misreading your behavior. In return, knowing what stress looks like in family members or others close to you allows you to dismiss some temporary offensive behavior instead of becoming hurt by it.

Kerwin was moving to a new city to work, taking his fiancée along with him. They were planning to be married the week after graduation. He had to secure housing and purchase a new vehicle that would be safe enough to withstand highway traveling. Additionally, Kerwin had to finish two papers and complete his final exams. When his fiancée asked him about his preference of food for the rehearsal dinner, he blew up and stomped out of the apartment, leaving her shocked and tearful at his unfamiliar behavior.

1. What were the major stressors for Kerwin?
2. How would they put pressure on his relationship?
3. What are some recommendations that would be helpful to Kerwin in order for him to avoid having his stress create major conflict in his relationship?

Building Healthy Intimate Relationships

Even when there are no major stressors occurring in our intimate relationships, they still are susceptible to the little rough spots of everyday life. In addition, neglect can starve a good relationship into nothing. There is no way around the fact that we are not perfect in our relationships. No two (or more) people can live together in eternal bliss. Knowing how to build and maintain a healthy relationship is a key ingredient in successful transitions. Consider the following guidelines:

- quiet the ego
- identify expectations
- learn from mistakes
- practice empathy
- accept responsibility
- operate from "now" thinking

Quiet the Ego

When we allow our ego to dictate what we want from relationships, we make issues all about our needs and neglect to see that the other person's needs are equally important. We manipulate, coerce, and browbeat others into meeting our needs. When ego rules, intelligent, rational thinking goes out the window.

Tia lived with her mother as she had since her father died. She sought a promotion to a high-profile job and wanted to be at the top of her game. She spent several evenings a week working late and often brought work home. Tia's mother began to resent this and wanted Tia to spend time with her like they had done since her husband died.

Two ego elements are apparent in this: Tia's desire for professional achievement at the expense of her relationship with her mother and Tia's mother's desire to have Tia mitigate her loneliness. In intimate relationships, the choices we make as individuals must be examined for their effects on those close to us. You can see here that the ego, being a very strong force in the personality, can lead one down a destructive path if allowed to get out of control. Healthy relationships balance ego with empathy, my need and your need too. This then becomes a win–win proposition for everyone.

Identify Expectations

If expectations are hidden, unspoken for whatever reason, the other person cannot know about them—that is, unless there is some mind reading going on, which is not likely. Verbalizing and clarifying all expectations allows the relationship to bloom in the light of awareness. Withholding your expectations can only harm the relationship.

Even people who are "soulmates," including brothers and sisters who have known each other all their lives, cannot possibly perceive or guess each other's changing expectations as they mature. Unmet expectations are great sources of hurt and discord.

Callie and Ramona were just getting into a relationship. Both had some fears because neither had been in a same-sex relationship before. Callie expected to be able to tell friends about Ramona and to go places as a couple. Ramona felt strongly about keeping their relationship secret. Both could be hurt terribly by acting on their individual expectations without consulting the other.

Interestingly, this problem of expectations extends to many aspects of relationships. We do not resent those from whom we expect nothing. Unmet expectations, however, from those we love can be the downfall of a relationship. Identifying our own expectations to the point of being able to verbalize them is more difficult than it may seem. This may be why couples who live together fairly amicably for years fall apart shortly after being married. Their expectations of each other and of the relationship outside the label of marriage were different than under that label. Uncovering and voicing these expectations allows people to stay in close relationships.

Learn from Mistakes

How many times have you heard someone say, "Every time I do this, my elbow hurts"? The logical response is, "Well, stop doing that." It seems like each of us could learn about cause-and-effect relationships where our own behaviors are concerned. This type of learning does not seem to occur naturally, however, because much of our behavior reflects past, habitual patterns instead of strategic action. Maybe that behavior worked at one time. But when we ignore consequences and fail to learn from them, we make the same mistakes again and again.

> Bev met her husband, Julius at a nightclub in college. After five years of marriage, Julius died suddenly of an aneurysm. When Bev finally began dating again, the place she went most often was a nightclub where she met and dated several men, all of whom turned out to have a drinking problem. When her friends suggested she look in other places for men where drinking was not the main activity, Bev resisted: "But I met Julius at a nightclub, and he was a wonderful man."
>
> She continued to patronize the nightclub near where she worked. Finally, she met Chris and married him. Three years later, she divorced him because of his alcoholism.

1. Is there a behavior pattern where Bev has not seen the cause-and-effect relationship?

2. What is Bev clinging to as the place to find a suitable life partner?

3. How can Bev learn from this mistake?

The cure for repeating past mistakes is growth. The steps to ongoing growth are:

1. Recognize the patterns or similarities in situations that yield undesirable outcomes. If you tell your boyfriend (or girlfriend) that you will meet at a certain time, and you get an "Oh yeah, right" look or a sarcastic response, then you should see that as a pattern you have some part in.

2. Ask yourself what outcome or situation with loved ones you want to create. For example, "I would like him (or her) to respond positively—to smile and be enthusiastic about meeting."

3. Backtrack to determine what behavior of yours contributed to the negative outcome. (Remember, you had some role in creating the situation that went badly for you.) For example, "As much as I hate to admit it to myself, I have forgotten or been late for our dates several times."

4. Focus on the specific behavior to establish a new pattern. Write yourself notes, leave yourself messages, program your pager to remind you, whatever it takes, but every time you commit to a time to meet someone, be there. New

behaviors evoke new responses. (If this is really a long-time pattern for you, you might want to make appointments with, or commitments to, yourself first until you become more consistent in your behavior.)

This process can be very enlightening. Tracking down negative reactions helps you learn from the past. It gives you the potential to learn and create positive responses that are more in line with your goal of maintaining a healthy relationship.

Practice Empathy

It is so easy to just focus on our own needs and ignore the needs or views of our loved ones. We get wrapped up in our daily lives and forget all about the other people around us. Developing the skill of empathy means that we think of what it is like to walk in the shoes of others. We not only observe what the other might need or think, but we directly ask what those needs and thoughts are. That does not mean that one has to meet every need or demand of the other. But by asking questions, we can begin the process of negotiation that will lead to a balance between our needs being met and the other person's needs being met.

Empathy, though, is more than negotiation in an intimate relationship. It is both allowing and respecting the other person's feelings or viewpoints if they are different from yours. Patrick's wife had been the victim of a stalker for nearly a year, sometime before they met. Though her life with Patrick had created no occasion for fear, she was still inordinately concerned with keeping the house lighted and locking doors even when Patrick just went out to take the garbage. Patrick became offended: "I'm there, why is she still so scared? It doesn't make sense."

Patrick's inability to feel his wife's fear, or even remotely to understand it, made him dismiss it as ridiculous. Though her fear was excessive in her existing situation, it was real to her. Patrick's empathy, though, would have shown respect for her feelings. Then, he could encourage her to seek counseling for the problem in a more loving way.

In another case, Darryl was living with his parents until he could recover from an accident. His parents were very active and had a full schedule of things they did on a daily basis. Darryl had a back injury that required him to stay in traction for most of the day. After some pondering, he decided to ask some of his friends to come over and assist him on the nights his parents had plans.

His parents respected his empathy for them and felt grateful for his consideration. Darryl felt a sense of self-worth because he, while having definite needs, was able to move himself past his needs and consider the needs of his parents.

Accept Responsibility

Whether we want to admit it or not, if we are to be in a relationship with others, we must become responsible for our part in making the relationship good. Conversely, if you are the type that does not like to put much effort into making a relationship work, think again. You miss a wonderful opportunity for your own personal growth. You miss learning how to balance your needs, and you miss helping the relationship grow to a mature and healthy level.

Merritt had directed most of his energy over the past year to finishing his degree. Having graduated now, he was ready to start a serious relationship with a girl he had been dating for six months. Merritt has to accept responsibility for two challenges:

1. The energy and focus required to make it in a new job.
2. The energy and focus required to grow a relationship.

This is one of the most difficult transition challenges because few of us can maintain simultaneous focus in more than one area. Merritt will have to invest in making his new job go well, getting to know the people, processes, and requirements of his position. Moving a relationship from casual to intimate takes time and effort. Most of our close family members, friends, or mates will tolerate and forgive our self-absorbed, new-job behavior temporarily, but only temporarily.

The difficult trick then is to determine the point at which the investment in work success should be tempered with a priority on relationship building. One person alone cannot be responsible for a relationship; both (or all) parties must accept responsibility for developing and improving the closeness and empathy that are so much a part of intimacy. It is highly likely that Merritt's girlfriend is experiencing the same demands on her time and emotional energy from her work. Both Merritt and she will have to accept responsibility for building the relationship; for either to expect the other to take up all the slack is unfair and generally only produces resentment.

In our society, this shared responsibility is still a somewhat new idea. Historically, women took responsibility for the relationship; men were responsible for the financial contribution. Today's world has professionals of both sexes, so the roles of financial contributor and relationship builder have to be balanced and shared in a different way. The old rules do not apply, and those who still try to run their relationships by these old standards (consciously or subconsciously) will likely be disappointed. ▪

12.2 ACTIVITY

Helping is different from sharing responsibility. If you take on responsibility, you either perform a task or ask someone to do it. If you help, you expect someone else to do it or to ask you to do it.

1. In your intimate relationships what do you take responsibility for?

_____

_____

2. What do you help with?

_____

_____

3. Is your relationship balanced in this area?

_____

_____

Operate from "Now" Thinking

Many of the relationships that have problems are ones that have at their core unmet childhood needs or conflicts that are transferred into the grown-up world. These unresolved issues reside in our unconscious and cause us to do things that we might never do if we thought carefully. For example, the man who had an emotionally inaccessible mother may marry a woman who is emotionally distant. What is going on here is not blatant sabotage. Subconsciously, he is hoping this person will, because she "loves" him, completely change and give him the love he wants. But, instead, the same theme is acted out with the same result. This is an example of "then" thinking.

If this occurs at a level outside our logical awareness, how then can we make good choices in our relationships? The answer lies in our ability to:

- behave in a "now" manner
- think, rather than let our unconscious programming take over
- ask for help from rational adults around us

"Now" thinking is using our intelligence to direct us in our relationships. That does not mean that we should intellectualize all relationship situations and never have any feelings. What it does mean is that we do not have to act on every feeling we have. We can, instead, think, "Is this feeling coming from the 'now' me or is it welling up from the 'then' me?" Taking time to ask that question will help free you from the damage that can be done by making unconscious choices that could be bad for you.

You need intimate relationships in your life. We all do. You can fool yourself for a little while into thinking that superficial lovers are desirable. You can make yourself believe that low-key associations, the ones with no entanglements, the ones that require little energy to maintain, are the best for you. But, in truth, you need the real thing, an intimate relationship—at least in some form. Some of these relationships come in the form of family, friends, and lovers.

There is a lot of work involved in building satisfying intimate relationships because:

- needs must be shared and met
- talking must be paired with listening
- respect must build trust

But, nothing keeps us going, keeps us alive, like knowing there is someone who cares for and about us.

ACTIVITY 12.3

Can you think of any instances where your "then" thinking interfered with your "now" relationships? Provide an example and describe how you are going to reconcile the two.

_____

_____

_____

Follow the Rules

No one ever goes into a relationship knowing all the answers; therefore, it is your responsibility to seek out the necessary knowledge. It is important also to understand that you are not a static individual. You are forever in process. So are the people you will be involved with. You will be affected by situations and events throughout your life. Transition events will naturally occur, and you will grow and mature as a result. So that your relationships grow and mature also, a look at a few basic relationship rules will keep you going in the right direction.

1. Respect each other's needs. This may be as simple as doing quiet activities in the late evening when the other person goes to bed early. Or it may be as complex as learning to work around a job where one of you is on call at all hours. In the case of children, it may mean asking them what boundaries they would like you to observe where their personal lives are concerned or what behaviors would demonstrate love to them.

2. Accept another's odd habits or differing beliefs. This does not mean you have to agree with that person, or embrace the belief or behavior. You must understand that no two people think or act exactly alike, and there are just some things that you may have to decide not to be upset about. When the other person makes clothing, career, or belief choices that are not the same as your own, you must grant that person the right to make those choices. If you do not take such choices as a personal affront, this should not be a problem.

3. Ensure safety in physical, emotional, and sexual intimacy. For sexual relationships, safety is a serious matter. Other concerns, though less profound, should be addressed also. Each person in an intimate relationship should feel that the other person will not try to inflict hurt—either physical or emotional. Each should feel that the other will use care in offering criticism that is constructive and not spiteful, that advice will be given in love and not jealousy or anger.

4. Affirm by saying, "Yes, I am with you; I believe what you are saying has value," or, "I liked the way you handled that argument with the kids today." Everyone needs a cheerleader, a booster. People in intimate relationships offer that boost out of genuine respect and admiration. Good things should not go without saying. Remember that the occasional "I am really proud of you" or "You look like a real winner today" should become a part of your daily conversation, not just a rare compliment.

5. Listen with focused attention. This can be a high compliment, while not listening can be a deadly insult. Have you ever been in a situation where you needed to speak to someone about something important, and the other person did not even look up from what he was doing to answer you? Or the other person repeatedly looked at her watch? Intimacy brings with it a commitment for time and attention. What each of you has to say is important—especially in discussions about feelings. Most conflicts can be averted or resolved with careful listening.

6. Be open about ambitions, dreams, fears, and concerns. Secrets can do irreparable damage. "He won't tell me what he's thinking!" "I know she must be angry about something, but I can't get her to tell me what it is." Openness says that you can feel free to try out a new idea or confess a secret lifelong dream and that it will be met with interest, not criticism.

7. Preserve closeness by making plans for calm and quiet time together. For some, the closeness is intellectual, based on ideas exchanged. For others, it may be more emotional, a lift from the sound of a voice on the phone. However it is manifest in your relationships, time for closeness should be a priority.

8. Be persistent in applying good relationship skills: working conflicts until they are resolved, not just silenced; regularly affirming something about your child, spouse, lover, or intimate friend; expressing confidence in the growth and potential of the relationship and the people in it; demonstrating with words and actions your love for them and an appreciation of their love for you. Finally, be persistent in striving to improve the ease and level of connectedness with those dear to you. A relationship that is not constantly evolving in the face of ever-changing life events is likely dying. Books, tapes, therapists, counselors, seminars, all of these are sources of information that can contribute to helping you build a satisfying relationship. Intimate relationships require persistence; intimate partners deserve it.

ACTIVITY 12.4

Think about the relationships in your life. Using the ideas provided previously, identify at least one thing you are willing to do to improve the intimate relationships in your life.

1. I would like to improve my relationship with _____ by doing the following:

_____

_____

2. I would like to improve my relationship with _____ by doing the following:

_____

_____

3. I would like to improve my relationship with _____ by doing the following:

_____

_____

Though separating work relationships from personal relationships is important for a balanced personal and professional life, the nature of human interaction lends itself to many ways and levels of involvement with people. Each relationship brings with it certain supporting elements. Professional relationships can have many similarities to personal relationships when handled in an appropriate way. Teams will expose you to a specific kind of professional relationship.

High-Performing Teams

Many tasks in your career area require the use of teams. Traditionally, companies have had hierarchical structures: power, authority, and responsibility filtered down through layers of management. Employees reported to a single manager who was responsible for the productivity of a functional area consisting of 8 to 10 people.

Today, however, more and more companies are depending on groups of employees from different departments to work together as a team to complete projects or reach certain goals for the organization. Often these people have no prior association with each other, yet they are expected to establish communication, trust, mutual support, and a high degree of interdependence. The characteristics of the most productive teams are described by Reid, Moomaugh and Associates, a corporate consulting and training organization, as follows:

TEAM MEMBERS:

- share a common purpose or goal
- build relationships based on trust and respect
- balance task and process
- plan thoroughly before acting
- involve members in clear problem-solving and decision-making procedures
- respect and understand each other's "diversity"
- value synergism and interdependence
- emphasize and support team goals
- reward individual performance that supports the team
- communicate effectively
- practice effective dialog instead of debate
- identify and resolve group conflicts
- vary levels and intensity of work
- provide a balance between work and home
- critique, regularly and consistently, the way they work as a team

- practice continuous improvement (see also Coach's Corner)

Amazingly (or maybe not so amazing at all), these sound like guidelines for effective intimate relationships. The best teams know each other's strengths and weaknesses; they trust individual team members' commitments to deadlines and performance levels; and they genuinely understand, like, and respect those on the team. Sometimes, teams become very close-knit, working long hours because they enjoy the association, and they even socialize outside work with their families. Because they share so many common experiences on the job, it is perfectly natural for them to be involved in each other's lives outside as well.

Note, however, not all teams are like this in the world of work. Many responsibilities of your job are now labeled as *projects* and are carried out by teams made up of people with multiple reporting structures. Team members may have a manager to whom they report for performance and salary reviews or promotions. In addition, they may be responsible for several teams, each of which has a manager somewhere up the ladder who is responsible for the overall performance of the team.

Yes, this kind of multidirectional pull on your time and energy can be very confusing and stressful, but a close-knit team can offer you satisfying personal connections and support in an often impersonal work environment. At some level, good teams have learned and practice the rules of good relationships. Perhaps, people involved in intimate personal relationships would fare better if they followed the guidelines for high-performing teams. Recognizing that an intimate relationship is truly a team proposition might encourage those behaviors that will lead to the highest levels of satisfaction and support.

ACTIVITY 12.5

Look at the list of characteristics of high-performing teams. Choose two of these and relate them to specific challenges that occur in close personal relationships.

Example: *Emphasize and support team goals.*

"Because we agreed to save for a trip to Jamaica this year, I'm going to put this travel brochure on the refrigerator to remind us how great it will be and to remind me to take my lunch to work instead of spending extra to eat out every day."

Characteristic: _____

To apply this to my relationship with _____ I intend to:

_____

_____

Characteristic: _____

To apply this to my relationship with _____ I intend to:

_____

_____

The closest personal relationships, the ones we call intimate, are necessary for our health and our spirit. We need to know we are cared for and we need to care for someone. Not all relationships are or should be intimate, but some have the potential to become immensely satisfying and fulfilling—that warm, comfortable, and loving place we all want to be. Those deserve our care and commitment. And we deserve the intimacy.

TRANSITION SKILLS SUMMARY

Quiet the ego
Identify expectations
Learn from mistakes
Practice empathy
Accept responsibility
Operate from "now" thinking

GOAL SETTING

My self-nurturing goals for my personal relationships are:

_____

_____

_____

My self-advocacy goals for my business relationships are:

_____

_____

_____

COACH'S CORNER

Team members really don't have to like each other, but they do have to conduct themselves in such a way that the purposes of the team are served. A respect and an appreciation for the value of differences are the cohesive elements.

1. Members have to feel that they can disagree and it will be handled constructively. All members have a responsibility to express views in order to have the most thoroughly thought out decisions and actions.

2. Set aside the "I must be perfect" attitude. Performing team tasks in a vacuum may make you hold up a project. The client may not need 100 percent; maybe only 90 percent is required. The real need of the team in this case is the timely completion of 90 percent.

3. Recognize limitations and ask for support when needed. If four people are required to lift and move a piece of plywood, then anyone getting tired prevents the job from being done. For anything you don't know, ask for help; don't drop your corner.

4. Value sharing over ego. Consensus and open communication lead to a better job for the team. Forget the past where the best grade or the most points scored gave you value.

5. Make space for someone else's ideas. Assume everyone has something important to contribute.

6. New team members should spend time with the leader to discover the three or four main things they need to know about the team's activity. If this support is not available, seek out the information from more mature team members.

7. Don't assume anyone knows when you are floundering. Only your lack of productivity is noted and no thought is given to why. Ask for help when you need it.

8. Devote time to looking at how your team can do better as a group.

ROBIN REID, Reid, Moomaugh and Associates; e-mail: rreid@improve.org.

CHAPTER 13

Launching
Your Career

T he big step, a new job: a first career position just out of school, a change to a new and better job, a return to work after years of child rearing, or a recovery from a layoff or being fired. Each of these presents its own challenges, but all require some standard, expected protocols to lead to success.

Employee selection is sometimes a very difficult process for companies. This is partly because of a shortage of skilled people from which to choose in certain industries. Even with this great need, for serious consideration you are expected to:

- locate job leads and potential openings, more or less on your own
- supply certain documents, such as resumes, applications, and letters, in prescribed formats
- showcase your abilities and demonstrate your potential in an interview

The Job Fit Challenge

Every company with a job opening wants to hire not just someone who could do the job, but someone who would be more: an asset to the company in many different areas. The company is looking for someone who will help them make money or help them cut expenses. That is the bottom line of what an asset really is. They also, however, look for a *fit*. With a temporary or contract worker, they pick someone to fill a short-term, specific skill need, based mostly on a list of competencies. However, for full-time employees, the standards are different and the process, more involved.

In addition to technical skills (this term applies to any specialized skill within a particular industry), a prospective employee must also be able to:

- work as easily alone as in teams
- manage time and tasks for meeting deadlines
- demonstrate a good work ethic
- add to the synergy that occurs in groups that work well together

The person in charge of hiring, however, must determine all of this from a resume, one to two interviews (maybe only three or four hours total), and a few references.

A mistake in hiring costs a company a great deal. In a company that offers just a basic benefits package, an employee's cost is considered to be one to two and a half times that employee's salary per year. In addition, anyone new has to learn the processes, procedures, and strategic priorities of the company as well as sources to secure information and services. This takes time, time that is not at maximum efficiency. If an employee fails within a year, that up-to-speed cost was wasted, and the company must bring in someone new, who will take several months to reach reasonable productivity. Many companies figure the average cost of hiring a new employee at $8,000 to $15,000.

This figure is necessarily higher at higher levels of the company and in cases of scarce expertise where an international search may be involved. Though professional search firms (sometimes called *headhunters* or *recruiters*) charge a fee to take on this responsibility, many companies feel that the fee is still less than the cost of the time spent by their own employees on the hiring activity rather than on their own jobs.

In short, employers need you, perhaps even desperately, and truly want you to be just what they are looking for. Your job is to make that decision easier for them, to show them that you can do what they need and that they can trust you to act in the best interests of the company. That includes getting along with your coworkers and showing initiative as well as good judgment. The previous chapters have oriented you to many of the expectations a company will have along these lines, and a review of the highlights of that material may help prepare you to present yourself in the best possible way. A candidate who can demonstrate *savvy*, an understanding of the challenges and inner workings of a position, as well as the general demands of the workplace, is likely to receive an offer quickly.

When you finally do find that perfect *fit*, the job and company that suits your professional style and values your expertise, the transition becomes one to:

- an opportunity to do something you enjoy in an environment that fosters that enjoyment
- a place where you can be productive and make a visible contribution to something larger than yourself
- a source of stimulation and support in the form of colleagues and experts
- an environment in which to apply your creativity to complex problems and grow in your knowledge and experience
- a notable step toward achieving your ultimate professional and personal goals

The Search

Several expressions describe the search process. One expression, "license to hunt," suggests that with certain credentials, you will find prospects available to you that might not be available to others without those credentials. For example, some jobs require a bachelor's or associate's degree as an absolute cutoff for consideration. Others may expect certain professional certifications or licenses to be held by their serious candidates, such as Certified Network Administrator or licensed physical therapist. In any case, some aspects of your background, experience, credentialing, or special talents will allow you into different ranges of jobs.

Where one company might be predisposed to hire people from certain colleges, others may offer a preference to minorities or to handicapped individuals. Though there are still subtle, but detectable, cases of conscious bias—either for or against certain individuals or groups—most large companies these days work very hard to preserve fair hiring practices, both in policy and action.

Many of the best jobs never show up in ads or on recruiters' desks; they are only discovered through word of mouth. Notes Blair Boyer, career counselor, "Most estimates I have seen indicate that the hidden job market (those that don't show up in ads) comprises approximately 85 percent of available positions." In special cases, a person who can give you an "in" to a company may offer freer access to potential positions than you might have found without it.

Your own search strategy should identify and target jobs that will be potential assets in your journey toward your life goals. Several different approaches to the job search are described below, but these are primarily approaches to finding suitable job openings or opportunities. Later in the chapter, guidelines for evaluating a job to determine whether it would be a good fit are discussed. The most common sources of job leads are:

- college career placement offices
- alumni
- ads in the newspaper
- ads in industry periodicals
- Internet postings
- career counselors or recruiters
- prospecting—networking, unsolicited approaches, company Web sites

Though each of these sources has led to many successful career fits, a combination of several usually ends up being the most effective.

College Placement Offices

Of course, the individual anticipating graduation from any educational program should consult the career services department of the college or institute, but a surprising number do not. Companies recruit from colleges; thus, the contacts your career services counselors have are some you cannot obtain other places. Career fairs hosted by your school or by a professional organization at your school may result in immediate offers. In addition, if there is a particular company you are interested in, a call from the placement representative of your school might be received more graciously than your own effort.

Many schools at the postsecondary level also offer career testing that allows you to discover the best places to direct your skill and operational style—job types you may not have thought about. When companies do large layoffs, many of them offer these same types of services, called *outplacement assistance*. Leads, testing, counseling and, sometimes, mock interviews for practice, as well as resume and clerical support, are all available at college placement offices. You can consult career offices other than your own college, particularly if you are trying to relocate. Many offer services to the public or to graduates from other colleges (e.g., colleges that are members of NACE often have reciprocal agreements to assist students from other NACE colleges).

Alumni

There is no better person on the inside of a company you might want to pursue than a graduate of your school. If the company likes the graduate's performance, they may favor applicants from the same school. If you do not know any alumni, the alumni office may have directories to consult, or career services coordinators can contact others they have placed. Active involvement in alumni groups and functions may continue to provide you contacts beyond your first job as well.

An extension of the alumni contact is the professional or service organization. Many of these have college or other educational branches. If you have participated in one of them, then you will be most welcome to move into the full-blown organization once you have left school. Because many of these organizations are national, such as IEEE or Alpha Phi Omega, members could be of assistance in helping you find your way into companies in cities across the country.

Ads in Newspapers

Many of these ads are looking for people with specified experience. However, ads can also give you a contact name or address for a future search effort. Ads give you some perspective on where the most job openings are, which companies are hiring, and the qualifications for particular positions. The latter information will help you clarify your goal-related activities. Companies that have strong training programs may look for applicants through newspaper ads. In addition, ads requesting two to three years of experience might be worth a follow up. Often someone may be promoted internally, making an entry-level position available.

In general, though, ads are not a good source for an entry-level position, except in areas where skilled professionals are scarce.

Ads in Industry Periodicals

Sadly, many graduates, even in specialized fields, are not familiar with the journals and periodicals of their chosen industry. Libraries have many of these, but the very best for their job-lead potential are likely to be those highly specialized insider publications (or Web sites) that only people in the industry subscribe to. These have the industry gossip: who's being bought, who's just gotten a big contract, who's partnering with whom on a new product or service, what trends the industry sees coming, all information pertinent to your job search.

Some have ads for job openings as well. Just be certain you have a recent version; check the date. If you do not know anyone who could give you one of these publications, you might check the library or pick up copies at trade shows.

Philip had an interview that was set up by his college placement office with a company in his field. The position was not his first choice, but he had agreed to go for the prac-

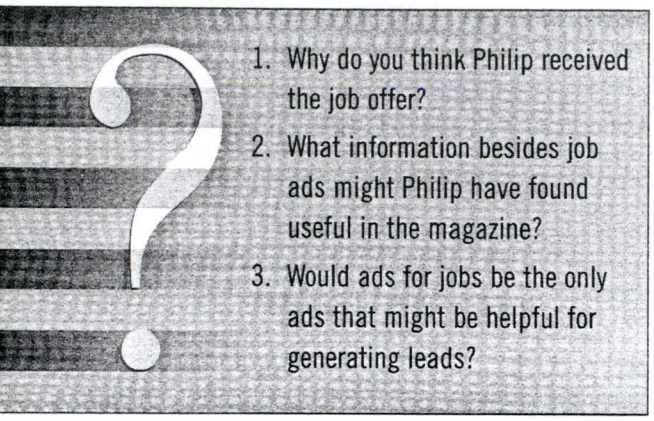

1. Why do you think Philip received the job offer?
2. What information besides job ads might Philip have found useful in the magazine?
3. Would ads for jobs be the only ads that might be helpful for generating leads?

tice. While he was waiting for his interview (he was put off for over an hour), he looked through the magazines on the table in front of him. None of the titles were familiar to him, but they seemed to be talking about products and issues in the industry. After reading for some minutes, he ran across an article on the company he was visiting. During the interview, he referred to information about the company that he had gathered while reading. When he left, he asked the receptionist if he could take an issue that was a few months old with him. Two days later, the company he interviewed with called him with a job offer. He turned it down because he was actively pursuing a company he had read about in an ad from the magazine for a job that was exactly what he was seeking.

Internet Postings

Certain Internet sites allow you to broadcast your resume in a *shotgun* fashion (no particular target, just thrown out onto a cyber bulletin board) with hopes that someone will be looking for just your qualifications. However, because of the availability of the Internet, the response rate is dropping on these types of sites. The best sources are those sites where you can apply directly to a company or link to a company's Web site and apply there.

Internet postings can be effective when you post on (or respond to ads on) sites dedicated to recent graduates or to entry-level applicants. You are assured in these cases that the company is looking for someone with your kind of potential and may be less concerned with a long track record. Many companies welcome fresh knowledge as well as the lower salaries they pay entry-level employees. It is not uncommon for a company that is doing layoffs also to be hiring new people for both of these reasons.

If you have experience, there are specialized sites and hard-copy publications where you can place your resume or position-wanted ad. Some are very discreet and protect you if you are searching for a new position while still employed. Be certain to look for the site's statement regarding its privacy policy.

Career Counselors or Recruiters

These professionals make their living by receiving a percentage of the starting salary for the employees they locate and bring to a company. Sometimes, the seeking company pays the fee to gain the convenience of not having to screen hundreds of resumes to find a fit. Other times, the placement person receives a fee from you—either a percentage of salary or a flat fee. Some just do resume preparation; others do employment testing, while still others place you on their Web sites or in their national databases; much like the multiple-listing services realtors use.

Two cautions: First, these people do not necessarily welcome entry-level applicants, and if they agree to take you on, they may put your search on the back burner. Second, some require an up-front fee with no guarantee of a placement. Be wary of these two scenarios. Read thoroughly before you sign anything to make sure you understand the fees involved, what you are agreeing to, and if there is any refund if the job does not work out.

Prospecting

The term *prospecting* is used because you are looking for "gold" anywhere you think you can possibly find it. It includes everything from targeting companies whose products you like and calling them *cold* (making unsolicited contacts for potential job openings) to telling everyone you meet that you are looking and what you are looking for. Job leads are everywhere! You may meet someone on the commuter train who works in the building of a company that interests you or in a city to which you are trying to locate. Standing in line at the car tag office or waiting for an oil change, you could begin a conversation with someone and find out the name of a contact or a networking group. People you know are the easiest, but not always the best, for finding leads in your field.

TRANSITION TIP   *Jasyn Banks, Inside Sales*

You have to see everyone as a potential job lead. Go places where there are people who are doing what you want to be doing. Introduce yourself to as many people as you can. Whenever you attend a professional function or even a club meeting, see how much you can learn about the people in the room. If you're hungry enough for the job you want, you'll overcome the fear of meeting people. Oh, and my advice to anyone for networking or for opportunities to get around the right people—learn to play golf. Executives and decision makers play golf; to get access to these people, do what they do.

Networking groups are formed for the purpose of exchanging leads and help. They can be taxing because every time you go, you feel like you have an objective of securing someone's assistance. The difficulty is that others in the room are doing the same thing. Get the host or hostess of the particular gathering to introduce you to the people you should meet—that is much quicker than casting about all night by yourself and much less frustrating. Some networking groups are on the Internet now, and you do not even have to go to meetings except for on-line chats.

Another source of leads from prospecting is your own curiosity. If you like a particular product, go the company's Web site, learn more about the product and how it is made, who the company partners with, how big the company is, and where the branch offices are. Investor Relations is another good section of the company (or their Web site) from which to obtain information. A letter or phone call from a knowledgeable person inquiring about joining a company because of a specific interest is better received than the general, unsolicited mailing. If you are interested in a technical position, call or e-mail someone in the engineering or production departments and ask for information or maybe even help.

In some companies, a salesperson is a good way in because salespeople are generally extroverts and like to talk to people. Many people enjoy talking about their jobs too. Questions such as, "What attracted you to this company?" or "What do you like best about what you do?" will often elicit lengthy answers. Trade show booths, especially when things are slow, are great places to meet people on the "inside" of the companies you would like to pursue. It is worth the money to find a large trade show in your field and make arrangements to attend. Solid job leads (and maybe actual offers) could be the reward; at the least you will meet many people who do what you aspire to do for a living, an important part of a career plan.

Preparation

Two types of preparation will best place you where you want to be: general and job specific.

1. General preparation involves building several alternate resumes that can be adjusted for a specific focus as needed, researching the industry and companies that interest you, asking your references for permission to list them, selecting and purchasing an interview wardrobe (one conservative, suit-like; one carefully tailored, business casual), choosing and establishing your professional look, having copies made as needed, creating a digital version of your resume, finding a computer with Internet access (or access

to one for an e-mail address), and getting a dependable phone answering system (not friend or family members).

2. Specific preparation involves a customized resume for a particular job interview, a list of job requirements matched with your qualifications and talents, a wealth of information about the company and its products and competitors, two or three leading questions you can ask the interviewer about the company or about her own experience with the company, affirmations and positive phrases to say to yourself on the way to the interview or a motivational tape to play, and a visualization of a successful interview.

If you need to develop the skills for introductions, answering difficult questions, taking tests, or the appropriate behavior in business and social gatherings, additional instruction or practice may be required. You should have enough understanding of the jobs in your field and a clear picture of how you fit into the position (and company) you are pursuing that you naturally exude that quiet confidence that wins the vote of the interviewer. As you begin your preparation, take a quick look at what you have. The resume is probably the first exercise you should consider as you begin to take a serious step toward that career.

Building a Resume

One instrumental tool in getting the job that starts you on your desired career path is the well-crafted resume. In this chapter, you will find several suggested formats. Each has successfully gotten job seekers to the interview stage, but you will need some guidelines to help you select the format best suited for your situation. A resume is laid out in sections. These sections elicit different levels of attention from the reader and must be strategically placed to achieve the most impact. If your resume is the commercial for the product (you), then it must be constructed with the goal of getting your reader to tune into what you have to offer. Each section of the resume must hold the potential employer's interest and pull him into the next section.

At the most basic level, you should have an attractive visual effect. Cheap paper and a type font that looks like an old dot-matrix printer does not impress anyone. If you do not do word processing, you will have to pay or ask someone to dress up the appearance for you. So many people today have access to desktop publishing and other word processing systems that employers expect a classy look. Your resume will be passed over and not even read if it looks hastily done or poorly presented. There is no need to get too fancy unless you are applying for a job in art or advertising. Neat and well-organized resumes do have an advantage.

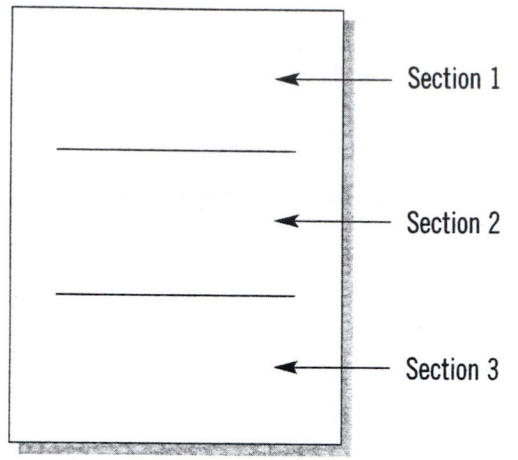

Section 1

Section 2

Section 3

The page itself should be well laid out, each section visually balanced; provide enough information to be meaningful, but do not overload the page with type. Also, as an employer scans the page, each section must hold her interest, both in relevant content and visual appeal. If you break the page down visually, into sections, each section should engage the reader.

Section 1

Section 1 contains **contact information** and your professional "introduction." Be certain that all contact information is current and correct. Also, be sure that whoever answers the phone you have listed or who records the phone message understands the need for appropriate conduct. A cutesy message may delight your friends, but an employer may not take you seriously.

Ann Allyson
406 Chadburn Ferry Road
Wierton, WV 57930
(406) 555-0095
annallyson@earthlink.net

If you provide an e-mail address in the heading be sure that it is professional sounding (no "surferguy@yahoo.com). Consider establishing an address to use just for your job search.

If the decision maker is over 40, he or she may require glasses to read small print. The resume in 12-point type that is easier to read without glasses could very well be picked up, with others skipped over. Of course, 14-point type would be overdone. Your contact information, especially, should be easy to read at a glance.

Also in Section 1 is the **professional capabilities** statement—what is great about you in 30 words or less. This is where you match who and what you are professionally with the specific job needs of a prospective employer. At one time, job seekers would include a "Job Objective" section. But job objectives often are too general to be helpful to a potential employer or too specific to keep doors open for the job seeker. You should know enough about the needs of a prospective job—at least about the job category—to be able to list your strengths that would qualify you for the job. These could be customized for various positions, thanks to the convenience of word processing.

Professional Capabilities: Problem solving and strong communication skills, including presentations, demonstrated in a customer-oriented environment. Familiar with database management software and fluent in Internet research.

This example might be a good statement of qualifications for a sales position. For a more technical position, a help desk, for example, you might arrange the information differently. Remember, in this section you should represent yourself as you want the employer in your chosen area to view you. If you have a unique or specialized skill or experience, or even professional certifications, placing relevant ones here would be helpful.

Professional Capabilities: Registered nurse with internship in critical care and four years' experience with a hospice organization. Can work independently in hospital or clinic setting. Familiar with computerized patient record management systems.

Section 2

By this point, the reader probably has some interest if the position needs fit and will read further for more detail. If there is no fit, then she is not likely to search your resume for something of value. She may retain or pass on your resume if she is familiar with other job needs of the company. Rarely does a reader look at a very general professional capabilities section and try to think of a place to use your skills. You must word that section to fit jobs you think are available. The same is true in the middle section of your resume, where you list all of the things you have done or know how to do.

For older, more experienced job seekers, a functional approach, describing what you have accomplished and how long you have been gaining skill in a particular line of work, might be best. List your accomplishments as line items.

Format A

Employment Highlights *[Some name this section "Employment Profile"]*

- Implemented client-server software system for 12-station local area network.
- Supported software programs as technical service representative for national accounts for major accounting software company.
- Demonstrated and conducted training on Excel in customer settings.

For less experienced people, or those embarking on a new career with mostly education to recommend them, a *managed page* approach is best. When people scan a resume, they generally lose concentration about two-thirds of the way down the page and are thinking about turning the page instead of focusing on what they are reading. In addition, those with little work history related to the job they are seeking seldom can impress a potential employer with their wealth of experience. So, the strategy is to direct the eye of the reader to those elements of your qualifications that fit the sought-after job.

This strategy includes putting achievements in school (recent achievements, not years before), honors in the military or civic and professional organizations, and course work during college, or grade point average high on the page. In addition, this strategy uses a "skills section" that shows all of the many talents and skills you have in a way that will impress the reader. Be certain not to overlook skills of a professional nature, though not necessarily in the specific field. For example, illustrating programs for the local theater group is graphics experience; it does not matter whether you were paid. Internships can also offer field-related skills, including projects completed in teams, and should be listed.

Format B

Education: Associate of Applied Science Degree

Graduation: June 2002 Major: Health Administration

Groves Community College

GPA: 3.8 out of 4.0

Accomplishments: Supported self 100 percent through school, member of National Honor Fraternity, Vice President of Toastmasters

Skills:

SOFTWARE	HARDWARE	PROFESSIONAL
Excel	Pentium III	Customer Service
MS Word	LCD (for presentations)	Speaking/Presentations
PowerPoint	Some MacIntosh	Technical writing (documentation)

A business-oriented resume plays up the managerial potential of certain skills or experience you may have. In this one, you give the skill, then where you acquired it.

Skills:

Project Management—managed relocation of telecommunication system to new facility.

Customer Support—maintained customer records and performed trouble call follow-ups in multimillion dollar business.

Budgeting—directed resources secured by fund-raising to programs in nonprofit organization.

Personnel—performed needs assessment, made recommendations, and secured services for training program in 100-employee company.

Technical—adept at business and market research on the Internet, Excel, MS Word, Adobe Acrobat; working knowledge of Visual Basic and client management system.

By this point, the reader is beginning to pay less attention to a line by line scrutiny of your resume. But, if he has seen something desirable, then there will be motivation to continue through your work history. Remember, this format is used when you have little or no actual work experience in the field for which you are applying. You are pulling desirable and employable features about yourself from other jobs, a prior career, or internships into the most visible portions of the resume, "putting your best foot forward" so to speak. Major school or volunteer projects can give you valuable skills and experience. Some companies are even beginning to look for community service experience in the well-rounded candidate.

Look at the following example and note the technical and nontechnical expertise required.

Rayana had just graduated from an associate's degree program in accounting from a community college. Her friend suggested she apply for a temporary job with the Internal Revenue Service for experience. She had never had a job in accounting, only her classes and labs. Just to quiet her friend, she read the description of the position.

Customer service representative—Internal Revenue Service

Expertise required: accounting, superior interpersonal and communication skills, problem solving in complex customer situations, ability to multitask, organization.

Because she had worked in customer returns at Sears since high school and had been given service awards twice, she realized that what was required for the IRS job was similar to her experience. Rayana put in her application, was called in for an interview, and was hired within two weeks.

Another format for this section of the resume is the classic "Work History" section. In this, you list your past jobs chronologically—from most recent to most distant. If you have worked only a few years, you might do well to use the preceding format and add a work history section afterward. You might have had a series of part-time jobs while in school, so your history might look erratic or undefined. If this is the case, you might want to sum up this time by saying, "Part-time jobs while supporting self through college included: fast food, teaching assistant, and retail clerk." Just as you try to put the strongest selling points highest on the page, try to put the least important information (such as dates of employment) on the right hand side of the page. This de-emphasizes them. (We read top to bottom and left to right.)

If you have gaps in your work history from layoffs, illness, or other reasons, the functional resume, Format A, is the best to sell your strengths before you have to explain why you were not employed for intervals of time. A general-format chronological work history follows:

Format C

Employment History:

April 2000–Present: Part-time jobs during college including Web page maintenance and database management.

March 1997–2000: Project Supervisor, Pacific Bell, Sacramento, California.

Directed installation of fiber-optic cable in two-county area. Brought two crews to deadline within budget.

June 1996–1997: Fiber-optic Cable Installer, Pacific Bell, Sacramento, California.

Worked up to crew chief in the first six months on job.

Prior to June 1996: Worked weekends and summers at sports park.

Section 3

This section can include whatever you deem desirable, whether it is professional organizations or achievements, awards, civic clubs, hobbies, or a willingness to travel or relocate. Every resume should have a "References" section, it seems, but most sources recommend that you simply say "References available upon request." Of course, you will have people in mind who have already agreed to say positive things about you. It is important to get the permission of those you submit as references. Do not press people into agreeing. If they turn you down, it is probably because they do not feel they know you well enough to answer questions from a potential employer.

This is by no means a definitive discussion of how to produce a winning resume. There are books and whole classes on the topic, but this discussion will get you started. (Note: www.myjobsearch.com and www.careerperfect.com have sample resumes for your reference.)

Remember that a resume is an ad for you as a product. You receive about 60 seconds of your potential customer's attention in the reading of your resume. Use strategy to put the good information about you in the most noticeable place. Allow each section to appear uncrowded and it will draw the eye of the reader.

You should show your resume to many people and get input. However, the resume has to sell *you*, so you have to decide what goes on there in the end. If the resume is "professionally" done (by a resume service), it is your responsibility to make sure it honestly represents you. And you should always proofread, even if a service has prepared it for you.

Keep in mind also what you have learned in this book. A resume is built to help you eventually command the job that will bring you joy. It is a document of the choices you have made on your career path and an introduction to the professional you wish to be.

A prospective employer generally scrutinizes a resume on four levels:

- *Level 1: Physical appearance*—notes at a glance type of paper, page layout, type fonts, clarity.
- *Level 2: Specifics scan*—looks for buzzwords, education cutoffs, and particular technical or customer skills.

(*Note:* These first two levels of scrutiny are generally completed in less than 30 seconds.)

- *Level 3: Initial approval*—likes qualifications and skills and may turn to second page or read work history or accomplishments area more closely.
- *Level 4: Final approval*—calls you in for an interview.

Interviewing

Many sources offer many approaches to succeeding in an interview: analysis of personality types, scrutiny of interviewer's clothes, practice with smooth answers to expected interview questions, and on and on. You are encouraged to check out the many Internet sources that offer hints on interviewing. (One definitive site is ww1.joboptions.com/careertools. This site even offers private question and answer sessions.) Also, talk to people who have recently interviewed successfully and secured a new job. Here, we will offer a few "nuts and bolts" to interviewing, along with some tricks.

Guideline 1

The person who interviews you may or may not be a professional interviewer.

The professional. This person understands the behavioral, legal, and financial implications of interviewing. She will not likely ask you any illegal questions, such as how old you are, if you are married, or whether you have disabilities. The professional interviewer will probably look at a variety of your qualifications including your personality type, your manner—how you conduct yourself—your overall approach to work, and your ability to work under pressure, in addition to the "technical" skills you have.

If a professional interviewer "likes" you because of an impression or "gut feel," it is likely because of his experience in the task of hiring. Many successful hires lead an interviewer to be able to recognize pretty quickly what a desirable candidate for his client or company is like. This person is less likely to have a personal reaction to you than a less experienced interviewer might; you may not even be able to tell if you have made a good impression due to his practiced reserve. Professionals (especially contract recruiters) know that their livelihood depends on successfully matching employees with companies. Mistakes of match or fit are costly to everyone involved and they know this.

The nonprofessional. This might be a person who desperately needs someone to fill a painful gap in skill, knowledge, or experience, but may see the interview process as time consuming and potentially frustrating. Because of these conditions, she may make a quicker judgment of you based on fewer considerations. After a long resume-screening process, an interviewer may feel that all candidates called in are equally qualified—she is just looking for someone who fits in with the work group or someone she likes and feels comfortable with. The questions asked may seem random and undirected or sound like they came out of the same books you studied to prepare. When the exhausted interviewer (who may be uncomfortable meeting a lot of new people) finds one she likes, then in her mind the search may be over, regardless of who follows in the appointment schedule.

Guideline 2

Interview decisions are often made in the first minute of the interview (some sources say as little as 20 seconds). In education, this phenomenon is called the *halo effect:* a good initial impression will carry you through several possible mistakes. Conversely, though, this halo effect can tarnish the interview after a bad first impression. Even if your skills and qualifications are a good fit, you may not receive a job offer. This is why grooming, carriage, manner, and introduction are so critical.

Guideline 3

The classic interview "uniform," the dark suit, may or may not be the most appropriate. Many companies are using a "business casual" dress code. You should try to find out what clothing is expected because part of making a positive first impression is to look as much as possible like the people who already work there. If you are working with a recruiter or career counselor, follow that person's guidance. If not, try calling someone in the office of the company you are pursuing and ask politely what the expected dress for an interview might be.

> "I have an interview there tomorrow, and I know companies have different dress codes. Can you tell me what might be the most appropriate to wear? I would really like to work there and want to make the best impression I can."

Another way to handle this is to visit the company (always a good idea so you can be sure you know how to get there) and ask if you can go to the breakroom for a snack or soft drink. On the way there, observe the employees to see how they dress and wear their hair. Though you will probably be expected to appear more conservative than some you might see, you will at least have some idea of the general style.

Says one placement professional, however, "I believe that most employers still say that interviewing is a game of sorts and the applicant needs to play by the rules. I also think that it depends on the position being interviewed for—if the position is a professional one (requiring a degree for example), then a suit is the best choice. This is versus a warehouse loading position where business casual in the interview is okay. Also note that how you dress for the interview does not necessarily correlate to how you dress on the job or how the interviewer is dressed. (Goes back to the game . . . you are expected to put your best foot forward)" (Boyer, 2001).

Women candidates might want to go to the suit department of a department store or specialty store and get advice.

Guideline 4

Your interview may not be in person. The phone interview is becoming more and more common as the logistics of interviewing candidates all over the country become more difficult. Phone interviews are particularly difficult for those who are used to making a good impression by watching the reaction of the other person throughout the conversation. Not being able to see the reaction of the person conducting the interview can leave you feeling anxious and tentative. Some larger companies have video-conferencing facilities, but that experience is not always a great deal better, due to the slight delay in the transmission.

Do as much as you can to encourage an in-person interview, even offering to meet someone at the airport on a layover. However, some people just do not want to take time for every candidate and might interview you from the car or airplane. Looking on the positive side, the phone does offer an exchange where you can ask questions and clarify points. Also, you can glean some reactions from the voice. Thankfully, sometimes a phone interview is only a *rubber stamp*, where the manager just wants to chat with the person his staff has already chosen. Either way, a relaxed, confident, and even manner is at least as important as the words you offer.

Look in a mirror while you talk and make sure you smile. A smiling person sounds different on the phone. Although you have the option of dressing casually because you are on the phone, if you dress as if you were going to the interview, it can help to put you in that frame of mind. It is very easy to get too comfortable on a phone. Also, you may want to stand up—it helps to project your voice. Do not eat, drink, or smoke while on a phone interview. Avoid the sounds of TV, radio, or kids in the background.

To stay focused have a notepad by the phone to write down notes. These should include:

- the main idea of the question just asked (keeps you from straying off the point)
- notes on the company or position (details you can review after the call)
- any names mentioned
- questions about the company
- the procedure for the next level of decision

Guideline 5

The interview may or may not be for a real position. Sometimes, companies talk to potential candidates to see what is "out there" in the way of skills or availability. This happens rarely to the entry-level person, but if it does, it is an opportunity to establish your value, to make the company understand that you are an asset that someone should find a place for. This kind of interview also may occur when a contact has gotten you in to a company to see someone who can make hiring decisions (or at least recommendations), commonly called the "foot in the door."

For this type of interview, do a great deal of preparation on the company and its products, directions, and values (often available in the financial statement or on the Internet)—this will make you appear to be keenly interested in the company's welfare. Additionally, if you can show what a match you are for the company, then the lack of a clearly defined position may not be such a hindrance to your aspiration.

Additional Guidelines

1. Manner. Your professionalism, reliability, poise, and intelligence may be gleaned from your manner and may be a large part of your evaluation. The elements that go into manner include: punctuality, tone of voice, diction, grammar, discretion and judgment (knowing what not to talk about), walk, handshake, facial expression, and social graces.

2. Punctuality. Always arrive early enough to locate a parking space and the office; do not check in with the receptionist until a few minutes before your appointment time.

3. Tone of voice. Nervous people speak in strained and flat tones. Relaxation of the throat muscles through yawns or voice warm-ups can help. Singing on the way to the interview (in the car, not in the building) is an excellent voice relaxer. Volume should be conversational, but watch for signs of the interviewer being overwhelmed or having difficulty understanding.

4. Diction and grammar. No one expects perfection in this area, but the ability to speak clearly, so that people from all parts of the country can understand you, is an important part of your qualifications. Poor grammar is often taken as a sign of a weak education or a lack of attention to polishing your manner. Strong regional accents and the incorrect use of verb forms are the most notable of these considerations. Adolescent phrases, such as "like" and "awesome," may make the interviewer see you as immature.

5. Discretion and judgment. Being too personal or discussing tasteless subjects can make a terrible impression, even when the conversation has turned casual and may even be taking place in a bar. Talking negatively about past jobs or other interviews is also considered inappropriate. If you have any doubt as to the suitability of any topic, stay away from it. You are being interviewed for a job, no matter how relaxed the situation is, and are expected to speak with integrity and candor. Lying and faking knowledge also fall in the category of things to avoid. Finally, if alcohol is offered over an interview lunch or dinner, just say no. You cannot afford to be impaired, even a little.

6. Walk. Striding forward confidently, especially when the interviewer is holding open a door or walking with you around the building, denotes assuredness with your ability to do the job. The interviewer should not have to wait for you to gather up things in order to walk in—be ready. It is possible to walk confidently, even when you do not feel that way; pick up your speed a little and you will move better.

7. Handshake. Practice, practice, practice. In Western culture, we often size up a person by the handshake. If you are from a culture that avoids this kind of contact or that believes a softer handshake is a sign of respect, remember that the expectation is a firm grasp of the whole hand. Eye contact is expected with the handshake as well. This is the moment you connect with the interviewer, if only for a second. An excellent rapport may grow out of a good handshake. Damp hands from nervousness may be tolerated in someone young or inexperienced, but try to dry your hands just prior to the greeting.

8. Facial expression. Relaxed muscles around the eyes and cheeks suggest a calm demeanor and a genuine interest. Note how your face feels when a song that evokes a pleasant memory comes on the radio; that is a good approximation.

9. Dress. If you do wear a suit, and you are a man, have the shirt starched and use a silk tie (synthetics do not tie as well). Though the classic charcoal or navy works in many cases, try to use a variation that works well for you. Image consultants can tell you the colors that best compliment you to give you that very "together" look. Also, make-up counters at many department stores will do a color consultation for free. When you wear colors that are right for you, you are more likely to elicit a positive response to your appearance; if you do not coordinate colors and shades, the interviewer may notice the clothes, but not remember you as "looking good."

Be certain that what you wear fits. Something too tight or obviously too large makes you look like you have bad judgment not only about your appearance, but also about how to behave appropriately in business situations. If your budget is tight, remember to check out consignment shops. The more upscale ones may have clothing that is still very much up to date and in good condition.

For both genders, minimal jewelry and cologne would be the guideline, and do not forget neatly trimmed fingernails. Women, keep earrings to quarter size or smaller; men, an earring is still considered somewhat unprofessional, at least for the interview.

10. Questions. Lists of sample interview questions are available many places for you to look over to prepare. Obviously coached and memorized answers will not make a good impression; however, you should certainly have already thought out some reasonable responses to standard questions, such as "Tell me about yourself" and "Why are you interested in a job with our company?" Amazingly, some candidates cannot adequately verbalize an answer to "How did you choose your particular field?" Trying to bluff your way through questions you do not know the answers to only makes you look more foolish than not knowing the answer and admitting it.

TRANSITION TIP   *B.D., Special Projects Supervisor*

Don't be afraid if you are a "tough case." I was older than most of the candidates as well as having a history of a felony conviction and alcoholism in earlier years. My prior employment background was in the arts, and I was applying for jobs in my new degree area, engineering. I also had been told that I had the kind of personality that just naturally rubbed some people the wrong way. But a professor agreed to coach me on the interpersonal stuff, and another of my profs called someone he knew at a large company that had hired many graduates of my college over the years with very good results. What really helped, though, was understanding very clearly what I had to offer—what skills and talent transferred from my prior arts career experience, and what my personality type was particularly suited for. I've found my niche here in a very short time and am doing well, with a couple of promotions already. My advice? Know what you bring to the job, get cool with who you are, and be able to explain what is really good about you. Finally, realize that a lot of people out there can, and are willing to, help you.

11. Social graces. This area is often overlooked by candidates preparing for an interview. Some companies may hold a reception for applicants to meet employees or may take an applicant out to dinner. This time is very much part of the interview because the hiring company wants to be sure an employee knows how to behave in polite company, especially in the company of a customer. If the interview moves to food, be sure you demonstrate table manners that reflect professional courtesy.

There is no specific do or don't regarding what to eat, but if you have the freedom to order, get something fairly small (so you don't have to spend all your time eating to get through the amount of food) and not too messy; you are there to talk. Bowtie pasta, for example, is easier to eat gracefully than linguini. If the company is large, there is a possibility that you might be taken to a really nice restaurant. A little research on foods and wines as part of your general interview preparation is not a bad idea. You really ought to know what calamari is before someone orders it for you. (Grocery stores are excellent for learning the names of things, as are cookbooks.)

What to say and what not to say at a business social gathering are important also. Never speak disrespectfully of anyone, even political figures. Remain positive in all that you say, and if you are in a group, monitor the volume of your voice. When you are nervous, you may tend to talk more loudly or more softly than usual. Avoid personal topics, like health and appearance, and if someone takes issue with a point you make, concede: "You have a point there. I'll have to think about that." Make sure you find out who the important people are in the room and introduce yourself.

Salary Expectations

One common complaint from employers is that candidates have unrealistic expectations about salary: they either have no idea about the "going rate" for their own industry or they have an inflated (and unsubstantiated) view of their own worth. A candidate who has done too little homework about the industry or about the type of position shows a distinct lack of initiative and seriousness about the process. An excellent source of salary expectations and hiring and salary trends is the National Association of Colleges and Employers (NACE) Web site, www.naceweb.org. Some highlights are included in Table 13.1.

Data for liberal arts and social sciences were not listed in this particular report (NACE, February 6, 2001). The site noted an increase in sales positions over information technology positions for the first time in several years.

TABLE 13.1	Average starting salaries for some professional positions.	
	AVERAGE STARTING SALARY	**PERCENT + OR −**
Accounting	$38,739	3.8%+
Business Administration	$36,314	1.3%+
Economics/Finance	$40,297	5.7%+
MIS	$44,879	4.7%+
Computer Engineering (includes both software and hardware)	$53,443	14.3%+
Civil Engineering	$39,852	9.2%+
Electrical Engineering	$50,850	6.6%+
Mechanical Engineering	$48,340	5.8%+
Computer Science	$51,581	5.9%+
Information Science	$44,251	1 %−

(Note: Communications companies hires received $47,583, which is 10.8% higher than last year.)

Data may be difficult to find for your particular field, but publications for industry or professional organizations will include some general figures, though you may find a great deal of discrepancy in the highest and lowest starting offers. Remember, averages are just that, averages; they take in the top and the bottom and include the prestigious schools as well as the small state colleges. Salary offers vary by region, size of company, capital constraints, and policy, and many other factors. Exceptions are found on both the high and low end. Just like a car, you are worth what someone is willing to pay to bring you on—no more, no less.

Occasionally, an employer will make a "lowball" offer (an offer lower than you would expect to receive). This could be for any of several reasons:

- strong feelings about probationary conservatism—to keep the risk low until your suitability is proven

- the company might want to see if you are willing to sacrifice and "invest" yourself in the company

- maybe you do not have exactly the skills they want, but they would like to bring you on with hopes that you will increase your value on your own initiative

Whether the reason is a budget crunch or simply seeing just how cheaply they can get their needs filled, you will have to make the decision whether the offer is good for you. Some considerations along this line include:

- future potential—for example, growth in a large company or significant additions to resume

- culture and conditions—the particular ambiance of the workplace or geographic location

- role in goal support—the degree to which the credentials gained from the duties or by association with a "name" company will contribute to your goal activity

- benefits trade-off—educational reimbursement, health plan, flexible hours, professional freedom, bonus potential, or company stock

- risk—the company is a startup in new technology that could flourish or flounder, company rumored to be up for sale or going public, highly competitive and volatile market, history of high turnover rate, or potential for family disruption due to transfer

Many of the considerations you have about your career in general will enter into the decisions you make about the right match between you and a particular job—money is just one consideration. If you are just coming out of college with student loans or if you are recovering from consumer debt or a job termination, you may not currently have the luxury of taking on an exciting, but perhaps risky, job. Relax. You will likely work for a minimum of 40 years. This gives you plenty of time to explore several job options.

TRANSITION SKILLS SUMMARY

Determine the job fit

Search all sources

Build a resume

Use interviewing skills

Understand salary expectations

GOAL SETTING

My self-nurturing goals to preserve my personal and relational health during a job search are:

_____

_____

_____

My self-advocacy goals to contribute to my career management in my job search efforts are:

_____

_____

_____

COACH'S CORNER

"Reading" an interviewer helps you determine your strategy during the interview. A lot of what the interviewer communicates may not be words. Preparation is essential, but eventually, it is just you and the interviewer. There are some ways to assess what is going on to determine how you are doing.

1. Determine the mission of the interviewer. If it is to screen 50 applicants, then the purpose is to get rid of the obviously unsuitable as quickly as possible for the next "real" round of selection. If you can find out in advance what the situation is, all the better, but if not, here are some signs that there is not much interest:

    a. When the interviewer sits down, he immediately (or almost immediately) looks down and writes or reads notes or questions. This could mean that the interviewer is inexperienced and needs the prompts on the paper for a guide, but it may suggest disinterest as well. A flat or monotone voice will signal lack of interest as will the interviewer's not making any attempt to show enthusiasm or to make you feel welcome.

    b. If the interviewer seems to try to "sell" the company and position to you, it may mean that you have made a good impression and would seem to be a good fit. It may also mean, however, that due to some element of the job (possibly undesirable location, travel, or salary), the interviewer knows it may be difficult to secure commitments from strong candidates who have many choices.

    c. An interested interviewer will lean slightly forward and may make eye contact intently, appearing to scrutinize you more closely. However, hands or feet fidgeting may show boredom or impatience.

2. If you establish rapport, the questions will seem more natural and relaxed. Be careful, however: that tone may be merely to see if you will let your guard down and say something inappropriate. The same applies if they leave the room. The interviewer may watch you from outside the room or have the receptionist look to see what you do during the time you are alone. You should pick up or take out company literature and have a question formulated for the interviewer about it when he returns.

(continued)

a. Some hints for establishing rapport: "I know that you have constraints on your time today, but I believe I have more than just a resume to offer. I am teachable and believe my background is just a launch point. I really look forward to expanding into being an asset to the company."

b. Note the room in which you are interviewing. Is it the person's office? If so, what is around? A family picture on the wall or desk might suggest a family orientation. Awards or artifacts can be conversation pieces. The more quickly you can move the conversation to the interviewer and his experience with the company, the more quickly you will have a "real" interview instead of a canned one.

3. If you sense that you have been dismissed in the interviewer's mind, you have a chance to "punt" anyway. You can stop the interview and say, "Look, I'm very new at this interviewing thing, but I have researched this company and its products and would really like to work here. What information can I give you that would show you what a good fit I would be?" It's a long shot, but sometimes that is just the thing to jog the interviewer out of a general boredom with so many candidates. Energy and interest are two very appealing qualities, and few interviewers would overlook either.

GENE MINOR, Interpersonal Communication Specialist and Executive Development Coach; e-mail: lgminor@mindspring.com.

Chapter 14

Lifelong Career Management

The following quotes reflect the experiences of a number of people who made significant changes in career direction after they had worked a year or so. In each case, they were hired for an entry-level position that their skill or knowledge qualified them for, and they used that position as a stepping-off point to explore other task areas and to develop new skills and experience. Experience is a great leveler: the clever and capable people bubble to the top fairly quickly, and the less capable eventually settle into their places as well. People who start out in the workforce with MBAs or engineering degrees may enter with a higher starting salary than someone with a bachelor's degree in business or technology, but the earning potential often evens out fairly soon, based on the talent and career management skill of the individual.

> "I didn't know what I wanted to do for the long term, just that I needed to build as much on my resume as I could as quickly as I could—computer skills, productivity records, etc. My first job was long and hard hours, and I didn't like it very much, but the experience looked great on paper when I was ready to change."

> "My first job was in a movie rental store. Imagine, me right out of college, a hotshot with a finance degree working in a video store. But I turned around three of the locations and made them profitable. With that record, I moved into a position

271

at a bank in the loan department. That experience introduced me to a client who was CEO of a high-tech startup, and she invited me to work there—no job description really, just carved out my own place. Now I'm doing business development and handling purchases and mergers—at 30."

"I got out of school and immediately went international. No husband, no geographic ties, and the excitement and money were all in the international arena. My systems degree opened the door, and now I direct overseas purchasing."

"Though my degree was in accounting, I worked an internship in a small company that let me try different things out. My interest grew in the area of marketing, and I focused my skill building there. I had a great mentor, so I really picked up the job quickly. That experience landed me in a major market research firm by my second year out of school—and last year I bought a house."

"My original focus was design. When I graduated, though, I was more interested in the business end and sought out a company that sold their designs through their own exclusive outlet stores. I was able to use my art background to get in, but I've since eased myself more into the marketing and strategic end of the business."

One interesting career management story is Michael's. He performed on Broadway for many years, got a degree from Harvard University, then decided he needed more "marketable" skills and sought a bachelor's degree in information systems from a technical institute. He is now the Chief Information Officer at the company where he works. Some people do a stint in the military for a career starter; some have a family first, then move into education and a profession later. For some, graduate school becomes a means to an end; for others, a sales position with a company or in a field that they want presents a threshold through which to pass into upper management.

Career Success

Arby's restaurants, in a survey of customers, reports that most people had their first real feeling of adulthood when they got their first full-time job. Perhaps, but *career success ultimately comes when you are being paid to do things you like and are good at, and when you are paid a wage that allows you to meet your needs.*

These statements are obviously subjective, contingent on a lot of individually defined words: "things you like and are good at," a "wage that meets your needs." How you define each of these concepts is truly an individual response. This chapter's objective is to explain how to reach that point, and perhaps more importantly for someone starting out, how you decide what that point is. As one career explorer phrased the idea, "I want to be able to work where I want, not just where they'll let me."

Understanding the keys to career management will give you:

- professional freedom
- autonomy with regard to your career future
- opportunities to contribute to the community
- time to involve yourself in meaningful relationships

In this book, you have up until now looked at how to make changes, how to solve problems, and how to maintain and enhance relationships. In the area of your career, the principles are the same, even though they may be applied somewhat differently. Whether you feel like you simply have not found the right place career-wise or are just looking at the beginning of your job path, the plain truth is: *You spend most of your waking hours pursuing work. If your job does not contribute to your life in a meaningful way, then you are missing a great source of personal fulfillment.* The following examples illustrate the point.

Jemal makes $26 per hour at the car manufacturing plant. He has been bored with the job for some time, but because he earns a reasonable wage and has great benefits, he feels he would be foolish to leave. Melaney is an insurance claims representative. Her job is to process client claim forms. Though she feels that she is paid well and is liked by the people she works with, she is not using her accounting degree and her job has no real value to her.

Both of these people are unhappy with their current career paths. Neither seems to know what to do about this struggle. Being unhappy, or maybe even just not being terribly fulfilled, often fails to motivate someone to make changes. Occasionally, it takes being laid off or fired to cause a close examination of the reason for a successful career choice.

Is the Job Fulfilling?

A lack of fulfillment or a failure in the form of the loss of a job are only two of the work or career problems you may face. Stress and a sense of struggle, of just not being in the right place, all of these are symptoms of a poor job and employee match. Work-related stresses invariably spill over into your personal life and can affect families and even harm personal health. So, problems with work life do not just stay at work.

Where are you now? As you have seen in prior chapters, *understanding your current situation is the beginning of a new direction.* Perhaps you have just decided to move to a new job, to a college education, to a different and more lucrative or satisfying career path. Wherever you are at this moment, you can use career management to guide you toward the most reward in your work. *Career management is a careful process of discovery and design—discovery of what you really want in a career, and design of the job that will bring you the most satisfaction.* The beginning point for designing a meaningful career path is to explore the attitudes you have developed over time about working. In Activity 14.1, you will be asked to begin a careful examination of what work and a career mean to you.

14.1 ACTIVITY

Answer the questions about your attitudes toward work. Where possible, give an example to explain your answer.

1. What impression do you have of your parents' work? Do they enjoy it? Do they think it is important? Is it just a way to earn money?

   _____

   _____

   _____

2. What experiences have you had with work? Do you work now? Have you worked in the past? Was it a positive experience? What is your strongest impression about it overall?

   _____

   _____

   _____

In a career, we often find the same cause-and-effect connections that we do in our personal relationships. For the most part, we receive what we expect. If we expect work to be a meaningful contribution to an overall satisfying life, then we make choices and direct our effort to that end. If our view of work is that it is a drudgery that has as its sole purpose to provide income and no more, then that is likely what we will settle for. The really seductive situation, though, is the one where we either expect or are receiving a substantial income, though we might not find the working conditions or job tasks ideal. Maybe the work is great, but the location requires a long commute or places you in a town or part of the country you do not care for.

TRANSITION TIP   *Jeff Tillilie, Buyer*

It's tough, the money or lifestyle choice thing. I have friends who jumped into the 70-hour weeks to either make a lot of money or to build a resume for a fast track up. For me, a smaller town situation suited better. I don't make as much, maybe don't have as much upward potential, but I like what I do and I'm living where I want to. Also, I chose a job where I could limit my time at work. My advice would be to have a life, a lifestyle you enjoy."

Dwayne was experiencing stress at work. He was absent more than other workers, and he seemed to have a lot of conflict with his coworkers as well as his boss. As a medical technician, he did testing and analysis tasks in a lab. Though competent at what he did, he showed no enthusiasm for his duties, and his behavior with friends and family was becoming more and more negative. One night he confessed to a coworker, "I want to work with patients more and be treated like a real professional." Eventually, it came out that Dwayne wanted to be a nurse, but with a disabled father to support, he didn't feel he could stop earning an income long enough to complete a nursing program.

Feeling trapped, Dwayne had become more and more frustrated with his job. He had become convinced that he had no choices about his current situation.

What about you? Maybe you have chosen a direction in your professional life and are now gathering credentials or skills that will prepare you to pursue that direction. Maybe, instead, you are embarking on a career with no clear direction as yet or understanding of what a satisfying career might be. Viewing your work as a set of choices that will lead you closer to happiness can give you a sense of freedom and joy.

1. What is Dwayne missing in his work every day?

2. Is his situation likely to get any better without some specific action on Dwayne's part?

3. How might his life be different if he were to redirect his career?

Does the Ideal Job Exist?

There may be a work area that will suit you but doesn't even exist yet. The world of work is changing all the time, so try to keep your thoughts open as you begin to choose your career path. Instead of a job name you think you should pursue, you might try to define a set of conditions you would ideally work within. Here is an example.

Not "I would like to be a lawyer"—instead, "I would like a job where I get to analyze problems and research the answers to those problems. I would also like to be respected for my ability to do my job well. I would like to be able to work with people (or alone). I would like to share ideas with other people in the same type of work."

This description could apply to many jobs in many different industries: real estate title searches, research assistant, marketing analyst, or troubleshooter. Because many of us do not know the names of jobs that we might enjoy, a great deal of self-assessment will help. (See the appendix for a list of self-assessment tools.) An ideal job for one person could be most unpleasant or stressful for another. The key is understanding enough about yourself and your professional needs to seek positions that allow you to capitalize on your strengths and preferences.

Chou went to college because his parents said he should and because he did not really have anything better planned. But as graduation neared, he still had no career direction. He was receiving a degree in business, but preferred to spend most of his time on his skateboard. When his parents expressed concern about this, he answered, "But Tony Hawk makes his living on a board and he's an old guy." Chou knew that only a few boarders are good enough to make a living at that sport, and he had never even entered a competition. Thus, his chances were pretty slim. He could not see himself in front of a computer all day or working construction full-time as he had one summer, yet he knew he had to move on to some type of job.

Lucy was a 15-year sales veteran with a major telecommunication company. She consistently got good bonuses for her sales and was highly respected at all levels in her company. The company downsized and began offering early retirement buyouts for people who wanted to leave the company voluntarily. Presented with the option of doing something different with her life at the company's expense, she took the opportunity to examine what she really wanted. Lucy is now nearing graduation as a physical therapist. She already knows, however, there are no openings at the hospital in her small town.

Both of these people have to do some serious self-assessment as well as career research—not just job research because that may become limited to just a survey of job titles and duties. Career research requires an investigation into what people actually do all day to carry out their jobs in different career areas. For example, a customer service person generally comes to the job enjoying contact with people, having good communication skills, and possessing the ability to learn about a company's products and procedures. Customer service representatives can be anything from retail clerks to software troubleshooters or client liaisons in many different and diverse fields. Both Chou and Lucy need to discover a career design framework to chart their career destination.

A Career Design Framework

Having a place to go for eight hours (or more) a day where you do things that make you feel valued is truly satisfying. *Meaningful work makes individuals feel motivated and enthusiastic every day.* Sometimes it takes a while to arrive at your career direction. After you figure out where you are going, though, the steps to get there are easier to discern.

A U.S. soldier was stationed overseas in a country that had quite a few American cars among its imports. One of the area residents had purchased an American-made van and sought out the serviceman for advice on operating it. Among other devices, buttons, and levers, the serviceman pointed out the cruise control, saying, "This manages the speed of the car and lets you relax while you drive." The resident thanked the serviceman and drove happily away. An hour later, heading down a long stretch of road, the driver set the cruise control and climbed into the back seat to have tea. He was discovered late that day with his vehicle spun out in the middle of a sandy plain. He was unhurt but covered with tea.

Stepping into the back seat while you put your professional life on cruise control is liable to cause more problems than just spilled tea. Applying a framework to your career design process will help you focus your efforts. To remember the steps in the process of developing your career plan, remember the word "ARRIVE."

- **A**ssess your skills, talents, traits, and interests
- **R**evive your curiosity
- **R**each for a goal
- **I**nvest in your journey
- **V**erify along the way
- **E**njoy your success

When you open up your thinking, you dramatically improve your potential for arriving at a satisfying career future. Just by expecting satisfaction from your career path, you are increasing your chances for achieving that satisfaction.

The first consideration in pursuing a career that will bring you fulfillment is to determine what work activities you like. Dr. Fred Ott of Georgia State University describes the process this way: Your primary goal in considering a career direction is joy. This idea, interestingly enough, is fairly new to our culture. For generations we have been told, "Get a good, steady job and stick with it until retirement." Nothing was ever said about enjoying that job.

Today, however, we are seeing so much stress-related illness that we are beginning to look to the workplace as a likely contributor. When your health is affected by emotional factors, then negative work environments can be a very real threat. Because you have begun the process of looking at your career path in terms of your own satisfaction, you will likely find problems that you have to deal with. Many of you may have already started this and are now in a new job, or in a college or a training program to make changes.

Assess Skills, Talents, Traits, and Interests

Throughout this book so far, you have been examining the elements that make up the package that is you. In addition to this examination process, you have been adding life-management skills. During your educational process and in the jobs you have had up to now, you also have established a repertoire of specific skills for your industry. If you have attended a career or technical college or training program, defining your job-related skills may be easier than if your education was in a broader university because of the focused curriculum at career-oriented schools. However, cataloging what you bring to the needs of the world of business is necessary for mapping out your journey.

Skills

Assessing your skills should include listing everything you know how to do: equipment you can operate, hardware, software, and interpersonal skills, such as customer service, sales, or training. Skills are sets of knowledge you acquire through experience or training that can be demonstrated in some observable or measurable way.

You must be very careful and objective in this aspect of your assessment. Note the comments by an agency whose job it is to assess and place contract workers in a specific field.

"People come to us right out of school, and we ask them to rate their skill levels in the various software packages used in this field. Most rate their knowledge as a 9, but upon testing, we find they rate a 4 or 5 at best. What happens is that they become very knowledgeable in one or two areas of the software, but have no exposure at all to other capabilities that our clients require" (Sherra Bell, Industry Resources Recruiter).

At job search time, you will be expected to substantiate your claim of a skill either by demonstration or by examples of jobs or training you have had. For this part of the process, though, you are taking an initial look at what you have to offer.

Talent

Assessing your talents may require some thinking outside your assumptions of what an industry might need for a particular job. Talents are abilities you are born with and may have enhanced through training, but not necessarily. Performance in many areas can be enhanced by skill training, but this section addresses those areas that an individual has a natural capacity for. Math aptitude, verbal ability, language acquisition, the talent of being able to read people and situations, creativity, music, visual–spatial awareness, fine motor skills, organization, simultaneous multitasking (not experiencing stress from a highly unstructured and busy environment—such as advertising), and written expression.

Many companies and specialists test for these talents and may uncover some you are not aware of simply because you have not been in a position to use them, such as a language acquisition ability. Even without elaborate testing, you already know some things just come easy to you. Those areas are probably where you have talent. As intelligent beings, we can learn to do just about anything. Our talent areas give us an edge.

Traits

Traits are those aspects of our character or operating style that we need to examine carefully. If they are not in line with the expectations of the workplace, immediate action toward correcting discrepancies is in order. Traits can describe our personal or professional self. Punctuality, dependability, self-discipline, persistence, affability, moodiness, energy level, distractibility, ethical orientation, and values; all of these are traits that you have to consider in your assessment. If you are punctual, dependable, and persistent, and have many examples of your past behavior to attest to these traits, then they should be part of your self-description. If, however, your energy level is low or you are moody, you need to take these traits into account when you consider work environments and activity or stress levels.

Performance traits are behaviors and, as such, lend themselves to changes in the pattern. If your value system dictates or allows certain behaviors (e.g., smoking) that potential employers would not find desirable, you might want to examine that value system. If you have not been punctual or dependable in the past, try to determine the reason and take corrective action. Personality traits can be observed in testing as well as in behaviors (e.g., tolerance for ambiguity, Type A behavior, introversion, extroversion, need for inclusion, locus of control). These are part of our personality or the way we view the world. Knowing your predispositions, such as a low tolerance for ambiguity (a complex or rapidly changing environment would be stressful) or extroversion (you prefer to interact with people rather than work alone), can help you look at jobs that suit your operating style.

Many assessments of personality traits are available to help you develop a vocabulary to describe the type of person you are: a discovery virtually impossible for an interviewer to make in a short interview when trying to determine your suitability for a job. Your chances of finding a satisfying and interesting job improve dramatically when you know what type person you are and know how to uncover the conditions at various workplaces. The closer a match you are with the characteristics of the jobs in your career area, the less stress you will experience and the more "at home" you will feel.

Interests

Curiously, though, our talents and skills are not always our interests, especially in multitalented people. A young woman who tested extremely high in math ability preferred to direct her career to her voice talent. A man who naturally can ride a horse well may never be interested in that and may use his body awareness for tennis. This is why we need to look beyond our skills and talents to our interests. Consultants can help people match the activities they seem to prefer to do with jobs that require those activities. You may be able to write computer programs and have a good math aptitude, but you enjoy more the part of your job in which you assess the needs of users and design systems to meet those needs. Therefore, if you are a programmer and only 20 percent of your responsibilities involve assessing user needs, you may actually end up spending 60 percent of your time with users because that is what you enjoy. Then, you will be stressed when you have to do the bulk of your job, those programming tasks you do not like, in less time.

Thus, knowing what your interests and motivations are may be at least as important in your eventual career success as your skills. You will be willing to invest more time and energy into those high-interest activities, and will, according to research, experience less stress on the job. What is a stressful set of work conditions for one person may be the place where another person thrives. While one enjoys sitting at a terminal writing manuals and reports all day long, another would consider that a maddening drudgery. Some feel much more energized when they interact with people, whereas others might find that much people exposure to be taxing (Kolbe, 1990).

When you actively and honestly assess your skills, talents, traits, and interests, you come closer to a realistic and workable description of the right career fit for you.

Revive Your Curiosity

Learning is a part of succeeding in any new activity. You must learn new skills and information to be able to progress in your life or your job. To do this, you might look at the style of the real experts on learning: children. Children live to learn and savor every new idea and experience because of their natural curiosity.

One way children express curiosity is through "Why?" questions. They want to know how a fire truck works, why the sky has clouds, and where the moon goes in the daytime. By being curious, children learn about their world. You have the same opportunity. When you see people who appear to be doing the type of job you think you would like, ask them how they like their work. Or, if you see an article on the field you are interested in, read about what others have to say. A product you use or a service you have contracted for recently could be starting points for researching new, potential job categories you had not thought of before.

> Curiosity is asking questions, wondering about issues, exploring ideas. It stretches the imagination. It makes "What if . . . ?" become real.

Reviving your curiosity may take some effort, but the returns are tremendous. Your curiosity will lead you to discover helpful information by asking questions and noticing things that might help you progress on your career path. Become nosy about public meetings and trade shows; attend seminars on things that interest you. Amazingly, sometimes a career path becomes lit with neon just because your curiosity led you into a particular room.

The best advice for someone who wants to move forward in life is this: "Be in the room." Of course, this sounds a bit cryptic, but the following situation will explain.

> "I had been in operations for an insurance company for a year, a decent job, just not very exciting for me. My hobby on the side was studying and trying to build an all-electric car. Out of curiosity, while on a vacation in New England, I took a morning to attend a conference held by a clean air organization. At one of the seminars, I heard about a company that was building electric buses. I talked to several companies to learn more about this interesting area. One I talked to was looking for someone for their operations department. I made a quick career change."

Maybe this sounds like "dumb luck," but the opportunity would have gone unnoticed if the person's curiosity had not led her to the conference. In addition, if she had attended in a passive way, she might not have learned some interesting information about her hobby. But, by asking questions, she became aware of the potential of what was being discussed. Otherwise, nothing of career benefit would have occurred.

Curiosity can make a party or even waiting time in a car repair shop a valuable career contributor. Listening to a conversation about market influences on a particular industry or asking how a particular company got started can enrich your career life on many levels. You are in the middle of a world of information and opportunity each day. A key to this process, though, is getting out and into new "rooms." Dennis Waitley, a noted motivational speaker, advises that the way to get into the career you want *is to be around people who do the kind of work you are interested in.* He recommends professional organizations as well as seminars conducted by leaders in the industry. Associating with these professionals can create opportunities and expand your knowledge. By knowing what factors will bring you closer to your goal, you can tune in to new events, people, and situations that will be helpful to you.

Chou read skateboarding magazines and went to shops, where he asked a lot of questions about distributors, designers, manufacturers, and consumer preferences. He developed a list of ideas to explore about companies that manufactured boards and about places boards were sold. He also looked at other products that were sold in the same places as skateboards and the types of people who competed professionally, as well as the ones that rode casually. That led him to extreme sports parks where he talked to shop owners and park managers.

Lucy's challenge was to think about her goal in different ways. She talked to physical therapists about their work and the equipment they used. That led her in two different directions: to therapy equipment distributors and to temporary agencies that managed contract workers. She discovered that many salespeople for equipment did not have a therapy or even health care background. She also discovered that resource agencies often handle all types of contract skilled professionals and many in her area had no specialists in the health care fields.

Many transitions in our lives began with wondering: "I wonder what it would be like to . . . ." Endless curiosity leads to the discovery of endless thresholds to new tiers of career fulfillment.

Focusing your effort toward specific career goals is a two-step process:

1. determining the focus
2. learning what is required to reach the ultimate job goal

Determine Your Career Focus

A good focus definition will make your changes work for you. A key point to remember is: *The job focus definition should be simple and attainable.* The defining and goal setting you will do in this case are somewhat different from the goal setting discussed in Chapter 2. In this chapter, you will narrow your vision down to focus on a specific industry or set of conditions. In addition, you will discern paths to those industry or condition goals.

Some people drown themselves in endpoint statements that are too detailed or limited or are intimidating in their size and complexity. An endpoint focus statement for a very intense law student read, "I will pass the bar exam in Texas and be admitted as a junior partner in ABC firm by August 2004 at the salary of $68,000 per year to include a company car and benefits." On the other hand, a housewife who wished to return to the workforce wrote as her defining statement, "I want to increase my accounting skills in order to secure a position where I can feel respected and can experience growth."

Chou began looking at his definition and focus: "I want to have a job that gives me time to skateboard; I'm not that interested in a 'people' position; I like a casual dress atmosphere and probably would rather be in a small company, without corporate hassle. I don't really care where I live."

Lucy wanted "to be in a health-care related position where I can use my degree and make a difference in people's lives in a personal way. I like being able to direct my own activities each day rather than having tasks assigned to me. My salary should be at least $40,000 per year to maintain a standard of living I am comfortable with, but benefits are important also. I would prefer to stay in this area."

ACTIVITY   **14.2**

Develop an endpoint definition statement for yourself—where you would like to end up professionally. It is okay to have more than one, but try to keep your statement simple and direct.

I would like to focus my energy in the direction of:

_____

_____

Later on, I would like to move into:

_____

_____

Learn What Is Required to Reach Your Goals

Now that your curiosity has been stimulated and your focus is becoming clearer, you are beginning to find out what is required to reach your goals.

Maybe schooling, training, or new experiences are needed. This is part two of reaching for a career definition: identifying the competencies required to reach your endpoint, then developing the process for acquiring those competencies. In many ways, you will leverage what you know at any stage in your goal pursuit to learn more or acquire additional skills that will help you achieve your end result.

Once you learn the competencies required, or maybe even the experiences expected, to reach your ultimate dream career situation, then gaining those competencies and experiences leads to your near-term goals. You may find that the career dream you desire requires that you have experience living in a foreign country. Though there are many ways to accomplish this—military, school abroad, job in an international company—you have a clear goal to reach. Thus, you will begin to invest time in acquiring the necessary competence.

One complaint from students and from those making a career change is that they cannot get experience in jobs to discover what they really would enjoy and what is involved in different types of jobs. An excellent aid to this discovery process is community service work. Many duties and responsibilities in volunteer and charitable work parallel those of industry.

For your own contribution to the community, Habitat for Humanity, United Way, Red Cross, an historical society, and public radio and television stations can always use volunteers. Whether your motivation for community service is for professional advantage or personal altruism, the net effect is that you gain visibility and acquaintances in many different fields.

Check out the boards of directors of the local arts councils or other service organizations. Being involved with a pet charity of someone important gives you the chance to be around others of importance, while doing a valuable service for someone else. Also, some large companies have particular nonprofit organizations they support with money and hands-on activities. You can meet people from a company you think you might enjoy and learn something about the company in casual conversation.

You will be able to practice, and become expert at, skills you have acquired, and you can learn new ones. From a personal perspective, you derive an enhanced sense of your own worth when you give to others. Working with people who are in need helps keep your perspective on the whole of live more grounded. You also meet some pretty terrific people who will enrich your spirit.

Invest in Your Chosen Area

Philip and Adrienne wanted to be in business for themselves, but they had heard that over half of new businesses fail. They were curious to find out the reasons for this high failure rate. They went to seminars, read articles in magazines, and talked to small business owners. What they learned is that most people who go into business know their product or service well, but know nothing about managing and marketing a business.

Time

Curiosity leads Philip and Adrienne to a guide for meeting their goal. One thing they must do to achieve their dream is to learn more about business management and marketing. So, their goal now has sub-goals that they can do one at a time. If they are serious about what they want to do, they will spend some time each day adding to their business knowledge. If your goal is important to you, you will devote time each day to activities that will lead to your achieving it. If this is not the case, you may lack conviction. This may be the time to analyze your goal to make sure it interests you enough to pursue it.

The summer after Chou graduated, his parents gave him the option of traveling for a month prior to starting life on his own. In preparation, he spent some time every day either on the Internet, looking through magazines, or sending e-mails to make appointments to meet with people at skateboard manufacturing companies, shops, and skate parks. He asked about what positions they might have open and what qualifications were needed. Then he planned a trip through several states to meet with people in the industry.

Motivational speakers will tell you that the only bad idea is one that you do not act on or that you dismiss because you think you can't make it happen. *Finding opportunity is helpful, but acting on opportunity is what moves you closer to where you want to be.*

ACTIVITY   **14.3**

From the information you have gathered, pick one of the elements needed for you to reach your career goal. Then, list one or more activities related to this element that you can spend some time on each day.

Element 1:

Activity: _____

How long will this activity take? _____

Time schedule for activity: _____

Element 2:

Activity: _____

How long will this activity take? _____

Time schedule for activity: _____

Conviction

Attaining life goals requires commitment and energy. You have to constantly give yourself pep talks to keep your level of enthusiasm high. Nothing important is accomplished without enthusiasm. Others may or may not understand your goal or your wish for the goal to be fulfilled, so, they may not be as supportive as you would like. This is unimportant. *You can be your own supporter. It is your goal, your joy, and you are entitled to feel good about it.*

You can do this by activating your goal in your mind. Use present tense statements such as, "My chosen career path is a source of joy," "I devote effort toward my goal," "My goal is vital and positive." By talking about your goal in terms of your "here and now" thinking, you make that goal part of your present reality. You invest thought and enthusiasm into the process as well as your time gathering qualifications along the way. Without a real emotional investment on your part, you probably will not see your way through all of the barriers it will take to reach your dream.

So many people stop goal activity because they talk themselves into believing that the goal is, after all, not attainable. Many goals are attainable over time that are not remotely in your realm right now. New jobs and new industries emerge daily; the conditions, salary, and position you ultimately aspire to just may not exist at the present. That does not preclude your finding it a year or 10 years from now. Your challenge is to keep the self-talk positive whether the day is good or bad, or whether your friends are supportive or not. Your goal has value and merit. Remind yourself of that often.

One thing you should do for yourself is build confidence in your goal activities. You do this by engineering successes along the way. On the way to your final goal of a fulfilling career position are many small goals that need to be accomplished. As you define these goal steps, it helps to make each one small enough so that you can complete it successfully in a limited amount of time. Few people achieve great things by huge leaps; more often, they win little victories as they go. These little victories reinforce a clear sense of purpose and give you the opportunity to affirm your progress on a regular basis.

Chou really wanted a job in the skateboard industry, but his friends who boarded worked at pizza delivery places or video stores and teased him about going for a "real job." But Chou wanted his own place and a high enough income to be able to travel to different sports parks around the country. "My goal of working a full-time job in the extreme sports industry will give me the personal life I want and a job I enjoy." Another affirmation Chou wrote for himself was, "With my degree and my knowledge of the sport I am well suited to a career position." On his mirror he taped in large letters "BOARD AND BUCKS."

Lucy received a lot of approval for her decision to pursue a health care provider position, but she ran into a barrier with the lack of full-time positions in her area. She resisted discouragement by reminding herself, "I have a lot to offer with my professional background and new specialized skills. Using a creative approach I will design or discover a position that will pay me for both." Still enthusiastic, she went to a half-day exhibit for personnel and contract worker agencies. One of the companies was promoting a new division in health care services that would be locating in the area. Earlier that week, she had attended a meeting of physical therapists where the conversation had centered on the lack of variety in the work and the unavailability of therapists for home-bound patients.

ACTIVITY   14.4

Describe how reaching your career goal will lead you to a satisfying life. Don't forget to remind yourself regularly about your potential. Many of the most successful people do it every day.

Reaching my goal will:

_____

_____

_____

Action

Talking to yourself in a positive way helps to keep you motivated in the face of all sorts of barriers to your goal-directed activity. Once you move your goal ideas to the status of goal actions, you are well on your way to success. *Daily action reinforces your quest by directing your energies regularly toward your desired end result.* In addition to this daily activity, you will become more alert to situations that might expose you to opportunities.

During his summer travels, Chou attended three extreme sports events, visited the home office of two in-line skate and skateboard companies, and did

Internet research on the size of the industry. At one of the events, he talked with the owner of a sports park and found that he was looking for an assistant manager to coordinate all of the separate activities and programs. The owner appreciated Chou's ability to understand the terminology and the types of activities a sports park offered.

He was also impressed with Chou's research on the industry as a whole and with Chou's good grades in his business courses. One of the "perks" (benefits) of the job was that Chou could skateboard any time he was not working, and he especially enjoyed being able to meet all of the "stars" of the sport when they came to do exhibitions or compete. He accepted the job on the spot. He was able to move ahead with his goal activities.

For you to do the same thing is quite easy. Here are the guidelines:

1. Define a short-term, intermediate focus that is relatively easy to accomplish.
2. Acknowledge your successes as they occur.
3. Affirm your progress often.

Accumulating small successes will give you the confidence to move forward and face the challenge of the larger steps. Successful action leads to more attempts and more successes. With many successes to your credit, temporary barriers to your goal activity will seem insignificant.

Verify Along the Way

Pursuing an ultimate career goal should be like mountain climbing: stop periodically to enjoy the vista because everything looks different from each level the higher you go. At the base, you see the beauty of the lower rock formations and the clouds further up the mountain. When you are in the clouds, you see only what is immediately around you, but you still know pretty much where you are in relation to where you are going if your compass and equipment are correct. Finally, from above the clouds, you see the sky and perhaps a distant peak. Two-thirds of the way up, you may decide that it would be much more satisfying to snowboard all the way down the mountain or to hang glide over to another peak altogether: choices you might not have even considered at the base.

The Endpoint

When you set your direction for your life, an occasional stop along the way, either by choice or by circumstances, allows you to survey the territory, to take stock of where you have arrived. Sometimes, because you can see something different at one level than you saw at an earlier one, you might want to redirect your climb toward this new destination. If your dream is happiness, be wary of defining that in a purely situational way; that is, as a specific set of circumstances. Each new threshold you pass through places you in a new position and a new prospect. When your view changes, so might your definition of what will make you happy.

The single-minded pursuit of a goal—a practice advocated by many motivational and positive thinking books—will likely do what those books promise: get you to the goal. But what happens if somewhere along the way an avenue or opportunity opened up because of a new skill acquisition or an unexpected contact? If that might redirect you from your original endpoint, in a strict sense of pursuit, you should ignore it. However, there is no reason for a focus so narrow that it ignores options or limits overall potential for dream fulfillment.

Verifying at regular intervals that you still want the original endpoint or direction allows for breadth of scope and creativity on your part as well as flux in the workings of the universe.

The Impact on Others

Another area of our lives that we should check every now and then is the effect of your goals on those dear to you. In your confident charge toward your career path of fulfillment, you must be cautious that you maintain balance. The people you care about are affected by your decisions and choices as well. Personal goals that are harmful to others bring negative long-term results. You must have a clear vision of your goal, but you must also have a heart.

Terence, a restaurant owner in a large city, reached his dream of opening a second restaurant. However, the children rarely saw their father unless they went to his restaurant. In this case, Terence's goal activity was succeeding, but at the risk of damage to his family.

Jennifer worked for two contract companies as a graphic designer in order to build her portfolio so she could get a position at a large ad company. She was able to manage because she worked at home most of the time. She and her oldest friend, Maria, for the year since they had started working, used to meet every Thursday night for sushi and mutual support. Though Jennifer knew Maria was going through an ugly divorce, she stopped going on Thursdays and ignored Maria's repeated pages while she pressed to meet a deadline.

1. Is Jennifer entitled to her goal-directed activity?

2. What price is her friend Maria paying for Jennifer's degree of focus?

3. What might be your recommendation for a way to maintain both career-goal focus and balance with those close to Jennifer?

Admittedly, it is easy to get lost in the pursuit of a particular definition of success, especially if things are going well. But, *personal relationships sustain us far more profoundly than professional accomplishments ever can.* It is a sad case, indeed, when a person begins to see work as the sole source of joy or achievement.

Achievement does require sacrifice, but sacrificing those you love for the sake of a goal may lead to an empty victory. Those who say it's lonely at the top may well have alienated friends and family along the way. This is just not necessary. Some of the most successful and busiest people in the world fiercely protect their family time and priorities.

You will have to make your own decisions about how you want to allocate your time. But, if along the way you stop long enough to include those closest to you in your goal setting and in the steps you are planning, you will find a solid support base. When they understand what you are trying to obtain and where they fit into the picture, they will be your biggest fans. Also, by including them in the process, you will prevent their feeling threatened or left out of your life.

Others' goals and needs have value just as yours do. You are not the only one going through transitions to reach higher levels of satisfaction in life. Verify where they are with the decisions you are making. To maintain connections with other people who also have goals and dreams, you will be required to give and take in all areas of your life. The ability to do this will make your arrival in *Success City* a celebration for everyone.

TRANSITION SKILLS SUMMARY

Assess skills, talents, traits, interests
Revive curiosity
Refine your career focus
Invest time, conviction, action
Verify the goal and its impact on others

GOAL SETTING

My goals for my ongoing emotional and relational development are:

_____

_____

My goals for my ongoing career management are:

_____

_____

_____

COACH'S CORNER

Many people these days want to know what the route to entrepreneurial success is. Of course, there is no formula, but there are a few common elements to those who make it.

If you are in a corporate environment, you need to find your way into P&L (Profit and Loss) responsibility, such as marketing, operations, or general manager jobs. Stay away from human resources, public relations, and administration. You need to have a track record of results—for an entrepreneur, results are all that matter. Be prepared to think outside the box and document successes doing that. While still employed, you will need to network with entrepreneurial types to stay fresh and on top of potential opportunities.

Once you prepare to go out into the entrepreneurial arena, there are two routes: create your own start-up or join one in the early stages.

Option 1: Your own venture. Ascertain the reality of the market. A great product does not necessarily invent a market. Is someone willing to pay to meet a need? Write a business plan (before you leave your regular corporate job) to figure out the necessary resources—what will it take to finance the business? The assumptions of the plan are more important than the figures themselves. How long is the sales cycle, for instance? If it takes one year to close a sale, then you need funding for one and a half years. Realize it always takes more time and more money than you expect. Circulate your plan and network with other entrepreneurs for feedback and advice. SCORE's retired executive volunteers will help you, and there may be similar organizations in your area. Consult books on startups and research details of the industry and potential customer target groups. If a 30 percent close rate is expected, that means you close 1 of every 30 calls, and one salesperson cannot handle it profitably. You also have to have a clear understanding of all cost and revenue drivers. Financing can come from friends and family, or an "angel" funding (a wealthy individual who looks to invest in early-stage entrepreneurial corporations). Another source of financing is loans from the Small Business Administration, but you will need collateral or assets to secure these debts. Venture capital is a less likely option; less than 10 percent of all businesses are funded by venture capital. Women generate many times more startup proposals than men, but less than 4 percent of all venture capital money goes to women. Finally, one very risky approach is to use credit card sources. (This has actually been done successfully with a $100,000 debt.)

(continued)

Option 2: Joining an entrepreneurial company that is already in business. Locate a likely company through events that venture capitalists and technology companies go to; call attorneys and accountants and find out what is going on. Read business papers to find out what's hot. How do you get in? You will have to demonstrate that you can produce results: generate more revenue, make more customers happy, or reduce costs. You might also get an edge if you are willing to work on a trial basis with no pay (a month) or will take a low salary in exchange for stock options. But you need to figure in the risk. The majority of new businesses fail, and people who invest in or are involved in them know this and expect it as part of the game or process. But greatness never occurs without risk. It's best, though, for your own peace of mind, or at least to arrive at a close approximation of the actual risk, to do your own due diligence, to investigate the same as a potential investor would.

Look at the market potential, the size of the customer base, product need, and buying power. Figure out what the sale price would be by studying sales of similar companies. There is, ultimately, a possibility that you are not suited to an entrepreneurial situation. Are you risk-averse? Do you need a lot of structure? Does rapid and unpredictable change bother you? Do you have little or no cash reserves or alternate income sources? If any of these conditions are outside of your comfort level, you would be miserable, and you just wouldn't be a good fit.

It can be a very rewarding experience whether you end up cashing in big or not. You have to consider the overall value of the experience, however. Are you in it for the final sale or for the excitement and creativity of the whole entrepreneurial situation—the team—people you respect and are inspired by, the win–lose element, the variety, the high energy level, the learning experience? There is also the chance to contribute, to have input due to the size of the company, to stretch and take on all sorts of different responsibilities. It's more than the small chance at hitting the jackpot that draws people to this kind of situation. I think the spirit, energy, and potential are at least as much of an attraction and reward.

KAREN ROBINSON, President and CEO, consultant and advisor for early stage entrepreneurial enterprises; e-mail: krobinson@npcml.com.

Appendix

Self-assessment testing should be used as a basis on which to build a personal and professional growth plan. Its purpose is not to determine what is good or bad about your personality or operating style, but to give you a framework for ongoing development.

The following SELF-ASSESSMENT EXERCISES, located on the Prentice-Hall Assessment Library CD-ROM, are loosely coordinated with the chapters. We suggest that you use all of the assessment tools. You will be better informed about your capabilities, style, and areas of needed growth, and this will be impressive to prospective employers.

Chapter 1: Self-assessment tools 1, 3, 5, 7, 43
Chapter 2: Self-assessment tools 9, 10, 11, 12
Chapter 3: Self-assessment tools 18, 19, 32
Chapter 4: Self-assessment tools 16, 17, 21
Chapter 5: Self-assessment tools 8, 15
Chapter 6: Self-assessment tools 22, 23
Chapter 7: Self-assessment tools 2, 24
Chapter 8: Self-assessment tools 27, 28, 29
Chapter 9: Self-assessment tools 4, 6, 36, 44, 45
Chapter 10: Self-assessment tools 13, 14, 37
Chapter 11: Self-assessment tools 15, 25, 26
Chapter 12: Self-assessment tools 40, 44
Chapter 13: Self-assessment tools 30, 35
Chapter 14: Self-assessment tools 38, 39, 41, 42

On the Internet site www.queendom.com/tests/alltests, you might want to match chapter topics with test-type groupings.

www.queendom.com/tests/personality/index Chapters 1, 2, 4, 5, 7

www.queendom.com/tests/relationships/index Chapters 6, 8, 11, 12

www.queendom.com/tests/career/index Chapters 3, 10, 13, 14

www.queendom.com/tests/health/index Chapter 9

This site also offers several I.Q. tests that attempt to help pinpoint areas of natural ability: verbal, visual–spatial, logical. They are not designed to tell you how "smart" you are, but to help you determine your cognitive strengths.

www.queendom.com/tests/iq/index

Suggested Readings List

Anger and Conflict in the Workplace: Spot the Signs, Avoid the Trauma, Lynne McClur (Impact Publishing, 2000).

The Art of Systems Thinking: Essential Skills for Creativity and Problem Solving, Joseph O'Connor, Ian McDermott (Thorsons Publishing, 1997).

The Body Language of Flirting, Dating, and Romance, Raymond C. McGraime (Gestech Publishers, 1998).

Building a Career Development Program: Nine Steps for Effective Implementation, Richard Knowdell (Consulting Psychologists Press, 1996).

Complete Job Search Handbook: All the Skills You Need to Get Any Job and Have a Good Time Doing It, Howard E. Figler (Henry Holt Publishing, 1988).

Difficult Conversations: How to Discuss What Matters Most, Douglas Stone, Bruce Patton, Sheila Heen (Penguin USA, 2000).

Emotional Vampires: Dealing with People Who Drain You Dry, Albert Bernstein (McGraw Hill Professional Publishing, 2000).

The Employee Handbook of New Work Habits for a Radically Changing World: 13 Ground Rules for Job Success in the Information Age, Price Pritchett (Pritchett Publishing Co., 1994).

First, Break All the Rules: What the World's Greatest Managers Do Differently, Marcus Buckingham, Curt Coffmen (Simon & Schuster, May 1999).

Get a Job in 30 Days or Less: A Realistic Action Plan for Finding the Right Job, Matthew H. Deluca, Nanette Deluca (McGraw Hill Publisher, 1999).

Getting the Love You Want: A Guide for Couples, Harville Hendrix (Harperperennial Library, 1990).

Getting Things Done: The Art of Stress Free Productivity, David Allen (Mass Market Paperback Reissue Edition, New American Library, 1996).

Here's My Card: How to Network Using Your Business Card to Actually Create More Business, Bob Poplk (Renaissance Books, 2000).

How to Become CEO: The Rules for Rising to the Top of Any Organization, Jeffrey J. Fox (Hyperion Press, 1998).

How to Feel Great About Yourself and Your Life: A Step-By-Step Guide to Positive Thinking, Martin English (AMACOM).

How to Get Control of Your Time and Your Life, Alan Lakein.

How to Get Organized and Increase Self-Confidence: A Task Management System, Ray Vitullo (Apostrophe Press, 1986).

I Could Do Anything if I Only Knew What It Was: How to Discover What You Really Want and How to Get It, Barbara Sher (DTP, 1995).

In the Spirit of Marriage: Creating and Sustaining Lasting Relationships, Robert Roskind (Celestial Arts, 2001).

The Leader's Edge: Mastering the Five Skills of Breakthrough Thinking, Guy A. Hale (Irvin Professional Publishing, 1995).

Learning Outside the Lines, Jonathan Mooney, David Cole (Simon & Schuster, August 2000).

Life Is an Attitude: Staying Positive When the World Seems Against You, Elwood N. Chapman, Michael G. Cresp (Cresp Publishing, 1992).

The Magic of Dialogue: Transforming Conflict Into Cooperation, Daniel Yankolovich (Simon & Schuster, 1999).

Marriage Lust: The 10 Secrets of Longlasting Desire, Pamela Lister (Hurst Books, 2001).

Master of Networking, Irvan R. Misner, Don Morgan (Bard Press, 2000).

Messages: The Communication Skills Book, 2nd Ed., Patrick Fanning (New Harbinger Publications, 1995).

Now, Discover Your Strength, Marcus Buckingham, Donald Clifton (Free Press, 2001).

Nurturing Yourself and Others: Learn How to Fill Your Life With Happiness, Lee Schneby (Fisher Books, 2000).

The Pathfinder: How to Choose or Change Your Career for a Lifetime of Satisfaction and Success, Nicholas Lore (Fireside Press, 1998).

Powerful Conversations: How High Impact Leaders Communicate, Phil Harkins, Phillip J. Harkins, Warren G. Dennis (McGraw Hill, 1999).

Real Life Guide to Starting Your Career: How to Get the Right Job Right Now, Margot Carmichael Lester (Pipeline Printing, 1998).

The 7 Habits of Highly Effective People, Stephen R. Covey (Fireside Press, 1990).

Strategic Thinking: The 9-Step Approach to Strategic Planning, 2nd Ed., Simon Wootton, Terry Horne (Kogan Page Ltd., 2000).

Success Through a Positive Mental Attitude, Napoleon Hill, W. Clement Stone (Simon & Schuster, 1992).

Taking Care of Me: The Habits of Happiness, May Kau Mueller (Insight Inc., 1997).

Who Moved My Cheese: An Amazing Way to Deal with Change in Your Work and in Your Life, Spencer Johnson, Kenneth Blanchard (Putnam Publishing Group, 1998).

References

Alcorn, Paul. *Social Issues in Technology: A Format for Investigation*. Upper Saddle River, NJ: Prentice-Hall, 2000.

Austin, Linda. *What's Holding You Back? 8 Critical Choices for Women's Success*. New York: Basic Books, 2000.

Berne, Eric. *Games People Play: The Psychology of Human Relationships*. New York: Ballantine Books (reissued), 1996.

Bradshaw, Pete. *The Organizational Impact of Self-Esteem*. (1985, out of print).

Boyer, Blair, Director of Graduate Placement, Interview, February 11, 2001.

Brislin, Richard W. *The art of getting things done: eight strategies for the acquisition and maintenance of power*. World Wide Web: smartbiz.com/sbs/arts/ exe2.htm, accessed January 4, 2001.

Cameron, Julia. *The Artist's Way*. New York: Jeremy P. Tarcher/Putnam, 1992.

Campbell, Ross. *How to Really Love Your Child*. Cook Communications, 1992.

Elgin, Suzette. *How to Disagree Without Being Disagreeable*. New York: John Wiley, 1997.

Flamholtz, Eric and Yvonne Randle. *The Inner Game of Management*. New York: Amacom, 1987.

Fulghum, Robert. *From Beginning to End: The Rituals of Our Lives*. Ivey Books, 1996.

Gardner, Howard. *Frame of Mind: The Theory of Multiple Intelligences*. Boulder, CO: Basic Books, 1993.

Geer, Carolyn T. Ready, Set, Quit. *Fortune*, August 24, 2000, pp. 82–110.

Ghattas, Raouf and Sandra McKee. *Practical Project Management*. Upper Saddle River, NJ: Prentice-Hall, 2000.

Hall, Donald. Operations Vice President, Interview, April 11, 2001.

Hallowell, Edward M. *Connect: 12 Vital Ties that Open Your Heart, Lengthen your Life and Deepen your Soul*. New York: Pantheon Books, 1999.

Iannuzzi, Patricia. *Teaching Information Literacy Skills*. Boston: Allyn and Bacon, 1999.

Kolbe, Kathy. *The Conative Connection: Uncovering the Link between Who You Are and How You Perform*. Reading, MA: Addison-Wesley, 1990.

Kübler-Ross, Elizabeth. *On Death and Dying*. New York: Simon & Schuster, 1997.

Lowe, Robert. *Improvisation, Inc.: Harnessing Spontaneity to Engage People and Groups*. San Francisco: Josey-Bass, 2000.

Ostrow, Ellen. Tooting your own horn: Practical strategies for developing your skills at self-promotion. *MidLife Mentor Newsletter*. World Wide Web: midlifementor.com/newsletters/issue17.html, accessed January 4, 2001.

Phillips, Shawn. Up Front. *Muscle Media*, October 2000, pp. 10–12.

Ruggiero, Vincent. *The Art of Thinking*, 6th ed. Denver: Longman, 2000.

Shaw, F. J. Transitional experiences and psychological growth. *ETC*, 15:39–45, August 1957.

Tannen, Deborah. *Talking from 9 to 5*. New York: William Morrow, 1994.

Walters, Brenda and Sandra McKee. *Life Management: Skills for Busy People*. Upper Saddle River, NJ: Prentice Hall, 1997.

Index